The Business of Trying to Keep

Rotherham United

The D.C. Years

Giles H Brearley F.C.M.A.

&

Gavin Mackinder

Typeset and printed on behalf of the authors by Shadowline Publishing Ltd, the print publication division of the Convecto Media Group.

First published 2009

ISBN 9781-904706-27-4

© 2008 Giles Brearley & Gavin Mackinder

FOREWORD

I received a telephone call from Giles and Gavin in late December to say they'd had a long hard think about who should do the foreword for this book.

After trawling through a long list of suitable candidates they had decided there was only one person for the job and that was Denis Coleman, especially as the book carried the subtitle of the "DC Years". It was a very proud moment for me.

My love affair with the Millers started in 1973 after moving from Belfast to Rotherham the previous year. I went to my first English football game when Rotherham United played Stockport County at Millmoor. I was hooked.

After following The Millers the length and breadth of the country for many years I'd just spent 6 weeks in Australia and Asia playing golf and having a good chill out before my next project commenced and returned to Rotherham to discover my greatest passion could be shortly coming to an end.

I contacted an old school friend Paul Douglas and asked him to assist me rallying a group of business people in the town to see if we could do anything to help. Whilst there was a lot of sympathy there did not seem to be anyone committed enough to go that extra mile, so drastic action was needed. Weeks of long hours and hard work, eventually found myself as Chairman and custodian of my beloved Millers (a dream come true), or so you might think.

The next two years were a real roller coaster as I m sure you will realise when you have read the book, a few ups and many downs" I do hope this now sets the record straight for a lot of folk because football is full of rumors, some close to the truth and some so far off the mark its bewildering.

I would like to take this opportunity to thank the supporters and staff of Rotherham United as well as the people of Rotherham in general (even those who follow other local teams) for the heartfelt support I received whilst in office as Chairman but more importantly the many kind words offered since (it really has been amazing)

A BIG THANKS

Finally I would like to show my appreciation to my fellow Board of

Directors who gave it their all for no financial reward but a lot of heartache instead. A big thanks to Dave Costin, Gary Hall, Giles Brearley and Gavin Mackinder. I don t know how I'd have got through those two years without you lads, and not forgetting my wife Helen who suffered more than most.

Denis Coleman (former Chairman)

Rotherham United Football Club

The Authors

Giles H. Brearley FCMA

South Yorkshire born and bred, Giles Brearley attended Mexborough Grammar school and qualified as a Chartered Management Accountant in 1983 following a National Coal Board scholarship. He started alone in Public Practice in 1984 building up to the five partner practice of today. He has undertaken assignments in many overseas countries as well as acting for U.K clients. He was elected as a Fellow of the Institute in 1997. He is an accomplished Author and Broadcaster on South Yorkshire's Historical past. He first attended a Rotherham United game in 1964 and was honored to be invited to join the Board to assist in what was to be a difficult task ahead.

Gavin J. Mackinder

Born in Sheffield in the early 1960's, Gavin teamed up with Giles almost 20 years ago, eventually becoming one of his business partners in 2000. He was actively involved on a day to day basis managing the cash flow at Rotherham United and liaising with the board of directors. He still believes that with the correct amount of financial investment, accompanied with the move to a purpose built community stadium, the club will prosper and repay those supporters who have remained loyal to their team through these very difficult times. "Up the Millers".

ACKNOWLEDGEMENTS

Giles and Gavin would like to thank the following for their assistance in the preparation of this book:-

Denis Coleman	Rotherham Advertiser
Gary Hall	League 1 and 2 Finance Directors
David Costin	Mike Brearley
Paul Douglas	Tobin
Jeremy Bleazard	Trevor Smallwood
Mark Hitchens	The Laird of Camster
Lisa Costin	Swansea F.C

A big thanks from the former Board of Directors;

Denis Coleman, David Costin, Gary Hall and Giles Brearley would like to thank the following for their financial and personal time contributions donated to Rotherham United over the 2006/7 and 2007/8 seasons, without whose assistance we would have struggled to see out 6 months.

Sheffield Site Services Ltd, Rotherham Surfacing, S D Block Paving, Brearley & Co Accountants Limited, M.J Hughes, J.B Doors, Ron Hull, Chris Cooper, ABS Industrial Resources Group, Shoparound Mortgages, Ben Bennett, Camwatch, Audio Vision, Stuart Aston Carpets Work House Gym, Lazer Products, Liam Wheeler, Wayne England, M & D Security, Sign FX, Mick Williams, Gareth Mayo, AFP Van Hire, Pete & Terry Snee, UK Doors, Gateway Auto Refinishers, Candy Corner Fisheries, Patrick Nortcliffe, Perry's, Horbury plc, Jumbo Partitions, Rosehill Press, Bee Quick Scaffolding, Tim Naylor, MKS Timber, Ace Fire Solutions, Top Tread Tyres, Dean Westbrook, Steve Bagnall, Himalia Take Away, Del Chambers, Bob Shaw, Neil Wheeler, Howard Webb, Rotherham United Supporters Trust, David Hinchcliffe, Roger Stone, Ben Mansford, Peter Wainwright, Ian Herbert, Rotherham Council, Neil Warnock, Sheffield United Football Club, Martin Green, Steve Saul, Redtooth Limited, Parkgate Retail World. Also a special thank you to Carol Brown and her staff (Carols Catering) for the excellent service provided looking after the various club directors, Guests, Referees, V.I P's and Sponsors throughout our term in office.

DEDICATION

This book is dedicated to the memory of Nicholas Duke (Fluke) lifelong Miller who sadly passed away in December 2008. God rest his soul.

CONTENTS

Introduction	xi
Chapter 1 Perhaps it was all Charlie's fault.	1
Chapter 2 Millers 05.	6
Chapter 3 Raising the capital.	11
Chapter 4 The points dilemma.	15
Chapter 5 The first board meeting.	18
Chapter 6 Lease from Hell.	22
Chapter 7 Ground problems.	33
Chapter 8 Cutting costs.	41
Chapter 9 Albania here we come.	52
Chapter 10 Boardroom skirmishes.	58
Chapter 11 Tobin emerges from the shadows.	68
Chapter 12 The big hitters.	73
Chapter 13 Millmoor Suite.	77
Chapter 14 The Watford Gap.	81
Chapter 15 It's Gaz Man.	87
Chapter 16 Possession hearing.	97
Chapter 17 Alan Knill.	103
Chapter 18 The council men cometh.	113
Chapter 19 Stamping on our rights.	123
Chapter 20 The crumbling foundations of the football stadium crisis.	127
Chapter 21 The Football League Awards.	130
Chapter 22 Fish, chips and mushy fees.	135
Chapter 23 Our credit card crunch.	137
Chapter 24 Robo the quiet man.	140
Chapter 25 You can tell Neil Warnock's gone.	146

Chapter 26 The Ensuing Court case.	149
Chapter 27 The Insurance claim.	167
Chapter 28 Creepy Crawley (the Pablo Mills Affair).	173
Chapter 29 I didn't think Ray would make it.	178
Chapter 30 I think he thinks he's Don Corleone.	185
Chapter 31 Hoax inheritances.	189
Chapter 32 Don Valley or bust.	192
Chapter 33 Shares, bloody shares.	196
Chapter 34 Accrington Stanley, who are they are exactly?	200
Chapter 35 The 50:50 turns into 3 to 1 as Bah Humbug sets in.	205
Chapter 36 The Darlington away game stadium experience.	208
Chapter 37 Dino appears out of nowhere.	216
Chapter 38 The Americans are coming.	219
Chapter 39 Butch Cartledge and the Sun Tanned Kid ride again.	224
Chapter 40 Are the Irish coming?	227
Chapter 41 Life in administration.	232
Chapter 42 Great, Grandfather would not be happy - Rochdale F.C.	240
Chapter 43 Mansfield Town, the last away game blues.	246
Chapter 44 The final hand over.	257
Chapter 45 So how did we compare? Giles's finance notes.	264
Chapter 46 Matchday antics.	289
Chapter 47 Rotherham United Statistics 2006/2007 and 2007/2008.	315

INTRODUCTION

League Football is one of the hardest businesses to manage. Other than the top Premier League clubs, few make a profit on a regular basis. You can be in profit one year and lose it all the next. There are so many external factors beyond your control that all the good you do can be unravelled overnight by an act of God, or someone else's whim.

On the other hand, there can be great rewards which other businesses would not give, like the euphoria when your team achieves a magnificent victory against all odds. Unexpected windfalls can occur. A talented youngster might suddenly hit dazzling form and be spotted by scouts from a bigger club. The transfer funds can uplift the balance sheet and turn a small club's finances around overnight. With a fair wind behind you and some good luck in the cup competitions you can bring in revenues way beyond the average budgeted figures used in your business plan; like Barnsley FC did in the 2007/2008 F.A. Cup competition, when they scooped more than an extra two million pounds.

Trying to keep Rotherham United in one piece involved us taking knock after knock, but we had to keep on getting back up and continuing the fight regardless. The club had a long history of undying passion for football that we all desperately wanted to preserve for the town and the fans.

The 'D.C. Board' was primarily set up to act as the caretaker and custodians while the hunt went on for an 'heir apparent' to take the club over and give it a much needed financial kiss of life and invest in its future. Many potential investors crossed our paths, hoping to wear this crown. Some gave us hope, but most were just not princes in waiting.

Once you become involved, football acts like a drug. It gets into your blood and your brain; it becomes an obsession and alters your life beyond belief. Like all hard drugs, it slowly eats in to your reasoning, and you can come out the other side a different person. You become prepared to undertake financial commitment and duties that you would have sneered at in the past. The club has to keep going, no matter what the cost becomes your only thought. The years you spent building up businesses is re-prioritised because suddenly the football club must always come first, only narrowly avoiding a clash with your moral duty to your family.

Whilst certainly the roller coaster 2006/7 and 2007/8 seasons were barely survived, they will remain part of the club's history. The fans, so loyal, were able to get their fix of football that would otherwise have been denied them. In our plight and in the ensuing battles we managed to take Paul Douglas our tortured chief executive to the extremes. He soon realised that his contract of employment consisted of blank pages wherever job description, responsibilities and terms and conditions were concerned.

A lot of the club's fans had no idea of even half of the problems that we faced during this period .Quite rightly at times, they were very critical of us. Unfortunately, business confidentiality often meant that we could only tell half the story to the fans; which probably made us look foolish. However, with professional business etiquette in mind as well as constantly being in the public eye it had to be that way. Loose talk often leaves one repenting at leisure and with the hauntings from the past, the vindictiveness of the few and down right bad luck at times it all combined to make life even harder.

We make no apology for the high business content of the book. That is what we were all about: the business of — Trying to keep Rotherham "United"

Giles H Brearley and Gavin J Mackinder

CHAPTER 1 (G.H.B WRITES)

PERHAPS IT WAS ALL CHARLIE'S FAULT.

So where do I start with all this? For me, the road of trying to keep Rotherham "United" began on Saturday the 29th April 2006. That night saw wife Ruth and me dining with our very good friends, Alan and Claire Downing of Harlington. They were taking us out as a treat to chill us out a little. We had been on tenterhooks all week waiting for the call telling us that daughter-in-law, Laura had gone into labour for the birth of our first grandchild. They had decided to eat Italian style and booked us all in at Galliano's at Wickersley, which unbeknown to me then was owned by Dino Maccio. I had visited only once before, a year earlier, and we all thought it would make a nice change.

We had just about finished the main course when my mobile phone rang. It was our son, Alex who announced that Laura had finally been admitted to Rotherham District General Hospital. We all went wild with emotion.

Alan said, "Come on; let me get you a celebratory drink." We walked to the bar near the restaurant entrance and Alan duly ordered two special ports. These were quickly followed by two more to wet the ensuing baby's head.

Suddenly the outside door opened and in walked Denis Coleman and Dino Maccio both wearing full length overcoats and looking like they had come to carry out a contract killing. They had been out on Rotherham United business, drumming up support from here, there and everywhere. I had read of their efforts to take over the club in the Rotherham Advertiser.

Although I had acted for Denis professionally on many occasions in years gone by I had lost contact with him of late and not seen him for a while.

Upon seeing me, he walked straight over and, wearing a large grin, vigorously shook my hand. Denis said that it was a remarkable coincidence that I was here as he had been discussing me with Dino. I did not really know Dino but Denis did the introductions.

He quickly outlined how he was trying to get a team of people together, who would donate their services to Rotherham United

Football Club. The finance and accounting services were unfilled and he wanted me to consider taking them on board. I explained to him that we were a four partner firm now and I would have to speak to the others. I agreed to ring him in the middle of the following week.

It was noticeable how people kept interrupting us to ask how it was going with the club, and wishing them well with the task ahead. They were treated like returning Kings. Denis told me that he had never known anything like this, everyone wanted to give something to the cause.

The crack of dawn, just 6 hours later, on a cold Sunday morning saw us picking up Laura's parents, Ralph and Ann from their home in West Melton and heading off to the hospital to get the first glimpses of our new grandson – little Charlie.

I whispered to him about all the fuss he had created the night before. One eye opened for a split second and shut as if to wink at me.

At our Partner's meeting on the Tuesday we discussed the conversation I had with Denis. It was decided that we needed to know a lot more of the details to establish what exactly was expected of us. To this end a further meeting was duly arranged at all haste.

The very next day saw me and my fellow partners, Gavin Mackinder and Mark Smallman, at Millmoor meeting with Denis Coleman, Dino Maccio and Dave Costin. Discussions centred on the need for doing the annual accounts and respective company filing obligations. Denis initially proposed that in return for our annual service we would receive a free advert in the programme and a discounted advertising board inside the ground. As our conversations progressed it soon became clear that the financial services they needed went well beyond an annual service. There was supervision of the quarterly VAT returns, monthly payroll operations, monthly management accounts, banking facilities to organise, accounting systems to review and there would have to be regular monitoring of the club's cash flow and reporting to the board of directors. It was also clear that there was still a lot of negotiating to be done with the 'legal boys'. We suggested we should adjourn and come back with a detailed proposal for them to consider.

Back at the office, we started to cost out the envisaged time it would take. It was frightening when considering the impact it could have on our practice. We either were for it 110% or we forgot it. After some debate we all felt we should go for it but the goal posts would have to be dug up and moved substantially before we could commit.

At Denis's suggestion we met at the Ring O' Bells pub at Kimberworth. It was a midweek lunchtime and Denis said that there would be no one there and we could talk undisturbed. After the fourth table move and the sixth "Hi Denis; how is it going with Rotherham United?" we eventually decided to sit outside.

We set our stall out to the assembled crew, including specific conditions (i.e. we would insist on a seat on the board of directors plus a share option at some future point). In return we would ensure our full commitment to the club's needs.

The seat on the Board was essential because the finance function was a crucial part of the business and needed proper director level dialogue and implementation. Denis was initially unemotional about our proposals. I think we had caught him off guard. It was suggested we should meet again after the board had more time to consider our proposals.

A further meeting was held at the George and Dragon Wentworth. This time, for privacy purposes, we all squeezed into one of the many alcoves and indulged ourselves first with the delicious Steak N Ale Pie before we discussed our proposals further.

We reiterated our concerns over the club's needs once the new season kicked off. It was decided that Denis, David and Dino would discuss it amongst themselves and then put it to the vote.

The next day I received a call from Denis: we were on.

We jumped straight into action. Fellow partner, John Hesselden, visited the ground that day and looked at the current financial systems and identified the accounting needs. There, John was well received by Claire Yeardley, who ran the accounting function. After we had done our initial work we agreed to meet again, but this time we could speak with more knowledge and have the basis for putting together a business plan.

It was essential that the Directors and ourselves bonded into a team where everyone's role was understood in the day to day operations with mutual respect.

Our next meeting was arranged at Millmoor in the cramped office of Paul Douglas the club's chief executive. Denis chaired the meeting and opened discussions, "United we all stand" and "United we all fall" was his battle cry, encouraging us into working together as one.

It was all agreed that:

David Costin was to look after the Stadium and Training Ground.

Alan Cartlidge was to look for sponsorship, advertising and other commercial opportunities, working alongside Dino.

Dino was to oversee the makeover of the club's shops in readiness for the new season and also to supervise the Millmoor Suite.

Brearley & Co were to overview the finances.

Denis Coleman would look after the players' side of the business and the strategic part of the Club.

But what about Paul Douglas? Well, he copped for everything else. He was very understanding about our allocation of burdensome duties, but he knew that after all he was the captain of the ship, sitting daily at the helm. There was a job to do and he wanted to do it. Paul in fact was the only salaried member of the board/executive.

One of our first jobs was to predict the future trading performance and tweak it to form a workable budget. Everyone needed to know what was expected of them if control was to be exercised. We asked for copies of all legal agreements affecting the Club and these were delivered the next day to Bridge Street.

When I saw the Lease and Hospitality Agreements my stomach churned. I sat in my office reading both agreements through, page after page right to the end. I had seen many agreements over the years but these were the worst I had seen from a tenant's point of view. I wondered as a club what predicament we were getting ourselves into.

It knew it spelled trouble... and was I right.

Gavin poked his head round the door and said, "You look like you've just seen a ghost"

"I have" I replied, "it's the ghost of Rotherham's Future."

"It can't be that bad" he said.

"Well, you take it home and give me your verdict tomorrow."

I rushed home from the office promptly at 5pm that day as we were having tea with our son, Alex, his wife, Laura and a first with little Charlie. With things like lease terms still exploding round my head I looked at Charlie as he lay there and thought, "Yes, I would not have been collared by Denis if it wasn't for you young fellow. If all this does go wrong I can say that perhaps it was all Charlie's fault".

Chapter - 2 (G.H.B.)

Millers 05

Millers 05, the consortium we took over from, featured so heavily in our period of office that we make no apology for retelling their story. It will give the background to a lot of the events to which we refer.

During the 2004/05 season, the long-time chairman, Ken Booth, on behalf of his company, C F Booth and the shareholders, sold the club to Millers 05, which was a company formed by supporters and proclaimed it was one of only a handful of football clubs owned and run by such a group. The board members of Millers 05 were:

Peter Ruchniewicz (chairman) – a Maltby-born solicitor and senior partner in the London law firm, Colins, Benson and Goldhill.

David Veal (vice-chairman) – owner of the Hellaby based Coffee Exchange Company and then chairman of RUST. David took over the responsibility for marketing

John Harrison – a chartered accountant in general practice who took responsibility for finance

Chris Dobbs – a landscape architect and the RUST representative of the previous club board, who took responsibility for community matters and partnerships

Trevor Smallwood – a former Millers director and ex-managing director of First Buses who took responsibility for operational matters as associate director.

Phil Henson – he had served the club as player, manager and chief executive through often difficult times, continuing in the role of chief executive and company secretary.

There had been various unsuccessful attempts to sell the club before Millers 05, so their intervention was well received by the Booths. The new owners were enthusiastic and pledged to have no hidden agendas and that all the revenue generated would be re-invested in the club for an improved playing squad, greater comfort for supporters and greater opportunities.

Ken Booth was made a life president. In one flyer it stated that:

> "He will be our landlord (through C F Booth Limited) but we have conventional leases such as many league clubs now have, which have been negotiated to be extremely beneficial for the club".

I wish that had been true. Who wrote it, I wondered?

The club was apparently losing around £20,000 per week at around the time Ken Booth handed the club over. Like we did, Millers 05 set an agenda to break even as soon as possible.

A loan made to Millers 05 by C F Booths was reported to be at a favourable interest rate. It was also stated that the Booth group would make no profit from the loan arrangement. There were also plans to have a new community stadium established within ten years.

£100,000 was invested by the board, mainly from Trevor Smallwood, Peter Ruchneiwicz, David Veal and John Harrison. It is amazing how we all start out at the same place in these situations, probably because there is rarely anywhere else to start from. Millers 05 reasoned that there were 100,000 people living in Rotherham itself (a number that grew to 250,000 when taking into account the outer lying parts of the borough), and that they needed to tempt back the missing fans and businesses.

The "New Stand" was a major part of the plans for the club to go forward. It was to generate new income streams. The idea was for the stand to be a single tier of 4,000 seats with hospitality boxes, banqueting facilities and a new club shop. It was confirmed that money was being raised through the Football Foundation as well as from other sources. A fundraising campaign was started in the summer of 2005 with the "Buy a Brick" campaign. Many fans invested in this and it later left a bitter taste in their mouths when the stand was not completed. This failure was to hamper our later attempts at fundraising. A new budget was drawn up by Millers 05 for the new season but, like us, they were plagued in that the players' wage bill was too high. This was a legacy of the previous season in the Championship league. As many players as possible were transferred or loaned to other clubs, but the remaining contracts still had to be honoured.

After a good start to the season, the team suffered a disastrous sequence of results, going 18 games without a victory (oh, doesn't history repeat itself!) and ultimately, the club parted company with the manager, Mick Harford. The assistant manager, Alan Knill, was appointed to replace him.

As a result of falling attendances, the budget predictions for match day revenue were not being met and Millers 05 realised that they were fast heading for a financial crisis. Trevor Smallwood loaned the club over £500,000 in an effort to ease the situation and they sold the leading goal scorer Deon Burton to local rivals, Sheffield Wednesday, for a purported £100,000. Ultimately however, an announcement was made in February 2006 that the situation was so dire that unless there was a major cash input of around £1 million, the club would cease to trade and the final game would be against Bristol City on Saturday, 25 March 2006.

The Walk to Huddersfield in March 2006 trying to save the Millers after Millers 05 ceased.

A fundraising effort was immediately launched with a fantastic response. At Millmoor itself and at grounds throughout the country, bucket collections were held as the realisation that the club could disappear, hit home.

In the month between the announcement and the date of the final game, around £200,000 had been pledged. This in itself was not enough and there were appeals for people to come forward to take the club over. Unfortunately, no-one came forth. The club's demise was a hot topic both on the radio and in the newspapers.

One loyal long term fan, Denis Coleman, thought about it long and hard and decided that although he didn't have the resources, he had guts and determination and would try to take the club forward, one way or another. He teamed up with fellow supporter and local restaurateur, Dino Maccio, and started campaigning to rally support for the club, to rise like the phoenix from the ashes. Denis and Dino officially took over the club on 22nd March 2006 and were welcomed by the fans on the pitch before the Bristol City game.

As the season finally unfolded with the possibility of relegation compounding the dire financial position of the club, Jeremy Bleazard a corporate recovery expert was consulted regarding the potential insolvency of Rotherham United. It was decided that a Company Voluntary Arrangement might be the only possible option to save the club. The timing would be crucial and this would also depend on if or when the club was relegated — the dilemma of which is covered in a later chapter.

The season finally finished with Rotherham United managing to survive relegation by the narrowest of margins. In the meantime, documentation was being drawn up to go ahead with the CVA. Meetings were arranged by Denis and Dino with the Football League and Professional Footballers Association (PFA). The proposal drawn up for creditors to consider was subject to the Football League share being transferred to them and for them to pay one penny in the pound to unsecured creditors. They also undertook to make payment to "football creditors" upon terms agreed with those creditors. In essence, the football debts had to be paid in full and would be taken over by the new club. The settlement of these debts was outside the scope of the CVA agreement. The duration of the CVA was to be for twelve months and had to be proved at the statutory meeting of creditors by the directors, pursuant to Section 3 of the 1986 Act.

CVA fees were originally estimated at £15,000 for the insolvency practitioner and £20,000 for solicitors and other legal costs. The assets of the company were charged primarily to the Nat West Bank. There were second charges by Paul Eyre and Trevor Smallwood, but they lay behind the Nat West in ranking and were unusable. The Statement of Affairs' list of creditors looked like a who's who of local businesses in and around Rotherham. In order to get the CVA approved, there had to be a sufficient number of supporting creditors voting in favour of the proposals. Herein, a problem lay. Without the support of the C F Booth group, the CVA would ultimately fail. Denis, in the meantime, had been having talks with the Booths, trying to thrash out a new lease; but suddenly, with knowledge of the CVA terms, his bargaining power was whisked away. The C F Booth group wanted the existing lease to be assigned to the new company along with the Hospitality Agreement. The club was to also take responsibility for paying all of the Booth's legal fees. It was made very clear to Denis that, unless he agreed to this, there would be no support for the CVA and that would be the end of the club.

Reluctantly, this situation was accepted; hence the lease unravelled its grip from the throat of Millers 05 and attached itself firmly on the new company, the difference this time being that there was no acceptance by the board that the lease gave the club anything other than a huge continuing liability.

Chapter - 3 (G.H.B.)

Raising the Capital

The rules of the Football League were that one needed at least £500,000 of share capital before taking over a League One football club.

When Denis, Dino and David initially took on the task of trying to save Rotherham United, they were unaware of the size of this requirement or, indeed, where the funds would come from. As they quickly familiarised themselves with the rules and needs of the League, they set about the task of raising the cash. To a degree, this had already started before the end of the previous season following the announcement of the Millers 05 financial crisis. Loyal fans had been carrying out "bucket collections" outside the Millmoor ground, on the streets, in pubs and even at other football grounds. At the D.I.Y shop in the centre of Swinton a donations bucket was almost a permanent fixture as customers were encouraged to make donations. The public and supporters were marvellous and over £160,000 of the monies pledged was collected. A few of the fundraisers never handed the money over and to this day we never discovered why. Perhaps their own financial plights were worse than the club's. Further donations were also received of £10,000 and £20,000 from two Rotherham businessmen but a large amount was still needed. Denis said "the response was unbelievable; people were throwing money at us wherever we went. "They spared us what they could".

To make up the shortfall, Denis and Dino started contacting various individuals they believed to be stalwart supporters of the club, never doubting that by hook or by crook, they would get the funds. Denis assumed the role similar to the one Bob Geldof did when he was raising funds for 'Live Aid'. The expressions "give me your money and "help keep Rotherham alive" got worked into just about every conversation he had and it was broadcast on the radio and on Look North and Calendar. Following these pleas another generous donation of £60,000 was received from an anonymous Rotherham businessman. When the euphoria eventually began to subside, Denis and Dino took stock of where they were. Despite their efforts a large lump of cash was still needed.

A Knight in shining armour who came to the club's rescue and without whose involvement, Rotherham United would most likely not be here today was none other than the former Millers 05 board member Trevor Smallwood O.B.E. Trevor paid over some £200,000 to us to help the club go forward With this final injection of cash the new company could finally meet the Football League's capital requirements. The phoenix was now rising.

Trevor's association with the club went back to his childhood when, at the age of seven, he with his Father, Grandfather and Uncle Bill would watch the Millers play. In the 1960s he used to help the club by selling programmes. He recalled that when Rotherham played Manchester United in the F.A. Cup, he was stampeded and had sold every programme he had within 10 minutes. His most memorable game was when Rotherham played Southampton and were losing 3 nil when all of a sudden The Millers got into gear and banged 4 goals away, winning the game.

Trevor went on to be very successful in business and no matter where he was, always followed the Millers ups and downs, as they were very close to his heart. After an invitation he agreed to be involved with the Millers 05 board but when that did not work out, the future of the club was still uppermost in his mind and he was concerned to see that it did continue. He appreciated the task ahead for the new consortium and without approach offered to make this large personal donation to assist. Trevor, being the private person he is, always wished us to keep his name out of the public domain ,to give him some anonymity. When I broke the news that we were writing this book I managed to persuade him that we should let the fans know that he was one of the main benefactors who helped keep the town's football club alive during this very difficult period.

He was a firm part of the Club's history, and without people like him the club would definitely not have survived.

We would report back to him periodically and at times, ask for guidance on other matters. I spent a good few hours chatting to Trevor and found that we had a lot in common in that we both went to Mexborough Grammar School. He would probably have been in the same year as my elder brother. He found his fortune in Transport. His involvement in the coach and bus industry evolved from the local 'Mexborough and Swinton Traction Company' of which his father was a former general manager.

Trevor started working there on leaving school and soon climbed the ladder of success. As the various companies were swallowed up by larger companies he was always deemed a management asset they wanted and he therefore became part of the new bigger picture.

This continued until 1986 when Trevor became the Executive Chairman of First Group plc. He led the management buy out (M.B.O.) of Badgerline from the National Bus Company. During the next 13 years he engineered the growth of the business from one with 800 employees to a worldwide network that employed several thousand people, had a £2 billion turnover and profits of over £100 million. Trevor oversaw the international expansion of the Group, which today has operations in many countries, operating some 10,000 buses in the UK, 14,000 US school buses and has 3 UK rail franchises. Once in semi retirement, Trevor took on some other Directorships like the Chairman of Bristol and Sheffield airports and of the Greater Bristol Foundation, a local charity. He was also a non-executive director of UKRD radio stations and Bristol Water plc. As Trevor's home base had become entrenched in the South West of the country and with his commitments it was not easily possible for him to attend many home games although we did meet up at some of the away matches played in London and the South.

Meanwhile back in Rotherham the funds raised were being held in readiness in a solicitor's client account The new company formed to go forward was an "off the shelf company" called 'Changing Finish Limited '. The opening of the bank account was troublesome because of the club's past history, but after some plea bargaining with our own contacts within the banking fraternity Barclays Bank eventually stepped forward. Some of the monies that the club held could now be used to pick up the pieces ready for next season and some had to be retained by the solicitors for the settlement of certain legal bills arising from the Lease and the Football League arrangements.

I will not go on about the early work carried out as this is referred to in detail in the 'Ground Problems' chapter later in this book.

The achievement of finally raising the £500k share capital, whilst a relief, was only a start, and now work had to begin to generate a substantial commercial income for the club. David

Costin in particular started beating the drum for more ground board advertising, sales and sponsorships. He began selling space in areas of the ground that had never been thought of before. Others started working on kit sponsorship deals and season ticket sales.

It became obvious very quickly that Rotherham United was a very hungry animal that needed constantly feeding with cash. Vigorous fund raising was going to be an essential part of our everyday life from hereon in.

Chapter 4 (G.H.B.)

The Points' Dilemma

As the 2005/06 season was coming to a close Denis had been rushed off his feet raising cash, getting people on board, organising the ground and handling the little matter of the 10 points that would be deducted by the Football League if the club entered into Administration. The Lawyers had also been looking at this along with the rules prevailing at the time.

The Millers' performances on the pitch in the 2005/06 season had not been good, and the relegation situation was not settled until the last game of the season. The dilemma for Denis was "Do we take the 10 point deduction in this season or the next?". If we were going to get relegated we needed to go into administration before the end of the game, so taking the deduction in the already beleaguered 2005/2006 season and clearing the decks for the start of 2006/2007. This would mean the Millers could start their new League Two campaign on a level playing field with the other teams. Unfortunately, the timing of this was not too convenient for the plans to move forward but had to be accepted. Starting with minus 10 points would have been a lot to handle particularly when coupled with relegation.

Immediately before the last game, Swindon Town, Walsall, M.K Dons and Hartlepool United were all jostling with us in the relegation zone, so on Friday the 5th May, before the last game, plans were put into action. Under the Football League rules that were then in force, we had until a minute before the final whistle to lodge the administration papers for the old company's demise to count as happening in that season, and for the club to suffer the points' deduction there and then. (The rule has been subsequently changed because of the number of recent administrations.) All the necessary papers were prepared, and fax machines were primed as six separate faxes would need to be sent simultaneously.

Saturday 6th May 2006, the last game of the season, saw Rotherham playing M.K Dons at home. There was a good crowd of 7,625 because everyone knew that important issues would unfold on the field that afternoon. It was the decider as to who stayed up and who went down.

Volunteers manned the fax machines, sitting nervously by them with one ear tuned into the radio and with their mobile phones switched on and fully charged in readiness. They knew Denis would only ring them to say "go, go, go!" if he thought we were going to lose. There was no room for error. If we won and stayed up the administration order needed to be made in the following season and so the phones would remain silent.

The League One positions and points before this last game were:

Rotherham United	51
Hartlepool United	49
M.K. Dons	49
Swindon	47
Walsall	47 (Bottom of Table)

As one can see if Hartlepool and M.K Dons won then Rotherham would be relegated.

The tension was high both on and off the pitch. Denis became ever more nervous as the second half progressed. He watched the game intensely with his mobile phone gripped firmly in his hand. He was also getting text messages of any goals scored in the Hartlepool game. The teams were locked at 0-0 so if M.K Dons scored in the closing minutes he would be dialling away the instructions to fax the documents.

Pete Winkleman, the M.K. Dons Chairman, also became very emotional. He left the directors' lounge and sat with the away fans in the Railway End as soon as the game started. Wearing an away shirt, he told Denis, that if they were going down today it would be sad for the supporters and he wanted to be with them. To go down was clearly not part of their plan; they had pumped a lot of cash into M.K. Dons F.C. over the past few seasons.

When the 90 minutes were almost up desperate whistles echoed around Millmoor, but the agony was prolonged even further when the fourth official announced there was to be 4 minutes of added time. For Denis those 4 minutes must have seemed like 4 hours

Such was the tension that Denis said afterwards those 4 minutes caused him to go grey overnight. The final whistle eventually blew and Denis could once again begin to relax. It remained a 0-0 draw with Williamson being named as "man of the match".

The other relevant results that day were:

Swindon Town	0	Huddersfield	0
Hartlepool United	1	Port vale	1
Walsall	1	Barnsley	2

The final league position was:

Rotherham United	52
Hartlepool United	50
M.K. Dons	50
Swindon Town	48
Walsall	47

It was for Denis "a tense day at the office". I must mention that the euphoria of the crowd that day was as if we had been promoted. There was singing, shouting and dancing all around, apart from at the Railway End that is. Denis spotted Pete Winkleman walking back around the pitch with tears streaming down his face. Denis put his arm around him and said "Bad Luck". Peter replied to Denis "Don't feel sorry for me. Wait until you see the new set up we have. You wait and see we will bounce back because good things are coming to the Dons." Having since visited the M.K. Dons Stadium I now know exactly what he meant. It is one of the best new stadiums in the country.

Chapter - 5 (G.H.B.)

The First Board Meeting

Everyone had been working so hard over the summer, taking up their individual assignments so that they could deliver what the club required to go forward. We had plenty of informal meetings and discussions but we needed to formalise it all. Signs of friction had started to show, some being quite critical of others' handling of certain duties. This was not untypical of a new regime after the honeymoon period was over. We desperately needed to officially kick start the machine, so a first formal board meeting was called on 11 August 2006 for 9.30am at Brearley & Co's offices in Bridge Street, Swinton. It was agreed that I would initially chair the meeting. In attendance were Denis Coleman, Dino Maccio, David Costin, Paul Douglas, Alan Cartledge, Gavin Mackinder (Advisor to the Board), myself and a large plate of sandwiches.

I started the meeting by outlining the essentials of punctuality and attendance at all meetings. I also went on to state that it was no good back-biting and that we should work as a team. Differences should be put aside and we should proceed harmoniously. I then went on to quote extracts from Shakespeare's St Crispin's Day speech, duly edited as appropriate.

> "Now my fair cousins, if we are to fail, there are enough of us to do Rotherham's United's loss.
> If we are to survive, the fewer men, the greater share of Rotherham's honour.
> He who has no strength for this fight, let him depart.
> Why we will not fight as a Board in that man's company, who will not fight for Rotherham with us.
> We will all be remembreth from this day forth ,
> we few, we happy few, we band of brothers ,we are the Board of Rotherham's Directors.
> Others will be reviled they did not fight with us to make this Rotherham's day.
> We are but the Director warriors for the working day.
> Our gaineth and our guilt are all besmirched ,but our hearts are in the trim.

*We must seeketh out the Investors from places far and wide.
Note my fellow Directors all things can be done if our minds are so.
You know your places and what you have to do
So let God be with us all".*

With the performance over, the next item on the agenda was the election of chairman. David proposed Denis and it was unanimously agreed. Dino was proposed, also by David, to be vice chairman again, this was passed unanimously.

The next item covered the directors' agreement that I had drawn up, which would act as the rule book for the conduct of the board. It included such things as: - expenditure over £1000 on behalf of the club must be ratified by two additional directors. No expenses would be claimed by any director unless authorised by the board. Contact with the media was to be channelled through Denis, who could hire and fire, etc etc. The agreement covered a whole host of situations to which everyone agreed and, so, the directors duly signed, binding themselves to a set of operational rules. This proved invaluable over the next two years.

The following item on the agenda was ratifying the actual duties of the directors. This was to be as we discussed at our first informal meeting at Millmoor with one exception that needed formally minuting. Overseeing the Tivoli or Millmoor Suite was to become the responsibility of Denis. He had ideas and wanted to exploit these. We agreed that board meetings would take place fortnightly and again, it was stressed that all should attend.

Further discussions then centred around the Millmoor suite, where we had already encountered some problems. We agreed to engage a licensed stocktaker because there had been problems in reconciling the bar sales with the stock count in the previous months. We recommended a company from Manchester (C.J. Dormer) who were extremely professional and would most certainly root out any problems. It was agreed that we (Brearley and Co.) would operate the payroll for the club for the next few months and then train the club's existing accounts staff to take over from us. The next agenda item under its own heading was the need to bring in investors A.S.A.P. or to find an outright buyer for the club. These discussions entered every board meeting from hereon in.

One disappointing item on the agenda was that the BBC wanted to cut the amount of royalties to be paid to the club for broadcasting rights. This currently was £5000, which considering it gave full radio broadcasting rights for all of the games was not a lot for them to pay. I believe Barnsley F.C. took exception to this and so there were no more commentary games transmitted from Oakwell. They would rather that than be insulted. When I wanted to use a thirty second clip from an old edition of "Top of the Pops" for a local History film that I was involved in, they wanted over £300 for the UK territory only rights.

Gavin Mackinder took to the podium and went through the budget and projections for the coming season, so that we all had a clear understanding of what was required. The figures predominantly centred on the number of "bums on seats", and that would depend on the performance of the players on the pitch. This even impacted onto commercial and selling advertising; sponsors want to know that their ground board and adverts are going to be seen by a good crowd and not just by a devoted few.

Everyone was greatly excited by the forthcoming season. So far it was akin to our having rebuilt a motorbike in the garage all summer but never having had the chance to take it out. From hereon in, it was, hold tight, here we go on the white knuckle ride they call "running a football club".

We then issued the following Press release:

A "Hello" from the new club director, Giles Brearley FCMA, (senior partner of Brearley & Co Accountants).

"I would like to say a big hello to all of Rotherham United's loyal supporters. It is an honour to be invited to join the board of directors and hopefully help the club go forward.

As a Chartered Management Accountant, I will be bringing on board some much needed skills to strengthen the team. As a local historian, I have a passion for South Yorkshire and dearly want the club to continue as part of it.

The amount of work put in by the other directors over the summer was remarkable and without them, the club would not have survived.

We now have to all concentrate on going forwards. It is

going to be tough but not insurmountable in the least. What is vital is the continued support of you all and if possible, luring former fans back onto the terraces. You must all know someone – lets show the football world Rotherham is back and back with a passion."

One or two of our larger clients turned out to be regular fans of Rotherham and had the skills, ability and connections to help the club. I have approached these and something positive has come out of it. Assistance can take many forms. I would love to meet up with anyone who has something they feel they can offer to benefit the club. The fan base is from all walks of life but they do all tread the same path as far as Rotherham is concerned. Please do take this request seriously.

Rome wasn't built in a day and turning Rotherham back to its former glory will be time consuming but should be fun as well. Former glories in my book aren't good enough and once achieved should be no more than a milestone in the relentless march to take the club to new heights.

Over the next few weeks, some major announcements will be made as we all strive onwards.

Giles H Brearley   FCMA

And it was meant...

Chapter - 6 (G.H.B.)

The Lease From Hell and the 'Inhospitality' Agreement

The Millmoor lease that was assigned to us after Millers 05 ceased to exist had come into force originally on the 1st January 2005. It was for a term of 26½ years and was to expire on 30 June 2031. This lease had C F Booth Limited as landlords and Rotherham United FC Limited as the tenant.

I knew from the moment that I first saw the lease that it was going to be like a millstone round the club's neck. It had certainly been professionally prepared with only one party in mind: The landlord's.

The Rental terms contained the following, to which the club was legally bound:-

Rent and other related costs per month payable as follows:

Millmoor	£4583
Training ground	£417
Changing facilities at training ground	£250
Tivoli Suite	£2600
licence fee	£5370
licence interest	circa £2700

All in all giving the monthly total to find of £15,920 (£191,040 per annum).

The licence fee was the balance of the loan initially made to Millers 05, which was still outstanding. We had to take responsibility for that, whether we liked it or not.

It was a large amount of money to find every month when you consider the close season and the number of times we actually used the ground. The rents were subject to reviews in the year 2011, 2016, 2021 and 2026. The Tivoli suite could be reviewed earlier. Another area of concern was that the rates would be set in line with the rents being paid, as is customary. At this level that would only add to the burden.

Other terms were as follows:

Repairs – SHARED AREAS

> The club had to agree to pay a fair and proper contribution towards the cost and expense of constructing, repairing, rebuilding, renewing, lighting, cleansing and maintaining any areas which were being used in common in the premises and other premises. This included the responsibility for the extended car parking area at the rear of the stand, which was technically not part of the lease.

I could live with this.

Repairs – THE GROUND and TIVOLI.

> At all times during the term, the tenant shall maintain the premises in good and substantial repair and condition provided that the tenant shall not be required to put those parts of the premises in any better state of repair and condition, the state of which is evidenced by the schedule of conditions. To keep in good and safe repair all conduits (power mains, sewers) serving the premises and to indemnify the landlords from any claims arising from any failure to repair or the misuse or overloading of any conduits of the premises.

This would normally have been a deal breaker. The club was fully responsible for all repairs regardless. There would be no help from the Landlord. The ground and Tivoli were in a decrepit condition and were in need of urgent expenditure.

Repairs – THE EQUIPMENT.

> To maintain and serviceable repair and condition, the landlords fixtures and fittings and all apparatus, plant machinery and equipment including heating, sprinkling systems in or upon the premises and to replace such of them as they may become worn out or lost, unfit for use or destroyed by substituting others of a like or more modern nature and of equal value or

quality to the reasonable satisfaction of the landlord.

The equipment right across the board was old and near the end of its useful working life. The central heating in the Tivoli for example was based on old large bore pipes that due to boiler problems had only a very limited heat output. To remedy that alone would cost thousands of pounds and it was all down to us to finance under the terms of the lease.

The Yield Up

At the expiry or sooner determination of the term, the club had to yield up the premises to the landlord with vacant possession in such state and condition that shall in all respects, be consistent with the full and due performance by the tenant of the covenant contained within the lease. If so required by the landlord, the club would have to remove all fixtures and fittings installed in the premises during the term. It would have to make good to the reasonable satisfaction of the landlord, all damages caused as a result of the removal of the tenant of fixtures and fittings and the landlord's adjoining land. The club also had to agree not to object to any planning applications in respect of a scrap yard or any development of the landlord's adjoining or neighbouring premises.

Millmoor was in a poor dilapidated condition in reality and we knew the annual expenditure on repairs would burden the club like a second noose around its neck. This certainly proved to be the case with repairs expenditure in one year of over £100,000. When the electrics failed on the ground the costs could have been high so we approached the landlord to see if they would be prepared to assist... ...but no such assistance was forthcoming.

Forfeiture

The forfeiture of the ground can occur if the rents shall be in arrears or unpaid for a space of fourteen days after the same shall have the conduce (whether

A view from the upper tier at Bradford showing the huge size of the ground. They paid more rent than Rotherham but the facilities they had to work with were second to none.

Hereford's Team coach waits in front of our Porta Kabin changing rooms at Millmoor. Not very welcoming facilities for the players after such a long journey.

Lisa Costin in conversation with Ken Booth (Senior) at a home game.

The Qatar advertising sign above the stand at Brentford fetched the club in a £100,000 a year. The ground was right under the flight path for Heathrow and it gave the advertiser a bit of "one-upmanship" over the other Airlines.

formally demanded or not) or if there shall be any other breach/non-performance of any of the covenants or conditions herein contained.

Not a long negotiation time if your landlord wants to get tough. Oh and guess who has to pay for the legal fees of all this? R.U.F.C. So the landlord goes and selects any Solicitor it wants, has the best partner in the firm, have meetings with them, sue us and we pay for it all. Great, isn't it?

Development of Neighbouring Premises

The landlords are entitled to carry out or permit the development of any adjoining or neighbouring premises and to build onto or into any boundary wall of the premises or to re-route any services in the premises without payment of compensation to the tenant for any damage or otherwise, any loss, access of light or air to the premises.

So this gave the C F Booth Group the right to build up to our boundaries and if they want, block out our light, and we haven't the right to object.

Compensation

Any statutory right of the tenant to claim compensation from the landlord on vacation of the premises shall be excluded as far as the law allows.

"Lovely jubilee"

Landlords Option to Determine

The landlord shall be entitled by giving not less than eighteen months notice in writing to the tenant to terminate this lease on 30 June 2016 or any anniversary of that date. Expiration of such notice (providing the landlord pays to the tenant the sum of £50000), this lease shall absolutely cease and determine without affecting the rights of either party.

I was concerned that any exit had to be strategised early on as it could prove difficult tying up this date with say a new Stadium and what about the costs that may arise?.

Tenants Option to Determine

The tenant shall be entitled by giving not less than twelve months notice in writing to the landlord to terminate this lease on 30 June 2011 and any anniversary of that date provided that up to the termination date, the tenant shall have paid the rents reserved by this lease and the lease shall cease and determine without affecting the rights of either party for any earlier breach of covenant.

So this was at least a lifeline get-out clause for us If we could ever manage it.

In summary, our view of the lease was:-

The rental commitment was far too high. I discussed the situation of rents with various clubs as we travelled around with the games and found that we were paying the second highest rent in both leagues one and two. The highest rent of all was paid by Bradford City. Their rent was in the region of £560,000 per annum but the facilities they got were very good but probably way too high for a club operating in the lower league. Other clubs received the support of their local authorities, Notts County, for example, paid only £20000 per annum for their ground, which had fabulous facilities. It was owned by the city council who wanted football in Nottingham firmly in place. With their banqueting suites, etc, they could really earn other revenue to assist the club's finance.

The Exit costs were outrageous. When the original lease was taken out, there was no new stand. The ground was complete (albeit with poor facilities) and if the landlord so demanded, they could insist that the part-built new stand was removed at our cost and one built and put back similar to what was there previously. They could also insist that the large pile of earth and rubble stacked up behind the stand be moved, again at our cost. This was put there by the contractors after they had dug out the foundations for the new stand. As you can well imagine, the exit costs on this lease could cost a fortune. This would apply if we used the exit clause.

The hidden Costs of the Family Package Attached to the Lease

Attached to the lease and fully enforceable, was the agreement whereby the club agreed to:-

1. Make Ken Booth Senior (honorary president of the club).

2. To give Ken Booth entitlement to directors' box tickets for every away game of the club at no cost.

3. The advertising hoarding of C F Booth Limited shall remain in its current position and size at the railway end of the Millmoor football ground at no cost to CF Booths.

4. An advertising hoarding of C F Booth Limited of the same size shall be located in a site of similar prominence at any new ground used by the club at no cost.

5. Ken Booth shall be provided with four tickets for seats located in such areas, from time to time, be reserved for directors and/or executives of the club and four boardroom passes for every home game at no cost and a complimentary parking space be provided. This was to continue should the club move to any new ground.

6. Ken Booth shall be provided with sixteen tickets in the Millmoor Lane stand or in the equivalent stand at any new ground, should the club relocate, for every home game of the club at no cost.

7. Mr Carl Luckock shall be provided with two tickets for seats located in such area that, from time to time, be reserved for directors and or executives of the club with two passes to boardroom hospitality areas at no cost and complimentary parking space also to be provided and the same to be at any new ground. (Carl had previously sat on the Board of Directors of the Club back in Ken Booth's days).

8. Mr Booth shall be provided with four FA Cup Final tickets from the club's allocation save where the club does not receive four or more tickets in which case, Mr Booth shall receive whatever number are allocated to the club.

9. Mr Booth shall be afforded use of the club's physiotherapists at up to half hour per treatment three times per week at no cost.

10. Mr Booth shall be provided with six tickets of every home game of the club in the main stand or in the equivalent stand at any new ground should the club relocate, at no cost.

11. Following Mr Booth's death, the entitlement to receive directors' box referred to above, shall pass to his sons Mr Kenneth Frederick Booth Jnr and James Henry Booth in equal numbers.

12. Should the club enter into any arrangements to sell all or a substantial part of its holding in the shares of the company, it should make it a pre-condition of such sale that prospective purchaser enters into a legally binding obligation to Mr Booth or his sons, as the case may be, and Mr Luckock and C F Booth Limited to continue to procure compliance by the club with all the terms above.

13. The term of this agreement shall be from the commencement date and continue for seventy nine years thereafter.

Whilst some of the agreement was of no concern, there was a further loss of revenue to the club. The advertising board fee above the away stand would lose us another £5000 per annum. Interestingly, Brentford raised a six figure revenue from their stand by having the Qatar Airline painted across the entire surface. The ground was directly under the flight path of Heathrow and it was a bit of a oneupmanship to the other airlines. A previous sign had said "Fly K.L.M. next time" so passengers looking out of the Aircraft were greeted with that expression.

We calculated the full cost of the hospitality package in lost income to the club was another £31,000 per annum average.

We were deeply unhappy with the seventy nine year rule and the transfer of all these rights, should the club move to another stadium. We knew this would cause immense problems. For example, with a new community stadium shared with the rugby club and for use by the people of Rotherham, how could we impose onto the community those terms and conditions? Why should it be appropriate?

There were clearly no favours being handed out by the landlords and my view was that things would just get worse.

In the summer of 2006, contact was made with the club about the FA Cup tickets due under this agreement. We were indeed, threatened with legal action by DLA Pipers (C F Booth's Lawyers) for our apparent failure to honour this part of the hospitality agreement. This was extremely annoying as we had never received any FA Cup tickets. There is a ruling that if a club has been in CVA, the FA do not allocate tickets until the year after. We had to contact the FA, asking them to provide us with written confirmation of this as our landlords did not trust us . This was just another example as to how keen all the clauses were picked over and looked upon to be enforced. Whenever legal costs occurred, it was always at the expense of the club.

So where would we go from here?

We did write to C F Booth's to see if we could buy the Ground. We had the backing of six people who would stump up the cash on behalf of the club acting as a Private loan provider. We would let them put a charge on the assets and they would enter into an interest only finance deal. This would cut our costs substantially.

The letter I wrote for our Chairman to send was as follows;

23 November 2006
The Directors
C F Booth Limited
Clarence Metalworks
Armer Street
ROTHERHAM
South Yorkshire
S60 1AF

Dear Sirs

Re: Rotherham United Football Club and the Millmoor Ground

Following recent discussions and correspondence concerning the above matter with the local council and your legal advisors. The board of directors would like the opportunity to meet you and establish whether or not you are prepared to sell the ground to them and if so at what price.

We would like to suggest meeting in the Tivoli suite at lunch time early next week and trust you will liaise with Paul Douglas, the Chief Operating Officer of the football club to arrange which day would be most appropriate.

Assuring you of our best attention at all times.

Yours faithfully
D Coleman
(Chairman)
Rotherham United FC Limited

As you can well imagine we never even got a reply. But at least we tried. !!

CHAPTER - 7 (G.H.B.)

GROUND PROBLEMS

When David Costin took over responsibility as director in charge of the football stadium and training ground, I suspect he new little of what he was about to embark upon.

Periodically, safety advisors from the league would visit the grounds of all football clubs and categorise work that they considered needed doing. Subsequently, certain items started as low priority but eventually, move up the list. Let us say that by the time David took over, the high priority items on the list had become "top heavy". Things had been put off and put off before, but now the league were cracking the whip to get ground improvements back on target.

A large schedule of work had to be undertaken and completed before the start of the 2006/2007 season. This would prove very problematic and costly indeed. There was money in the bank but we had to stretch it as far as possible. Contact was made with many people trying to persuade them to do their little bit for the club preferably for free. This couldn't happen with everything that needed doing, but the response to the club's needs was terrific.

In particular if it was not for the support and donation of services given by the directors of Sheffield Site Services Ltd, the season may not have even kicked off. One item which had now come to the top of the list was the asbestos roof on the family stand, which had to be replaced. This would have cost thousands, which we could have ill afforded considering everything else. By the time we found out about this there was only four weeks left before the start of the new season. David was set to go on holiday for two weeks to Cyprus with his family. He was prepared to travel on later and let them go alone so that he could supervise everything, but we persuaded him not to in the end. Whilst away however he did spend a lot of his time on his mobile phone directing works from afar.

Sheffield Site Services not only attended to the roof for the club, they also concreted new areas where the toilets were, installed new dug outs and craned in new toilets into the ground. These were the toilets that were situated where the two lady stewards used to sit, one used to say "Mind the step, please" and the other one would say "Hello again". In addition to the donated time and materials we spent £150, 000 on other items essential to bring the stadium up to the league's acceptable standard..

The full work undertaken was:

New signage's all round, boxing in above turnstiles, decorating the front of the ground, redecoration to back areas of the Tivoli stand, putting all the toilets back in full working condition and decorating them, removing old electrical ducting and renewing wiring , tea bar refurbishment , safety markings being put in correct areas, re-newing all the red and white paint inside the ground itself, new nets and goal posts, new drains and repairs to existing drainage system at Millmoor Lane stand, 100 seat repairs, removing rogue trees and bushes, repairs to outside gates, bought the marquees and fitted them out, roof repairs to away supporters' club, erection of segregation fence behind the Railway End, repairs to gymnasium roof, repainting of Railway End stand, refurbishment of players tunnel area, fence off new stand at front and side, construction of new steps up the side of the new stand, provision of cabins for changing rooms, install electrics and plumbing facilities to cabins, new shale to edge of pitch area, creation of new advertising boards areas, new equipment for groundsman, new dugouts, reconcreting and step rebuilding to various areas, numbering all seats. New drains between old Tivoli stand and main drains, refurbishment of shop interior including new counter and shelving. What a list!

As the start of the season approached and with just three days left tradesmen were hurriedly finishing off their works. David and Lisa Costin were down at Millmoor following the tradesmen around, working every hour, carrying out cleaning works on the Wednesday, Thursday and Friday.

As the fans arrived for that first game on Saturday they had no idea of the efforts that had gone in to achieve the oracle so the gates could be opened up to them.

One problem for David was unfortunately the ground manager was on long term sick leave and did not return again. In the meantime, Liam Wheeler had been set on to assist. David stated that he would never have survived the tasks without the

David Costin at the Chesterfield game.

Finishing touches being put to Millmoor by Neil and Bob in a race against time to be ready for the 2006/7 season. They volunteered a lot of their time, undertaking many tasks.

The view from the Community stand of the adjoining C. F Booth's works.

A view across the pitch at Millmoor just before the 2006/7 season commences, highlighting the unfinished main stand.

dedication of Liam, who worked like a trooper and put in extra unpaid hours to ensure the stadium met the deadlines given to it. Quite rightly, Liam was offered the Stadium Manager position when it finally became vacant and was duly accepted.

As the ground was not in good repair, David was constantly challenged with a whole host of problems. The electrics became an ongoing nightmare and cost the club thousands in repair bills.

Another problem occurred following a visit by the safety advisor in that he insisted the marquee, which we had purchased from Rudy Enos for £30,000, be dismantled after 28 days and then re-erected after a short break. David argued on this point for many months. It would be completely impractical to comply with this request. In the end, the safety advisor accepted the position and the marquee remained in place. The floor of the marquee was loaned from a friend of Denis. As time went on the friend realised that he wouldn't get his boards back and that we weren't in a position to hire them, so he good heartily turned the banter into "I would never have used all them floor boards anyway"

Surprisingly, after Millmoor was vacated, the marquees were left in place to the benefit of the C F Booth group as landlords. They would have been saleable and I am surprised the new owners did not try to capitalise on them.

The marquee was subject to vandalism attacks periodically when mindless, wanton morons would enter the ground, cut their way into the marquee and smash up televisions and anything else that took their fancy. I never can understand the mentality of these idiots. Looking after the stadium was the kind of job that could not be taken on light heartedly. David often found himself down at the ground, working in the wings for long hours, to remedy problems. All in all, we directors felt he did a fantastic job and made the facilities for the club acceptable.

There was one incident in May 2006 that made us smile for many months after. David was passing the ground one evening, he noticed a white van was backed up to the shop and this gave him great concern. With no further ado, he swung his car into the car park and went to challenge the two men and a woman who he discovered were removing stock from the shop. He demanded to know who they were and how they had gained entry. It became clear they had gained entry by a member of staff

Paul Douglas at Dagenham and Redbridge. Note the small crowd facilities in the background. We won the game 2-0 in front of a crowd of only 2091 which included 414 Rotherham fans.

secreting a key for them, which they then used. They had driven down from Newcastle and the company was "Just Sports". R.U.F.C had given them a concession whereby they supplied stock to the club for sale in the shop, having their own dedicated area to do so. Once sold there would be a profit for all. David challenged the legitimacy of what they were doing and asked them to return the stock to the club and approach the club properly with any proposals.

Their attitude turned rather abusive and the lady jumped into the van, started the engine and started to pull away with the stock inside already secured. David ran across and turned the engine off by placing his arm through the window and grabbing the key. The lady claimed injury, saying that David had assaulted her. The two men then turned on David and a "battle royal" ensued. Dave Douglas (Paul Douglas' brother) had just called at the ground and seeing the fracas ran across to assist. Being the big lads they both are, the joint force proved insurmountable and the two men started to back off. The police had actually seen the incident taking place from one of their street cameras and instructed officers to arrive at the scene.

The timing of all this was rather unfortunate as upstairs in the Millmoor Suite, Paul Douglas was addressing a group of parents who were in the process of allowing their child to be signed to the Rotherham Youth Team, so becoming a future prospect for the club. As Paul was reassuring them that Rotherham United was a caring, family club that took its responsibilities seriously, out of the window, one could see flashing blue lights pouring onto the car park and the club's director in the middle of a melee of flying fists and a punch up. Paul said afterwards that the situation was unbelievable. "I was trying to portray the club's true image when all this was visible out on the club's car park. I didn't know what was happening at the time and was torn as to whether to dash out immediately or try to cover matters up." As it transpires, the parents were very understanding of matters and no-one left.

The lady who had claimed David had assaulted her whilst she was trying to drive the van had her claim rejected outright by the police. They had the incident all down on CCTV and saw what happened, so there was no case to answer. So for David, this was just another day in paradise. I am glad that he took on the stadium duties and certainly not me!

The upkeep of the ground was a constant running battle. You would often be accosted at the most unexpected times to have a repair notice verbally slammed on you. One night I was in the Travellers Rest at Swinton when Colin (a great R.U.F.C fan) told me the speaker at the far corner in the Tivoli was still not working. The week before he had told me the toilets were blocked again. In the Ring o Bells on the Friday another fan told me his seat was split and could it be sorted out. One certain bank manager, who I came across with clients from time to time, would always apologise to the client for diversifying and would then engage me in ten minutes of banter about the Millers with recommendations for some ground improvements or essential repairs.

Once whilst Denis was on a Radio Sheffield phone-in a lady called up and said "I have had the same seat for 15 years at the edge of the uncovered section of the Tivoli stand and every time it rains I get soaked to the skin. What can you do about it?" Denis hastily said that because of the ownership issues surrounding the ground the board could not sanction any further ground improvements but he would gladly find her another seat undercover.She wasn't happy about that and said she wanted to stay where she was, so what was he going to do about that then? He paused for a second then in total frustration said "Well in that case I suggest you bring an umbrella". It may not have been the most politic response one might have expected from the chairman but when your hands are tied and people ask the most ridiculous things then human nature takes over and in this case she got what was coming to her.

Chapter 8 (Joint)

Cutting Costs

One of our (Brearley & Co's) first jobs after being appointed was to despatch partners Gavin Mackinder and John Hesselden to meet with Clare Yeardley who ran the accounting systems at the club. They were operating a Sage accounts system, which Clare handled competently. But to have a more meaningful management tool we needed the accounts to contain specific cost centres. Reorganising the monthly accounts would give us a more detailed breakdown of departmental performance and activity. This would help highlight problems. There were many sources of income but unless we could line up the relevant expenditure we did not know how profitable each department was.

The Club's income was generated from:
- Football League sponsorship
- Season ticket & other ticket sales
- Cup runs
- Concessionaires
- Shop sales and catering
- T.V & radio
- Grants & donations
- Player sales
- Raffles & draws
- Programme sales and programme advertising revenue
- Corporate hospitality, Rotherham Utd Suite, bars & activities
- Match day bars
- Royalties
- Website advertising
- Centre of excellence
- Ground boards & perimeter advertising.
- Commissions
- Sundry

Once the monthly accounts and revised cost centres had been implemented there were other matters to attend to. There was a legal requirement to issue contracts of employment to all the staff and to

Mark Hitchens setting out the new stock in the Millers club shop.

carry out a review of the payroll procedures and scrutinise all suppliers' contracts and finance agreements. When one becomes involved in a new business you need to spend some time studying closely its operations and the complexity of its procedures before you can seriously make any productive changes, and that is just what we did.

It was clear from the start that the costs were far too high for the club to be a viable proposition. We had prepared a budget based on the existing financial figures, which were very much a carry over from the Millers 05 regime, but it needed major surgery. After interviewing much of the management team to establish their individual cash requirements, it became obvious they were over burdensome and if left unchecked could put the club's cash reserves in jeopardy. We revised the business plan several times before we came up with a model that would just about get us by. Part of this model involved major cost cutting. Over the next few months we changed power, heat and light suppliers, changed telephone service providers, terminated certain equipment rentals, replaced some other rentals with less demanding agreements, made enquiries with new insurers, cut back on pre-match entertainment expenditure, returned motor vehicles we were paying for and borrowed others for free, insisted on old stocks being utilised before fresh orders were made.

To tighten things up further, we put a system in place that no-one at the club could commit to expenditure above £500 without authorisation from ourselves. Unfortunately at first, this did not get implemented too easily and some people carried on regardless. Clare would telephone our office to inform us that an invoice had landed from out of the blue, above £500 and to askwhether we were aware of it. At first about 99% of Clare's questions were about purchases unauthorised by us. This would then embroil us in a series of disputes, in which the unofficial networking between staff would kick in accusing us of stopping people doing their jobs. We stood our ground on this point and eventually it was accepted.

One area that we constantly found ourselves having to agree to funding was essential repairs on the ground. The dilapidations were extensive and urgent work needed to be done on a regular basis. The directors, David Costin in particular, helped minimise the effects of this problem by persuading local businesses to donate their services in carrying out the repairs. David was very good at convincing them that their contributions were paramount in keeping the club alive. We always tried to reward these firms in other ways as a thank you, bearing in mind these requests were in addition to those previous pleas for help when the ground needed a complete overhaul to meet the Football Leagues requirements. David also seemed to know what skills he could best utilise from the hundreds of people he came into contact with. There were many times when the father of one of the youth team's players would be seen at the ground with his toolkit after finishing work. It was like one big happy family.

Because we did not have any formal banking facilities as such, we deferred the credit payments, which helped us increase our day-to-day cash flow requirements at the club. No cost was overlooked, we even stopped payments being made for the match day mascot and instead Paul Douglas found a volunteer. I also asked Paul to approach Jimmy Carroll of Radio Sheffield to see if he would terminate the contract he had been given for half-time entertainment in the marquee. Fortunately he beat us to it and decided the contract was too onerous and asked if we would agree to terminate his services. This was music to my ears as I didn't want to upset him. I have met him many times and seen him perform as an after dinner comedian. He was very good.

Clare's job was relatively high pressure. She was not just carrying out daily accounting duties but also had to use her cash management skills and report to us where and when she felt variances to our budgets were appearing. This was not always popular with the other staff.

Certain aspects of the costs were out of the club's control and, as such, we were subjected to large price increases without much notice. The policing costs increased substantially. We were told in advance what the costs would be for the forthcoming season; there was no room for negotiation. A further examination of whether the policing cost could be lessened by using extra stewards soon proved that any saving would be minimal. Another escalating cost was South Yorkshire Ambulance Service, again without much notice. In this case, we found that the East Midlands Ambulance Service would willingly come into South Yorkshire, carry out the same service and save the club money.

Policing costs skyrocketed without warning.

They had a depot near Eckington and were keen to come on board. .

Clare, however, had become frustrated with her job and decided to leave. We tried to persuade her to stay but she had clearly made her mind up. It was the summer of 2007 and after several years service to the club under 3 different regimes she had finally decided the stress of managing the finances on a day to day basis was too much. She handed in her notice to leave at the beginning of August, just as the new season was about to commence.

To be honest I couldn't blame Clare. She was in her mid twenties and had taken on a huge amount of responsibility for a person so young. She had done a fantastic job but the wand she found herself waving and wishing upon every day had finally lost its magic and for her it was time to move on.

This left us with the problem of her replacement. Gavin had the idea of bringing in David Ness, who had worked for one of our client's and had proved himself to be very competent. He was much more experienced than Clare in overall accounting and had management skills. He was, to say the least, a little surprised when we called him, but he agreed to meet us at Millmoor, later that week.

At that meeting we explained all the ups and downs "warts and all" from the day we became involved 12 months earlier and also what we knew from when Denis and Dino originally took over the reigns back in March 2006. The most poignant thing about David was that he relished a challenge and this was the main factor that had recommended him to us. I could see as the meeting unfolded that he was getting more excited about this new opportunity and the rewards it may bring for himself, the club and the community if he could help turn things round. He was not an entirely money motivated man but expected to be paid fairly and reasonably for the job he did. He wasn't after a quick buck and would not try to make a killing even though he realised our situation was rather desperate. After careful consideration he said he would be willing to come on board and agreed to meet with Paul Douglas and the staff the following Monday. David came at a higher cost pro-rata than Clare, but he brought with him a lot of skills the club urgently required.

In addition to overseeing the day-to-day accounting activity, we asked him to carry out a further review on management areas and systems to implement and further reduce overheads.

He recommended a new management structure for the club, which was presented, to us at our board meeting. It entailed some merging of duties, which would generate further cost savings. To take matters further, new job descriptions were provided and the staff were then invited to apply for the new positions. The Rotherham Advertiser picked up on this and reported that we were making compulsory redundancies, which wasn't the case. Some staff took this as their opportunity to leave by not applying. We were limbering up and sharpening the pencil. I think that some of the board thought that David's proposals would put too much strain on people at the club but Gavin and I pointed out it was crucial, as we still needed to reduce costs. Eventually the proposals were accepted and a new enthusiasm was shown by the staff, who realistically knew something had to give.

When David Ness first arrived, Denis said he was like a breath of fresh air and wished that we had been able to use his services earlier. He was given the nickname "Elliot Ness" the untouchable by the board members because of his very forthright approach to getting the job done. We all knew he was not taking any prisoners in this crusade to get the club firing on all four cylinders. He would report to the board once a month on the progress he had made in various areas. After a few meetings the report showed that certain areas were not bringing enough revenue into the club for the time and effort that was being expended on them. We always followed these up. Many viewed David as being a hatchet man. He reviewed suppliers' terms, looking for alternatives. and he was instructed by us to look to renegotiate where possible. He would upset people who often went crying to Denis. These issues would be reported to me as Finance Director but I backed David up when his actions were raised in Board Meetings. Paul and Gavin often joined me in defending his corner.

Things started to become more difficult when David challenged some of the board of directors to stop interfering in the day to day matters he was looking into. Both Gary Hall and Dave Costin argued with Nessy as invariably his reviews crept into their responsibility domains. That made things a little harder as at times I would be the only director who wished for him to continue.

When I sat people down and talked them through it, I did win back some support. A big part of the problem was that David's world was black or white with little or no grey. Although his new management systems had given everyone an opportunity to prove themselves, some staff had responded but others had not. Unfortunately Denis was beginning to form a dislike for David especially when he challenged the chairman on one or two issues. Denis was now starting to believe everything that he was told from his confidants down at the club. At one point a heated discussion about a new supplier's services that David wanted to introduce and that Denis thought was a waste of money turned into a blazing stand up argument in the car park, with the chairman finally telling him to leave the premises immediately.

David called me at my office to explain what had happened and that he wasn't sure if he had been told to go home for the day or stay at home for good. I suggested he did go home to avoid any further confrontation, and that we would speak to Denis and hopefully smooth things over, as we didn't want to spoil all the good work we believed he was doing over a simple misunderstanding.

David Ness did a great job for the club and it was unfortunate that his and Denis's personalities clashed. I had trouble at times explaining that David had nothing to gain by his actions and was only serving the best interests of the club. The suppliers may well be very nice people and may have been involved with the club for years, but just maybe a few of them were now serving the best interests of their own profit margins, which we could ill afford. During the administration of the club, David stayed on to assist Jeremy Bleazard, but when he and the new owner Tony Stewart did not see eye to eye they parted company shortly afterwards.

Another area we got involved with was scrutinising sponsorship packages sold by the commercial department. We found that one of the commercial managers had done a deal for the club where, in return for a supply contract for goods, a supplier would undertake certain sponsorship deals. We discovered that the increased costs to the club nowhere near matched the sponsorship pledges. The statistics on some commercial managers' reports may have looked good on paper but the bottom line effect was the opposite.

The role of commercial manager was a difficult task that needed ingenuity. There was always the temptation to keep hounding the same sponsors, the ones who had always been very good with us in the past. They however often complained that, whilst they did their bit, they could not help but notice that it was always the same old faces and that there was no new blood supporting the cause. I did once confront Tobin (a character later introduced in this book) about this problem and he subsequently did take a corporate table for his firm and really enjoyed his experience. But in true Tobin style the booking was made under his wife's maiden name. Of all the commercial managers we employed, Bob Gorrill probably generated the most income. However, it was just not quite what the hungry Rotherham United needed and you could sense the rot was setting in when the reports to the Board became so transparent.

Even the press saw little cup prospects.

One of Gavin's jobs was not only to prepare the budget but to keep them under constant review. If the variance to budget was becoming too adverse we had to react immediately. It was no use adopting the attitude "something will turn up in the end". We needed to be pro-active. From time to time the variance would even be in our favour when the club qualified for certain windfalls like the Carling Cup draw, when Sheffield Wednesday came to Millmoor and Sky TV decided they would like to cover this local derby event. This gave Rotherham (and SWFC) an unexpected £50,000 bonus each. I know Sky plan their viewing schedules keenly but I don't think they do enough for the lower league clubs. More coverage of games would help generate much needed cash resources and help clubs with advertising. There is no better selling tool than pointing out that your advertising boards will not only be seen by the crowd attending the match but by a T.V. audience as well. This is particularly important with the shirt sponsors. There is a growing audience worldwide of U.K. football and the exposure of all clubs to the world opens up opportunities. Look at the Accrington Stanley sales of membership packages to the fashionable Chinese economy (covered in a later Chapter).

A few months before the Sheffield Wednesday game, Denis and Dave Costin had a meeting with the people from Sky T.V. to enquire why we hadn't been selected for broadcast recently. Amazingly Sky indicated it was because the stadium manager had upset one of their top men. Denis and Dave realised that this was a former employee and confirmed to Sky that he was no longer at the club, assuring them they would be well looked after

A good crowd in the away end at Millmoor in the Carling Cup game against Sheffield Wednesday. The local derby crowd was good at 6,416 but not as high as we had hoped even with Sky TV coverage. None the less if only it was like that every game.

Sheffield Wednesday Director's at Millmoor. Chairman David Allen is seen consulting his programme. Following his resignation from Sheffield Wednesday a few weeks later, we approached him to see if he would come on board at Rotherham. The match was on 16th August 2007 and we lost 3-1 .

under the new regime. The meeting ended with the promise from Sky that an opportunity would soon be forthcoming, which it was.

In 2007/08 we received some much needed extra cash from the Premier League as a solidarity payment, which we had been calling for at the Football League's finance meetings for quite a while. The number of insolvencies occurring in football clearly sent the message that the funding arrangements were inadequate and that unless something was done there might not be a League Two in the future. It was a case of too little too late as far as we were concerned but anything was welcome especially when it was not in our budget and would help ease the pressure on cash flow.

In the January 2008 transfer window there was talk of another gem of a sale for us from our aspiring youth goal keeper. Chinese whispers were all around with talks of Premier Clubs eyeing up our young protégé with a good deal for Rotherham United to come from it. We had already had a bid from Sunderland for him previously of £50,000 up front with add ons possibly taking the fee up to £250,000. Denis turned this down knowing it was not enough. One had to appreciate that as a lower league club we were often seen as nothing more than a feeder club for the higher leagues. It was disappointing for the team manager, grooming his young players to see them whisked away, to fetch in survival cash. The fans only get a few seasons worth, watching the new blood develop, but not as a long term member of the team taking the club forward. Without the lower leagues the Premiership would struggle to fill its hungry demand for top class players.

Speaking of players, the budget was always a bone of contention. I felt certain players were well overpaid and this impacted on the business plans. When a good, young player was approaching a contract review, there were many issues with the dreaded Football Agents, who with their knowledge of what other young pros were earning, would put the club under great pressure to offer something well over our budget. I hated the interventions of these leeches and proposed at a Board Meeting that they not be granted free passes to games. If they wanted to come to the ground then let them buy a ticket like everyone else. They were only there in my view to make mischief.

CHAPTER - 9 (JOINT)

ALBANIA HERE WE COME

Mike Williams was a friend of Alan Knill's who came to a few of our home games. He had quite strong links with some overseas countries including Albania. He had set up his own football agency and was developing strong links with a view of introducing quality overseas players into the English Football League. Worldwide, the English league is seen as the kingpin, and any footballer worth his salt has an ambition to play in it.

In conversations Mike had with Denis, it came to light that football in Albania was quite big business; the clubs there were keen to forge links with overseas clubs and they had funds to invest along the way. Various letters went back and forth from our club to Mike Williams and Albania and, at the end of June 2006, arrangements were made for Denis and Paul to fly to Albania to meet various football personnel and potential investors.

Ruth Brearley (left) in deep conversation with Debbie Knill at Scunthorpe with the Rotherham Directors in the background.

They flew out late on a Friday morning and checked into their hotel late that afternoon. Paul remembers that it was blistering hot. That evening, a meeting was arranged between them, Mike Williams, the Albanian contact Freddi and another gentleman with strong UEFA contacts and who owned a group of hotels. The talks seemed to go well and Freddi was very interested in forging further links. His son, Franzi, was to have trials with the Rotherham youth team.

A further meeting was arranged the next day in Tirana, and while they waited for the meeting to start Denis and Paul were accosted by the press for some interviews. They wanted to know all about Rotherham United and football in England. At the meeting were four Albanian businessmen, one of them in particular appeared extremely dour and foreboding, which gave him a menacing persona. Denis and Paul explained Rotherham's predicament and they outlined Rotherham's long football history, whilst they described the current football scenario in Albania. The idea of being a director of an English club seemed very appealing and they hinted that if this occurred they would possibly be able to broker a deal for TV rights in Albania for Rotherham United's games and perhaps the Millers would become Albania's adopted son. They had indicated that funds were available to invest for the right proposition. One of the businessmen Sokol Abdalli was managing director of MBA Sh.p.k who owned the national Mercedes franchise for the country as well as other high profile businesses. When Denis told them the £3 million estimated cost to complete the main stand, they didn't bat an eyelid.

The Albanians explained that Rotherham United could be the key to open the door for them into the much cherished English Football League. They hoped to nurture and develop their home grown talent through a club like Rotherham despite Paul pointing out there was a lot of red tape and special rules regarding overseas players. They also discussed briefly their intentions to establish various businesses in South Yorkshire in the near future. After the meeting, they went for dinner in a nearby restaurant and got to know each other a little better. As they started to depart from the evening, Denis was accosted by foreboding when he remembered some further questions he wanted answering. Paul gestured over to Denis to come on and he hastily excused himself from the discussion. That evening, Freddi contacted them and asked whether they could meet more journalists. They agreed and they were taken by limousine to a TV studio. Paul kept thinking "where the hell are they taking us". Eventually the car stopped and they were ushered inside. This was a bit of a shock, as they never expected anything like this.

Once inside, they were taken to a studio where a live broadcast was taking place. They waited until the light over the door turned green and they were then whisked in. The announcer readily introduced them to the watching audiences and they then took part in a live three hour chat show being transmitted on Albania's main T.V Channel. It was a Football programme and was showing the Colombian 2006 World Cup game. Denis and Paul were frequently asked for their views on the game etc.

Thoroughly exhausted at the end of it, a taxi took them back to the hotel, where they caught up with some much needed sleep. The next morning when Denis and Paul went for a stroll along the city streets, people were constantly stopping them and shaking their hands. It seemed like everyone had watched the T.V show the night before and recognised the duo. There were also photographs and articles about them in the national newspapers. On Sunday, a further meeting took place and they agreed that the best way forward would be for the Albanian's to visit Millmoor, see a game and then engage in further talks. At the airport going home, the fame of Denis and Paul continued and they were whisked through as if they were diplomats, avoiding passport control and customs.

The first game the Albanians could attend was at home against Scunthorpe United. They arrived on Friday 18th August 2006 and booked their own flights and accommodation and duly flew into Manchester, where they were met and chauffeured to Rotherham to meet the board of directors.

Denis arranged for them to meet Roger Stone and Mike Cuff at the Rotherham Town Hall and a special dinner was laid on for them. The language barrier was a slight hurdle but they did understand a little Italian and Dino could converse with them and answer certain queries they had.

I had explained at a previous meeting that if we were successful in getting the Albanians to invest in Rotherham United, we would need to hire a firm of international accountants with an Albanian office to provide us with an audit certificate to confirm that the proceeds of the sale were from legitimate sources and accountable and that tax had been paid on the sums. Under money laundering regulations we would have to get them to 'prove the funds'. A meeting had been arranged later that afternoon at Carlton Park Hotel, which Gavin attended. The directors arrived with their guests about 4pm travelling straight from the town hall reception to the hotel where a meeting room had been set aside. Introductions were made and after a few light refreshments the business commenced. As well as Freddi and Sokol two other associates were in attendance, Artan and Adrean were two well connected businessman one of which was a merchant banker and had financed mergers and acquisitions in Albania and Europe on many occasions. He was a major shareholder in the bank and and was very keen to interrogate Gavin as to the true financial state of affairs at the club.

The meeting lasted at least two hours and we provided as much information as we felt necessary to wet their appetite even further. One had to realise that whilst Albania was a country often cut off from the rest of Europe due to the regimes in power over the last fifty years or so, the new found liberal thinking had given these businessman the freedom to explore new areas and generate wealth which had been stifled in the past. They were very shrewd entrepreneurs and wouldn't be carried away with the euphoria of owning or part owning an English football club. The amount of money they were initially prepared to invest wasn't quite as much as had been intimated during talks in Albania.

The merchant banker seemed to be the one who would be underwriting the funds and indicated that maybe an initial sum of £200,000 followed by further investment over the next three years. We couldn't pin them down as to what the total investment might be as they were hedging their bets as to the level of achievement at the club and I guess would wish to re assess the position in 6 months time. It was also unclear what they wanted in return for their investment. We suspected a minority share initially; building up to a significant holding if all was progressing nicely. This however was not apparent from the discussions, as they seemed more interested in having a seat on the board as consideration for their financial input. It was agreed to put together a more detailed business plan based on our discussions and email this to them within the next 4 weeks for

Left to Right Artan Abdalli, Roger Stone, Sokol Abdalli, Mike Williams, Denis Coleman, Dave Costin and Freddi.

their consideration and the meeting was drawn to a close.

The following day was our home game against local rivals Scunthorpe United and the return of Billy Sharp our ex youth team "jewel in the crown" who was transferred to Sheffield United several years earlier then subsequently sold on by them a few seasons later. Both our own Will Hoskins and Billy Sharp were currently on fire and leading the goal scoring charts for League One so it was a game we were all looking forward to. The Albanians were given the VIP treatment and sat with the directors to watch the match. After only 5 minutes Sharp scored with a near post header from a set piece to put Scunthorpe ahead. The Millers rallied the troops and for the rest of the game looked the better side throughout. Goals from Pablo Mills and a screamer from Eugene Bopp secured the points for Rotherham in a 2-1 victory in front of a 4,700 crowd. It was good to finish on a positive note, the fans went home happy, the Albanians had enjoyed the experience and we were very hopeful that the last few days had been time well spent in securing potentially the financial future of the football club.

Alas despite all our efforts including the revised business plan the Albanians never followed up their interest in the club. We never got a proper explanation. Maybe they didn't have the funding that was needed or perhaps they expected a larger slice of the cake. Whatever the reason, it was back to the old drawing board for us and realistically we should probably be looking a little closer to home.

Chapter - 10 (G.H.B.)

Boardroom Skirmishes

Just after I agreed to become the financial director I got a phone call at my office. It was Dino. He wanted to meet up with me, alone, so we could have a chat. He wanted to tell me his views on how things should be run at Millmoor while we looked for an investor for the club. It was decided that we would meet at the Earl of Strafford pub in Hooton Roberts as it was about half way between us.

We found a quiet table and had a good chat. He certainly had views on many things which he talked about with a passion. It was obvious that Dino was passionate about the club but I sensed that perhaps there were some cracks starting to appear in his relationship with Denis. Over the next few months, those cracks began to resemble deep crevices.

Dino Maccio sat with his young son Livio at the Bradford game on the 26th August 2006.

Dino was also pushing for Alan Cartledge to be formally made a director of the club. Alan had been working in the wings for some time and had attended board meetings, He felt that he was acting in the capacity of a Director and that this should be duly reflected. I think Dino originally met Alan through his being a regular customer at Dino's restaurant in Wickersley. In the August 2006 Board Meeting Dino was minuted as saying "Alan has been with the board of directors from the start and has put a considerable amount of time into the club. The offer of a directorship should now be made as he has not actually received any gratitude for the work he has done".

One September day I was in my office when reception rang to say that Alan and Dino had turned up and wanted to see me for just ten minutes. "Just ten minutes" I scoffed "The number of times I've heard that before over the years." I agreed to see them although I had another appointment within 30 minutes. They again reiterated Alan's case as to why he should be officially brought on board. I did raise the subject of Alan's appointment at the next board meeting as agreed and he was duly accepted. I must say this was with some reluctance by Denis. Perhaps he realised that Dino was lining up an ally for himself in the event of any future conflict?

As the weeks went by board meetings at times became quite stressful as Denis and Dino clashed openly. David Costin knew Dino from years gone by and had a little mistrust of him. David would raise points in meetings and Dino would often fly back at him. Denis would rally to David's defence and it would all kick off again. Whilst the other board members knew each other well, Gavin and I were the new kids on the block and were often left in the unenviable position whereby our vote could swing the balance either way when controversial matters were at a stalemate.

The main dispute centred on the then Tivoli suite. Originally, this was put under Dino's control. He had the experience of running bars and functions through his restaurant, and was the obvious choice. He frustrated us, though, by informing us of deals he was doing regards the suite, many of which never materialised. The suite was also a source of many complaints and was not operating properly. Some of the problems were down to the antiquity of the equipment. More importantly though was that it was losing money. That was something we did not need.

It was decided that Denis would take over responsibility for the suite's operations. Denis' answer to the suite's problems was to negotiate a deal with a brewery, get some cash and tidy the premises up. Denis and David called in some big favours, trying to get the suite looking right. Several friends of Denis took a week's holiday from work and toiled every day for free to assist. One of them was a big Sheffield Wednesday fan named "Chappie". At the end of the week Denis presented him with a Rotherham United watch that had been found in a drawer upstairs. His nickname from thereon was "Johnny Miller".

Dino's beef with the renovations was that he could have done all this, but was put off doing so, as it was getting the club into further debt. His other beef was that the total capital expenditure was well in excess of the loan amount, and taking up valuable extra cash from our scarce resources. Friction continued; each party often accused the other of interfering in its responsibilities. The suite proved to be a headache from start to finish as far as I was concerned. The overall structure was sound, but years of neglect meant the heating was inadequate and would cost thousands to update, and the electrical equipment installed there (the pa system and stage lighting, etc), worked only intermittently and ruined a few bookings as the entertainers were left with a very poor sound and light show.

One irritating thing Dino did, I believe to try and prove himself to us, was to make wild claims, like arranging friendly matches with top Italian sides as fund raisers, matches that always fell through for the most bizarre reason. He once told us that he was talking to Alex Ferguson and we were having a friendly against Manchester United. This info was passed onto the local Newspapers and proved a little humiliating for the club, as Manchester United seemed to know nothing of it?

Dino would also tell us he had lined up Armani as shirt sponsors, but as with the Italian games, we were let down again and nothing came of it. I could never grasp if it was all in his imagination or he was making statements before he had actually really approached anyone and got anything agreed. Some people are like that.

I always found Dino to be mild mannered but some R.U.F.C staff were terrified of him. There were a few incidents where certain staff members were reduced to tears. Paul would step in to console them and stop them from leaving. I was concerned that we may end up at an Employment Tribunal and I would regularly remind the Board that civility was essential. I could sympathise with Dino's frustration, as clearly staff were not toeing the party line and were doing us a disservice at times.

As Winter 2006 came, Alan Cartledge began to miss a few board meetings for personal reasons and, so, Dino stood up at every meeting alone to labour on about the Tivoli Suite. Denis would equally demand answers to issues over the ticket office and the stocking of the club shop that had raised a few problems. It was becoming unbearable and unprofessional. At one meeting, Denis and Dino nearly came to blows. It could not go on like this. I asked Alan if he was going to start coming to board meetings again and he snapped at me. Dino, unfortunately in my estimation spoiled himself when it emerged he had used the club credit card, that he held in good faith to pay some sizeable private expenditure nothing to do with the club. This was in breech of the shareholders' agreement we had all signed. When we questioned him on the subject, it fuelled another row. He did pay the money back, as he claimed he always intended to; but after talking to him privately I advised him to offer his resignation and bow out quietly for the good of the club.

The board meeting on the 21st December 2006 centred on Dino and Alan. It came to a crescendo when Denis and David realising the hopelessness of it all said they would both resign immediately and leave Dino and Alan to run the club. After much negotiation and arbitration between private meeting rooms Dino and Alan reluctantly agreed in the best interest of the club to tender their resignations forthwith.

I genuinely wanted us to part on friendly terms. Dino had worked hard from the start and it was a shame for it to end this way. Dino may have personally felt justified in using some of the clubs funds as he had probably lost a lot more by being prevented from operating his business, putting so much time into the Millers. Although I tried to keep matters amicable, it was obvious that the clock could not be turned back and the original friendship of Dino and Denis and David could never be rekindled. It was a shame all this had occurred. I did not know Dino sufficiently well to formulate any real opinion of him. I did think, though, that he had perhaps let himself down at this point; unfortunately worse things were to come.

A few weeks earlier Gavin had received a call from Clare Yeardley informing him that Alan Cartledge had been in the accounts office going through the clubs financial records. This amazed me as it was our department and, if he had a query, he should have come to us first. I did talk to him about this and he was a little non-committal as to what exactly he was doing. As previously stated, shortly afterwards Alan resigned as a director of the club along with Dino. He probably felt his position may have become untenable. He had some good marketing ideas, like the sale of flags to hang around the ground with Rotherham's colours on but decorated with different company logos. During the first year, the revenue would not have been high because of the costs of the flagpoles but in the second year, it would generate a good commercial income. Unfortunately, this never got past its original blueprint.

One thing that often frustrated us at the board meetings was when Alan announced he had mystery backers who he was working on to come forward and invest in the club. He was repeatedly asked for their identity, only for him to tell us that he could not reveal who they were at this stage of the negotiations. Well, if you can't reveal this to the Board of Directors then it is a sad state of affairs.

After Alan left there quickly followed a bombshell. An invoice dated 12th December 2006 arrived at the club for £93,345.26. in respect of commissions supposedly owed to him from sales and marketing revenue generated by his company Gloo Marketing Ltd. It landed on our desk in the first week of January and so it must have sat on Alan's desk a few weeks before he dispatched it.

There we all were, working for zilch, trying to save the club when along comes this outrageous demand from an ex-director who had agreed with us all that no fees were to be paid to members of the board. As you can imagine it was not well received. Later, after letters were sent from the club stating it did not recognise the debt, Alan appointed a lawyer from Leeds threatening court action for recovery. The written threat contained the reason why the debt was due. It claimed the existence of an agreement, lawfully executed and signed by the club, which was considered enforceable and was a proper bone-fide agreement.

Denis recalled that at the outset, Alan had handed over some heads of terms for consideration for a proposed contract, but said that they were rejected outright. It was completely unacceptable; the club's cash flow couldn't have possibly stood this. The whole matter then just got put to one side and was not really discussed thereafter. Everyone just got their heads down and got on with what had to be done and it didn't get mentioned again. Of the amounts now being demanded, a large amount, which was referred to as commissionable income for the club, was simply the loyal fans renewing their season tickets and advertising boards and nothing to do with Alan's marketing strategies at all.

His invoice claimed:

> 10 % of the Commercial department sales of £248,430
> 10% of the Red and White shop sales of £103,643
> 10% of Season Tickets sold (£477354 – first £35000 ?)

It is possible that when he was approached to get involved with the club he looked on it as yet another marketing job for his company. He should have realised that being involved with Rotherham United would not generate income but would actually cost him dearly. One has to wonder why an experienced businessman with no agreement signed would go charging in with expensive lawyers to try to force the club to pay? Following a request from our lawyers a copy of the legal contract to which they referred was sent for our inspection. Alan Cartledge on behalf of Gloo Marketing Limited had signed it on the one part and Dino Maccio on behalf of Rotherham United on the other part. If Dino had signed this in good faith, he was in breach of his shareholders' agreement. I had expressly inserted the proviso that no-one could contract the club for a commitment above £1000 without the board's express approval.

Denis went ballistic about this contract It was never in force, he maintained; it would have been madness. After more scrutiny the authenticity of this document was now being questioned. It certainly looked to have been signed by Dino, but it was dated well before the proposed heads of terms that Alan had emailed to the club for consideration in the first place.

So how could that be? – it clearly was a try on! Walker Morris our legal team wrote back to Alan's lawyer in no uncertain terms rejecting the claim and stating the reasons why. Alan knew we all worked as directors for free and, although he had not signed the no secret profit agreement that I drew up, he was aware that we had all signed and worked to it. If he thought any differently, why had he carried on and joined us as a director? As you can well imagine, the demand then died a death and nothing more was heard.

After Dino and Alan had left the board, it was like a ton weight had lifted and meetings returned to a pleasurable experience where the urgent business of trying to help Rotherham United continued.

I decided to tighten things up a little by writing to all Directors concerned reminding them of the procedures we put in place at the outset which had begun to slip following the recent skirmishes.

Our ref: GHB/JR/3148
26 February 2007
Mr D Coleman
Rotherham United FC Limited
Millmoor Football Ground
Millmoor Lane
ROTHERHAM
South Yorkshire
S60 1HR

Dear Denis

I am writing in order that the board meetings can become more productive and meaningful.

To this end, I wish to change the system. Twenty-four hours before a meeting, all directors should pass on details of items to be included in the meeting agenda. The chief executive will list these together with any other items he may wish to raise. The team manager should be invited to do a fifteen-minute presentation at every alternate board meeting. The agenda will be stuck to rigidly but there will be an "Any Other Matters" as part of the final schedule. An example of an agenda could be:-

Meeting to start at 12.00pm prompt.

Apologies for absence.
Minutes of last meeting.
Accounts
Team performance (Alan Knill).
Training ground – proposed by David.
Tivoli suite – Gary.
Marketing update – Gary.
Staffing matters – Paul.
Legal update – Giles.
Any other business.
Close of meeting.
Yours sincerely
G H BREARLEY
Brearley & Co Accountants Limited

The only other disharmony among directors (and I am going to call it that rather than skirmishes) was in the last few weeks of office when we were all running off in opposite directions trying to find an investor for the club. Because of the demands and intensity of this, we weren't communicating properly and updating each other as often as we should.

Oh, there was one other long-standing unresolved matter, Denis' inability to wear a tie

Extract from the directors' meeting minutes voted and passed: -

> "It was discussed and agreed that the dress code for Home and Away games for Directors and Chief Executive would be Trousers, Jacket, shirt and tie. Paul was to make all visiting Directors aware of this requirement. Directors should also make all their guests aware of this dress code too."

For some reason, Denis just hated wearing ties. By not complying and doing so, it gave him, at times, the persona of arrogance although he did not wish this to be the case. There were a few occasions when clubs made strong representation to Paul that our Chairman was in breach of their dress code and it wouldn't be tolerated next time. Notts County really kicked up a fuss about it. The wearing of a club tie gave respectability to the procedures, gave it some style and

The Board of Directors; (left to right) David Costin, Gary Hall, Denis Coleman and Giles Brearley.

showed a mark of respect. A shirt and tie was always a requirement in every Football Club's Directors' Lounge. We did put pressure on Denis and at times he did comply.

One of the most agonising Board meetings I remember was one of our last when Mark Robins (at that point unaware of the looming financial predicament) addressed the February 2008 board meeting to seek authority to enrol on the Summer 2008 Higher Coaching Course being offered by the FA, which he thought would "up his skills" and benefit the club. I really felt for him; he more than deserved it. I knew we certainly could not fund it. Denis explained that the budget was spent but we would ask R.U.S.T if they could help out and we would do what we could. He thanked us and left. I have every respect for Mark Robins and think he is a well-dedicated professional who didn't say a lot but most certainly thought plenty.

After Mark left the meeting somewhat disappointed, Sheffield Site Services came in to discuss investing £100,000 in return for shares in the club. Directors Kevin and Shaun were very keen to help out.

Most of the board meetings were held in Swinton but latterly in 2008, we held them at Denis' offices. The rule was that whoever hosted the meeting provided sandwiches at his own cost. There was a lot of banter as to who did the best sandwiches. Considering everyone's comments I think we just about won that one.

I became famous in the board meetings for saying "But we have no money" as various requests for expenditure were made and David Costin became famous for comments such as "If I can get five firms to put up £500 each, do you agree we can go ahead?" David never ceased to amaze. He was so passionate about the cause, I don't think people could refuse him.

Chapter 11 (G.H.B.)

Tobin Emerges from the Shadows

When I became a Director of the club we arranged some press coverage of the event.

After the article had been published, I was sitting in my office when a phone call was put through from reception with the message "it is something to do with Rotherham United". The caller introduced himself very professionally as an ardent Millers fan called Tobin. "Could we meet for a chat sometime?" the caller asked very respectfully. About a fortnight later I met the gentleman in Rotherham where he ran his business and I listened to all he had to say, which was quite a lot. I did not know him personally but I had heard of his business.

Tobin was very knowledgeable on the Millers and on the ins and outs of football. "If ever you want a second opinion on any matter feel free to ring me." he said. He kept himself up to date on the Club's affairs and would often write to me setting out matters and solutions as he saw them. In the past he had not been given much "street cred" probably because of his obsessive manner and at times his bluntness of delivering the truth as he saw it. He never forced himself onto you; he was just there if you needed him.

Meetings with Tobin always had to be undercover. He did not want us to be seen in public together. For reasons best known to himself, he thought it would be very unwise for the media to know we had met. He did not want any publicity other than the advertising board he had in the ground. Over the next 24 months we met up in pub car parks, remote inns and even once in Leeds city centre. Tobin had a good business mind and was very up on the laws of the land. He had plenty of connections amongst lawyers, accountants and other business professionals that he would call upon to clarify situations. He must have called in more favours than anyone else I know for Rotherham United's cause

Well, maybe not as many as David Costin in those early days.

Even as I got to know him quite well he would not let me take him as my guest in the directors box at away matches. He would go to most games but always travelling under his own steam, a little bit incognito. He did have a good friend called Terry who I gathered was just an everyday working lad. He travelled with Tobin quite often. They liked to be part of the background. In his presence Tobin adopted a completely different tone and discussion topic. Once when I was in deep conversation with Tobin, Terry came over and interrupted us. Tobin quickly changed the subject.

Tobin was very keen on the Court case we were embroiled in and believed we did have a very genuine case. He wanted us to use his lawyers in London who he utilised from time to time for larger clients. He said it had taken him about £300,000 in legal fees and ten years to find them, but now he was happy to recommend them. We were so deep in at this point with our existing legal team that changing would not have really been practical in any case. Tobin laboured the point that the land the ground sat on was originally donated by the railway company for sporting purposes to the people of Rotherham and he viewed the transfer of ownership to the Booths as morally wrong.

He had in the past had a lot of respect for Ken Booth but felt that the attitudes of certain members of the family towards the club had suddenly turned the fans against Ken, in effect from hero to zero in a very short space of time. Tobin had crossed swords with the Booths in the past, having been involved in some business dealings.

On the opening day of the court case unbeknown to me Tobin went to Leeds and positioned himself in earshot of the Booth's and their legal team so he could listen in to what was being said. When I walked into court and saw him I thought "You dark horse" as he had never mentioned his plans at all the night before. The look on his face said it all. "Do not acknowledge me or attempt conversation." After about 15 minutes he got up and disappeared. He rang me on my mobile phone to wish us luck and tell me what he had overheard. The reason he left so soon was because of the arrival of a few R.U.S.T. members who also came to observe the proceedings. I once asked him why he had not joined R.U.S.T. in the past. "Because" he said "I am a Lone Ranger. I can work better with my own agenda." It was never mentioned again. I did ask various people just in a passing conversation if they knew Tobin to see what reaction I got. On the whole I got little response, perhaps he was that good.

He had known many of the previous Rotherham United directors and managers over the years and clearly had some dialogue with them at some point. Some he did not like and would not "set them on" to quote him.

He did explain that being involved with the Millers was at times a thankless task. This however I already knew from my own short experience.

He would recall how he had a go at Sid Wood back in 1984 about the manager not fetching substitutes on late in a game, after saying that Sid was probably more interested in saving on the players appearance money. He apparently knew Sid's brother Len who worked as a purchasing manager at the N.C.B. H.Q. in the late 1970s. I think Tobin did business with him. He had a similar run in with the Pursehouses when they were in control over similar claims.

Of the players, he knew Richard Finney quite well and was fond of him as a player. I think Finney went to Thomas Rotherham College with Tobin's brother. Tobin also knew Alan Crawford who went on to become one of the club's highest scoring wingers. Trevor Swift, he told me, was as good at cricket as he was at football and could have gone to Everton, but didn't. He always said that one of his fondest home games was when he watched the Millers despatch Arsenal in a second round Football League Cup match in 1979 with a great goal from John Green. He went to Wembley for the Auto Windscreens Shield final in 1996 when the Millers beat Shrewsbury 2-1. As for the managers he loved Ronnie Moore and Ian Porterfield. He was quite emotional when Ian passed away in 2007 and that we had featured him in the match day programme.

Decision making with your directors hat on brings far more matters for consideration than you might at first envisage. These decisions do not always please everyone but may be essential to move things forward. The fan may scream for something to happen but you have to be more realistic. As Directors we soon established that whatever wisdom was used to solve a problem, someone would still come along and stick the knife in. For example when we were pushing the boat out with the school's initiative "a kid for a quid" to help get more bums on seats and introduce them to Rotherham United, we were berated by some because they had paid for a child season ticket and now "little

Johnny" next door was seeing a game for only a £1. Even though you explained it was a one off event for that particular school it did not seem to matter. They only saw it from their own position and not the betterment of the club in the future.

Fans' disharmony also manifested itself when trying to decide on season ticket prices. This took up more boardroom time than I care to mention. You sensed that whatever prices were agreed, they would be wrong. Tobin did give me his views on season ticket prices but I did not always take heed as some times I thought he was too close to it all and was unaware of some of the problems it entailed having first hand experience.

I quickly learned that you could trust Tobin implicitly when it came to matters of strict confidentiality. I did on several occasions delegate tasks to him to research and undertake on my behalf, which he did on most occasions with zest. Occasionally business pressures would intervene and he would be a little slow, but not that often. His knowledge of individuals around Rotherham was amazing. I did let him have my personal phone numbers so we could confer occasionally in the evenings, much to the frustration of his long suffering wife (and mine). He would often ring me as I was leaving to go out, and Ruth would be dancing up and down making gestures reminding me that we were already late. When he rang the office he would always tell the receptionist who answered the phone,"tell Giles it's his Uncle Tobin."

Tobin had a great memorabilia collection of Millers' mementos from the past. He had all sorts including programmes, photos, and team sheets. They went back years. He had a room in his large Victorian House dedicated to the storage and partial display of his collection. Only a few people have been invited into this hallowed inner sanctum. He was paranoid about burglars gaining knowledge of what his house contained. There was also a whole host of antique furniture ,pottery and books .

As a Local Historian, this part of Tobin interested me . There were things he had that I did not know even existed. When Tony Stewart's consortium first got mentioned as a possible saviour for the club Tobin sent for a copy of ASD Lighting PLC's accounts. He sent these to my office with a note saying "what do you make of these?".

As this book is about trying to save Rotherham United it is only fair I do mention Tobin and his efforts. He most certainly rallied to the cause. Since I ceased to be a director of the club Tobin had become much harder to contact. Telephone calls are not returned as enthusiastically, but I persist and I do get him. He is not getting off that lightly. I have work for him to do - proof reading this book for a start.

I wonder if he has called Tony Stewart yet and been allowed the honour to introduce himself? Put him off once and you have lost him for good! I was certainly glad to have him as an ally during a very frustrating but interesting period.

Chapter - 12 (G.J.M.)

Bring on the Big Hitters

Early one morning, towards the end of November 2006, I was awakened to the sound of my mobile phone ringing out. By the time I got to the phone, it had cut off. "Who could be ringing me at this hour?" I thought and soon discovered it was Dave Costin.

Later that morning, I returned David's call and he told me that he had not slept a wink during the night, thinking about the club and its long-term financial needs. Everyone was happy with the performance on the field but, at the same time, we were all conscious that further investment was necessary to stabilise the club. He asked whether Giles and I would support him on an idea to invite a small number of discreet, "high net worth" entrepreneurs based in Rotherham to a meeting where all the facts and figures could be laid before them and hopefully they could be persuaded to pledge support for the club financially. Dave had a list of names, some of whom were known to him personally and others who weren't. The one common denominator was that they all had some financial clout. Many of them were already sponsors of the club in some way, shape or form but what Dave was going to be asking for was much more than an advertising board or sponsoring a match.

I spoke to Giles and we agreed that, although there had been meetings in the past, this was more of a personal invitation for a select number. He did show some concern though that we could damage our position by going cap in hand to these businessmen too often. When Denis first took over he had meetings with some of these entrepreneurs and only got three positive responses so he was not too optimistic. We were hoping that with almost a year under our belts, this time our position would be taken more seriously and achieve the desired results.

The letters and invitations were drawn up and sent out to approximately 25 "Big Hitters" as we called them the letter read as follows:

22 November 2006
Dear Sirs
Re: Rotherham United Football Club

You are probably aware of the situation at the Club as it has been well publicised.

We have made great in-roads in reducing the losses incurred by the previous regime and managed to reduce the potential deficit but, the final part of balancing the books was always going to be the hardest.

The performances of the team this year have been particularly outstanding considering the cloud that was hanging over us at the start of the season. If it was not for the ten point deduction, we are confident we would have been in, at the very least, a play-off position.

In order for us to move forward, we urgently require financial backing to enable the Club to continue unabated and give us further time to reduce the trading deficit and reach breakeven point by the end of the 2008 season.

We are only writing to a few selected parties who we believe may have the financial clout and acumen to assist us in our needs. To this end, we wondered if you would be prepared to attend a confidential meeting with ourselves and other interested parties in order that we can sit and discuss the matter in full.

We appreciate with the Christmas period fast approaching people's diaries are starting to fill up but we would prefer the meeting to take place sooner rather than later and would like to suggest 6th December 2006 at say 12 noon. The meeting should last approximately two hours and we will arrange a local venue where we can hold the meeting privately and without any disturbances.

Please confirm if you will be available for this meeting, addressing your reply to:

Giles Brearley, Brearley & Co Accountants Limited, 39/43 Bridge Street, Swinton, Mexborough, South Yorkshire, S64 8AP. Tel 01709 581667.

Yours sincerely

| Denis Coleman | David Costin | G H Brearley |
| (Chairman) | (Director) | (Director) |

Rotherham United FC Limited

The meeting was set for 6 December 2006 at the Courtyard Marriott Hotel in Rotherham for 12 noon. Giles and I spent hours preparing a power point presentation, highlighting the problems that we had inherited at the club, showing the management figures to date and our budgets to the end of the season, along with our hopes and expectations for the next couple of years or so. We were open to offers as to how this extra investment could be justified by asking what they wanted for their money – was it shares, a seat on the board, corporate hospitality or would they prefer to be silent investors? Whatever was required, we were prepared to negotiate.

Despite the disappointing turn out, all the businessmen who did attend applauded the work we had done so far and hoped we could turn the club's fortunes around and stabilise the finances for the future. However, it seemed that the underlying problem in all cases was the fact that the club didn't own the ground and training facilities and on this point, it would be difficult to raise investment when potential new buyers have nothing to "hang their hat on".

Those in attendance included the board of directors, Denis Coleman, Dave Costin, Gary Hall and Giles Brearley and the local businessmen included Ron Hull, Ben Bennett, Chris Cooper, Richard Brewin, Shaun Dawson and Phil Bunting. There were apologies from the now Rotherham United chairman, Tony Stewart of ASD Lighting, Brian Beckett of ABS Industrial, Ian Henry of Ledger Holidays and Paul Shaw of Northern Engineering. There were others who didn't even respond and on that note, shall remain anonymous. The meeting was very relaxed and after my initial presentation, it was open for questions and answers at which point, we all tried to be as honest as possible in the circumstances. It was noted that Dino Maccio was absent from the meeting and questions had been raised as to whether or not there was a split in the boardroom. I did admit that things had been fraught at times recently at the board meetings but at this stage, whilst they were not all seeing eye to eye, the underlying desire to see Rotherham through this period took precedence. Dino in fact, was away on a family holiday at this time and was, I understand, a little miffed when he found out about the meeting on his return.

One of the questions asked was "What potential transfer income could be generated from the sale of Hoskins and Williamson", which was being speculated upon in the media at that time. We could only comment that at that time, there had been no interest shown by other clubs and although a new contract had been offered to Hoskins, we were becoming doubtful as to whether he was prepared to accept. One of the big hitters stood up and actually said that if they didn't want to play for the club, then we should cash in now and use the funds to secure the immediate future of Rotherham United. On leaving the meeting, we promised to allow people time to mull things over before we followed up with telephone calls within the next week or two. The board of directors and myself sat in the bar downstairs to discuss the meeting. David , who was sure we would get a positive response from the local businessmen, was a little less optimistic now , he realised at that point that we were in this thing alone and would have to fight tooth and nail to keep our head above water in the forthcoming months.

Please don't get me wrong; the people who came to the meeting have over the years supported the club financially by way of donations, sponsorship and advertising etc in the hundreds of £000's, but what we were asking for now was a commitment of more than just the money. No one at the club has worked harder than Dave Costin. He has provided vehicles, free of charge used by the coaching staff and youth teams, etc. He has also provided labour and materials in order to maintain and repair the ground and meet the Football League's high standards for health and safety at the same time. His idea to try and get the " big hitters" in Rotherham on board with us wasn't going to be easy. He must have been wondering at that time, with a wife and young family, what he had let himself in for.

CHAPTER - 13 (G.H.B.)

THE MILLMOOR SUITE

There were no negotiations regarding the acquisition of the Millmoor Suite in the lease; it was obviously part of the stadium and had to be incorporated with the Ground. Although it was put onto a separate lease, it would have been extremely difficult to operate in isolation with another party due to access problems to the upper offices, etc. It may have been separated from the main lease of the stadium as a way of justifying a higher rent.

In fairness, it was used quite extensively but did cause us tremendous problems along the way. We had to do something with it due to the rent that we had to find week in, week out. The problem of the suite was attacked on all fronts; organised functions, private hire and public openings. It suffered from a succession of bar managers who all had to leave for various reasons, which at times put us under tremendous pressure. Denis had researched the possibility of providing Sunday lunches at the suite. He decided that there was certainly scope for another venue to provide a lunch service and thought it would be a good idea to incorporate one at Millmoor.

The organisational wheels turned and for the launch, Denis, his wife and children accompanied by David Costin, his wife and their children, turned up for the inaugural dinner with the intention of having an enjoyable afternoon. When they arrived they walked into complete chaos. For whatever reason, most of the staff had failed to turn up; there was only one cook and one member of waiting staff. There was no other choice but for Denis to man the bar and David became headwaiter. Helen acted as a further waitress and Lisa went into the kitchens to assist. The kids took it all in their stride and played happily together as though nothing had happened.

David had also invited some friends to join them for this launch and they duly turned up. There was Andy, his wife and three children, his sister and 76-year-old mum. David apologised profoundly and explained the predicament they were in. Pressure started building as more and more people came in wanting their "Sunday Roast". As they were still seriously understaffed, Andy's mother, dressed up to the nines volunteered herself. She rolled up her sleeves and went into the kitchen to assist the cook and Lisa. As 3.30pm loomed, they were finally all able to relax, realising that they had not eaten themselves.

With all good intentions, similar ideas were put forward to try and utilise the suite as much as possible but many fell by the wayside, like the Sunday lunches did after a few short weeks.

To try and prevent problems on the bar, we instructed a national stocktaking organisation to take control and report on the bar's performance. There were many reports received highlighting various problems, which we suspected might be the case. This really angered me as all the directors were working their socks off for nothing. On one occasion I witnessed it first hand, being an accountant and long sighted too, I often read the price list and worked out my bar bill before it was rung into the till. This particular evening, I had ordered two pints of lager and a brandy and dry ginger. The bar tender served me the drinks and then went to the till, punched the order in then returned to me for the money. That'll be £7.80 I placed a pile of coins straight in his hand. "Oh, hold on" I said "I've paid you short". The figure he

A good pre-kick off crowd in the Tivoli suite

told me was higher than I had calculated, I thought it was strange but I put another 60p in his greasy palms. I studied the price list again and found my initial calculations were bang on. The till was also correct; as it transpired he was adding on to every sale when the opportunity arose. I did not say anything but watched him do this four or five more times. The next day, I had him removed; this just couldn't go on.

As the suite was an entrance to other parts of the offices and a natural meeting place, people thought nothing of helping themselves to soft drinks if they were thirsty, not realising it would show up in the stocktaking reports. We put all sorts of manual systems in place and partly computerised it, which tightened things up a little.

David, always being very charitable, approached me in September 2007 to see if I would make a donation towards the Elysha Roberts Fund, which had been set up to help pay for treatment for the young child stricken with a very rare disease, which locked her inside her body. She was 5 years old and had

The presentation of the cheque to Elysha's parents for her trust fund, to the left is co-organiser Councillor Ken Wyatt with Giles Brearley to the right.

been close to death on a number of occasions. She had lost the use of her arms and hands and could only communicate through her eyes.

As patrons of Swinton Heritage, Councillor Ken Wyatt and I were about to organise a fund raising event for the newly sited town's cross in Swinton. We agreed that we would make this a joint event and share the proceeds, 50% to Swinton Heritage and 50% to the Elysha Roberts Fund. To this end, we organised Gerry Trew (the number one Rod Stewart tribute act) as the star turn for a concert on the 16th November 2007 at the Millmoor Suite. Ken and I alone sold all the tickets for the event, and the Club did take a table in supporting the good cause. Ken also arranged for the Deputy Mayor to attend. We received generous donations for Auction items etc and the event was a great success despite the heating problems.

The faltering audio equipment also caused problems that night when Tony Styles, having donated his services as compare and DJ for the evening complained that a lot of the equipment was not working, in particular the lights and some of the sound system. Gerry Trew had not fetched lighting, as we had indicated on his booking sheet it was already on site. I jumped in my car and went round banging on the doors of entertainers that I knew borrowing the necessary equipment so that the evening would not be ruined. Visitors to the event would not have known anything was wrong but it was a very tense time - yet another example of how dilapidated the suite had actually become.

Denis, David and Gary organised their own fund raiser for Elysha via a football match at Millmoor. The event was a success and each of them donated a thousand pounds to her cause.

To try and further the Suite's profitability we took the gamble and arranged for Sky T.V. to be installed. Denis and Gary had noticed that some regulars were going elsewhere to catch some of the early games. It also gave us the chance to open up on big match nights and get more bar revenue. We opened the Suite at 12-00 noon on match days and we did have some success.

CHAPTER 14 (G.J.M.)

THE WATFORD GAP

In January 2007, Rotherham United had no alternative but to sell its crown jewels, namely Lee Williamson and Will Hoskins, in the transfer window. This caused much debate within the fans' forums, pubs, clubs and internet chat rooms. Within the media, varying amounts of monies were bandied around as to what the actual deal was and how much it was worth to the club.

The following chapter will hopefully close the gap between the speculation and reality of the Watford transfers.

Towards the end of November 2006, after a fantastic start to the 2006/07 season, we had managed to cancel out the ten points deducted by the Football League and move out of the bottom four relegation places. The next plan was to move forward and if we could finish the season on the verge of the play-offs or mid-table, then all concerned would agree that this had been a fantastic achievement.

Unfortunately, there were rumblings in the background concerning two of the club's shining stars this season ie, Lee Williamson and Will Hoskins. Lee had been transferred to Rotherham two seasons ago from Northampton Town and had always looked a decent player, he was the main driving force in the midfield, supporting both strikers and defenders and seemed to cover every blade of grass during a game. Will Hoskins, on the other hand, had progressed through the youth academy after being transferred as a junior from Notts County several years earlier. He will probably be best remembered for his brace scored at Wigan Athletic after being brought on in the second half by Ronnie Moore as a new raw talent at the club. Rotherham went on to win the game and from that day onwards, it was believed that Will would bring something special to the club in the years to come.

Before the start of the 2006/07 season, Denis Coleman and Alan Knill (Manager) had a difficult decision to make, whether or not to keep Will at the club. Since those heady days at Wigan Athletic in the Championship, Will's form, had been very up and down, along with his attitude and commitment to the club. It was finally decided to offer him a further twelve month contract to the end of the season, but he was told in no uncertain terms that things had to improve if he was to have any future at the club. Lee Williamson's contract was also up for renewal in the summer of 2007 but because of the previous financial problems at the club and with a new regime on board, it was felt his position be best reviewed nearer to Christmas.

As previously mentioned, Rotherham were on fire at the start of the 2006/07 campaign. Williamson was playing out of his skin and Hoskins was banging goals in for fun. He was the joint leading goal scorer with Billy Sharp at Scunthorpe United who eventually went on to win the Golden Boot for League One that season. It was decided by the Board of Directors that Denis Coleman and Alan Knill should commence contract talks with the two individuals and try to find out whether they were happy to stay at the club or were planning to move on. With the January transfer window looming some six to eight weeks away, it was agreed that now was the time to start talks with the players.

It became obvious very early on in the talks that Lee Williamson was intending to leave the club at the end of the season and, all bar a miracle, he would definitely be on his way.

In the case of Will Hoskins however, things were a little more complicated. Alan Knill had several meetings with him and his parents who respected Alan for looking after their son and helping him develop as a player and, at the same time, had managed to iron out some of his demons. On the face of it, it looked like we were going to secure his services for several more years. That was until his agent, Imre Varadi, decided otherwise. Will was ready to accept the deal offered to him by Denis and we were hoping to get his signature before the next home game the following Saturday.

On the Thursday evening Denis received a call from Knilly asking him to ring Varadi as the deal looked as though it may be off. Denis was in the Manor Barn at Kimberworth at the time but eventually called him sometime after 10.30pm. Denis was still standing in the car park after midnight arguing with him when the pub lights were turned off; everyone else had gone home. After telling Varadi what a nice man he was for the umpteenth time suddenly Denis' phone battery went flat ending the call. Worst of all he was stranded and couldn't call a taxi. He ended up walking the 3 mile journey home on a freezing cold November evening.

It's an agent's job to plant the seed in a player's mind that they are probably better and worth more than is actually the case. No exceptions were spared in Will's case by his agent and therefore, from the brink of accepting a new contract with the club, he now believed that his future lay elsewhere. Despite the financial constraints of the club the Board did not want to lose Will and so a revised offer was made to him. Varadi recommended rejection of this forthwith. After further heated discussions as to what effect on the crowds would be if our form deteriorated a final generous offer was made to him. Just like the previous offer it was rejected outright. Alan Knill tried talking to him. He felt that Will was leaving Rotherham too early. He needed to build on his skills with the team gaining more consistency. It all fell on deaf ears.

Once the Board were aware of the feelings of the two players in question, they had to accept their decision and from a financial point of view, get as much money for them as possible to reinvest in the club. The January transfer window was looming and with the threat of the Bosman Rule kicking in, especially in the case of Lee Williamson, it was decided there was no alternative but to sell now, otherwise, we could be left with virtually nothing for our two prize assets. In the early part of December 2006, the media were speculating whether or not Williamson and Hoskins would be sold and for how much money. Although there had been rumours that Barnsley FC were interested in Lee Williamson with transfer fees being bandied around between £100K and £300K, nothing concrete had been put forward and it was later confirmed by Denis that only West Brom had actually made an offer for Hoskins of £500K i.e. £300K up front and the rest on appearances. In the meantime, on the quiet, Alan Knill had met with Ady Boothroyd and other officials at Watford FC who had shown an interest in both players but, as we approached Christmas with no further interest being indicated, we assumed that this might be another winter of discontent.

To our amazement, during the first week of January, Denis Coleman was contacted by the Watford FC chairman wanting to thrash out a deal that would take both Williamson and Hoskins to the Hornets during the transfer window. Denis spent a full day, to-ing and fro-ing in order to try and get the best deal possible for his beloved Rotherham United and arguably, had his best day at the office as chairman by securing funding that was to keep the club afloat for a further twelve months. The players were quickly ushered down to Vicarage Road in order to have a tour of the ground and facilities, meet the staff, players, etc, and negotiate their own financial packages and personal contracts through their agents. Once personal terms had been agreed then the real business commenced.

Not unsurprisingly, with it's recent run of bad luck, on the morning that the sale agreements were being faxed and emailed between the two clubs, there was an electrical power failure at Millmoor. Emergency electricians were rushed down to the ground in order to restore power. It was at this point that their investigations revealed the inadequacy of the power supply at the club with one engineer commenting that "this was a disaster waiting to happen". We thought we were fully aware of all the problems we had inherited at Millmoor but were seriously caught with our trousers down this time due to the extent of the dilapidations at the stadium. This again, proved to be another massively expensive cost, which had not been budgeted for.

Paul Douglas rang me at 8.00am on Friday 5th January 2007, pulling his hair out, and asked if he could temporarily move his office into ours in order to conclude the transfer business. The electricity supply was likely to be disconnected at Millmoor for between two and three days but fortunately it was the FA Cup 3rd round and we didn't have a game that weekend. He was most concerned, however, that any delays in signing the paperwork could put these transfers in jeopardy. He arrived suited and booted at Brearley & Co's offices in Swinton just before 9.00am. As all of the fortnightly board meetings were held at our offices, we didn't look at this situation as being an inconvenience but more as a matter of necessity. Paul and I spent most of that morning faxing, copying, telephoning, reviewing and revising the various sales contracts in order to ensure that what Denis had agreed was going to come to fruition. After a final review by the club's lawyer, Ben Mansford of Walker Morris, the final papers were signed and faxed back to Watford somewhere around 4.00pm that evening.

The following Friday, Clare Yeardley rang me to confirm that

Will Hoskins.

Lee Williamson

£900K had been transferred that day into Rotherham United's bank account. You would have thought we'd won the lottery; never before had so much money been available in the cash flow during our time at the club and although certain creditors needed to be paid from these funds, we were confident that the cash reserves would carry us through to the end of 2007/08 season. I left the office that evening after Clare had confirmed the funds transfer and believed that this was the turning point for the Millers not realising that around the corner was a landlord who was quite determined to take possession of the ground and leave the club in financial turmoil.

The actual deal with Watford was as follows:-

	£	£
Total Transfer Fees for both players.	900,000	
Plus VAT @17.5%	157,500	1,057,500
Funds Received 12.01.07	907,500	
01.08.07	150,000	
Less Payments made from funds :		
VAT Paid to HMCE	157,500	
Sell on Clauses		
: Notts County	96,875	
: Northampton Town	25,000	279,375
Net Proceeds from Transfers		£778,125

The club also received a further £20K net following Lee Williamson's first 15 appearances and would receive a further £100K if Watford FC regained promotion to the Premiership whilst either player remained at the club. A 15% sell on clause was also attached to each player on any profit Watford made on future transfers.

The sell on clauses agreed with their previous clubs were: Notts County 12.5% for Will Hoskins and Northampton 20% for Lee Williamson.

CHAPTER - 15 (G.H.B.)

DE LE , DE LE, DE LE, DE LE , DE LE, DE LE, DE LE , IT'S "GAZ" MAN

Gary Hall told me he had followed the club home and away for 30 years. I quickly calculated this meant he was probably about 86 years old seeing as he wasn't allowed out on his own till he was well into his fifties. He would always try to help the club whether it was by buying a season ticket or buying a brick during the 05 campaigns. He had a career in banking and finance, spending a lot of time previously with the Bradford and Bingley. He was a little upset when they did not pick him as the lead figure in their new TV adverts to rival the Halifax's "Howard". He was even prepared to wear those dreaded round glasses if needed. During 2006 he set up his own company and as the business grew was able to offer more meaningful help with sponsorship at the club.

His first real professional help for the club was during the pre season of 2006 when, of his own initiative, he found a finance company that could help supporters buy their season tickets on credit. Gary provided, at his own cost, the leaflets and postage and sponsored the mail shot to over 8000 supporters on the club's database. To Gary this seemed quite an easy sponsorship and he waited for the mail drop to go out. The weeks went by and it was obvious that the club was not in a position to do this, rather large marketing campaign. He therefore put his own staff to work, and by working round the clock managed to get the letters out. It worked, the club started to see people take up the offer. Little did Gary know at this stage his first bit of work with the club would soon become his main focus each and every day regardless?

Gary agreed to more sponsorship, paying for a gigantic advertising hoarding taking up a third of the Railway End stand. He remembers the day he went down to look at it for the first time. He walked in to the ground and couldn't wait to see his company name emblazoned onto his beloved club's stand for all to see. His business partner had got their some 5 minutes before him and as Gary arrived he came out laughing, shouting to Gary, 'You are going to love this.' Gary walked through the Tivoli expecting to see his company name 'Shop Around Mortgages in all its glory. Wrong!!! The sign guys had started placing letters on from the back end and had run out of time and left the job unfinished with HOP AROUND MORTGAGES.

Gary was then informed that the sign writers had finished for the weekend and would return first thing Monday morning. This wasn't great news as the first game of the season was the very next day; Gary had also sponsored the match and invited his staff and larger clients for the unveiling. It would have been very embarrassing. He was directed to speak to Dave Costin who promised that it would be sorted even if he had to get up the ladder himself. True to his word David resolved the problem. To this day Gary still cringes about what could have been.

After this meeting Dave Costin introduced Gary to Denis. He had seen Denis at many of the matches but never spoken to him, as Gary said "well you wouldn't would you". Gary explained to Denis that if he could help in anyway, he would, as RUFC was one of the most important things in his life and still is. At the next board meeting a letter was presented from Gary. It was decided I should meet up with him and vet him before involving the full board. I thought a lunchtime meeting would be appropriate for all so I phoned him that afternoon. On the following Thursday, we went to the Manvers Arms at Adwick on Dearne for a bite to eat. Gary explained that he was meeting his lady friend, Amy, that evening and they were going to a new restaurant, so he just settled for the steak and ale pie with chips. We didn't get to talk properly until after the pie was consumed, as if I got too close to him, the flashing blades swishing up and down may have caused some permanent damage.

In a nutshell, Gary was prepared to make RUFC a profit share partner in his company. He would donate 5% of his profits to the club and also pay £12,000 up front. In return he said that in the future, he would like the club to acknowledge his input in some way. He felt his connections in the local business community and with other bigger corporations he could help with the Clubs regeneration. He seemed very sincere and had ambition. Oh and just for the record, I bought lunch.

Back at the office, I rang Denis, "I like him. I think he is genuine and I think we should get him to the September board meeting."

The board room patter got interrupted by our receptionist, Nicola, announcing that Mr Hall had arrived. We hurriedly hid the uneaten sandwiches, cleared the table and asked him to come in. Gary had brought his business plans and notes for our consideration.

A question and answer session then followed. After 15 minutes Denis brought out the secreted sandwich tray and put it on the table. "Would you like to join us" he invited Gary pointing at the tray? It was agreed that Gary should draw up his more detailed business plans and proposals for aiding the club and liaise with myself. A week later Gary appeared at my office with all his paperwork for scrutiny. His presentation went down well and I told him we would be in touch.

Dino in the meantime had told the rest of the board that Gary's business partner had been banned from Millmoor and that they should look very seriously whether they even wanted Gary's sponsorship money. This information proved to be incorrect; Gary's business partner was deeply offended and ready to take the club to court for slander. Gary managed to calm him down and David and Denis agreed to meet up with him again at the Golden Ball in Whiston. Gary explained that the information we had received was absolute rubbish and so the proposition was back on. Dino defended himself by reiterating it was only what he had been told in confidence and in good faith. From there on in, Gary was with us every inch of the way. The commercial function was struggling again and he agreed he would immerse himself into it and put some of his suggestions into practice reporting back to the board. At the second October 2006 Board meeting it was decided that Gary was to be given a trial period as a director designate. Although he could attend board meetings, he couldn't vote. It was made plain that he could not hold himself out to be a director at this stage. As a team member, he worked very hard. So hard in fact that at the meeting in November 2006 it was passed unanimously that Gary should be made a full serving board director of the club commencing December 2006.

Gary said that this was the proudest moment of his life; nothing else touched it. He was going to be a board member for his beloved football club. We arranged for Gary to meet the press and be interviewed for Millers TV at the training ground. To Gary it all seemed too surreal. He remembers waiting for the

Advertiser to be published on the Friday confirming his appointment. His family were as excited as Gary. Friday was to be an unforgettable day. Early that morning, he received a phone call from one of his mates "Aidy" who kept asking to speak to Mr Mills. Gary didn't understand what he was on about but was notorious for winding people up. Then his brother Andrew phoned and asked to speak to this mystery fellow. This was followed by another call from Phil also chasing Mr Mills. The mystery was eventually solved when Gary's mum phoned him spitting feathers.' Gary' she said 'after all you've done, the Advertiser have got your name wrong they have called you Gary Mills'. He was gutted It was his big day and they had christened him Mr Mills. This stuck with Gary for months at board meetings and with his friends. But by January 2007 Gary had contributed £12,000 to the club as promised as a first profit share.

As the new director Gary was formally seconded to look after the commercial department. He jumped at the chance as with all his experience in sales he thought how easy it would be to sell Rotherham United. Gary was surprised at just how wrong he was; it was hard work. He was amazed at the set up the club had for administration in its commercial department. This area of the business had been inherited from Millers 05. There was no structure or targets and there was very little focus. It was obvious that the department was just doing what it always did. This was not the staff's fault they had just not had any real guidance or motivation. The Tivoli suite was continuing to cause problems and with Gary's enthusiasm overflowing he was also asked if he would take this on too. He commented to me that at the time everyone on the board was keen for him to look after it; it would become apparent very quickly why.

The first thing Gary did with the Commercial department was to put in a system of Key Performance Indicators which would show what everyone was doing and where we could create extra income. To our surprise the commercial manager at the time Bob Gorrill decided to resign. This meant that Gary was therefore now looking after a department without a manager and guess who did all the work on his own over the next few weeks, yes that's right, our Mr Mills.

Gary after liaising with Paul Douglas decided that we had to get a manager who would take the club forward and bring new ideas to the table. It didn't have to be a football man, as it appeared that a lot of Commercial managers were set in their ways and were not flexible enough to accept change. They decided to put an advertisement for the role in the Yorkshire Post and we were somewhat surprised at the response, with some excellent candidates.

Gary and Paul started the interviews and were very happy with the candidate they chose. He had a superb CV and excellent past performance in sales and marketing. They were confident in making the right choice. He started promisingly enough and had some great ideas. Gary backed him 100% and hoped that we would soon start to see an increase in revenue in the most important part of the business. He certainly got the board's back up when he appeared at our meeting more concerned that we sign as guarantors for a finance agreement he had for his new company car. This made me quite annoyed as he remonstrated he had spent two days trawling the local area trying to set this deal up. I thought he was going to tell us of his early achievements. Denis ordered him out of the meeting.

The final nail in his coffin was when he organised a concert by a tribute band he was especially fond of. He was confident that it would work and as the concert got closer he told us that over 200 tickets had been sold and we were already in profit. This information was incorrect. On the day less than 100 turned up and most of these were his friends who had not paid for their tickets. The bar was run as an inclusive and hotel rooms had been booked for the band at a further cost. It was a financial disaster. Soon afterwards he decided to hand his notice in which, was a good thing as Denis was considering suing him for the losses.

Gary and Paul felt very let down but none the less set out once more to search for a replacement commercial manager. There was one thing that our last man did that looked as though it was going to help us and that was set up a meeting with Adidas UK. This excited Gary as further negotiations got them to agree that Rotherham United could be the first club outside the Premier League to wear Adidas kit. Gary even had agreed a launch date, the last game of the season, at home to Barnet. We were looking at opening an Adidas shop in town and everything was looking good to really increase sales for the coming years. This didn't come to fruition, as we never saw the new season in.

The minute's silence for well respected friend of Rotherham United: Dave Nicholls.

Gary then appointed Tony Stiles as the new man in commercial; Tony was 100% Miller and started the role well. Gary was confident that he would have been a complete success if he had the infrastructure around him in support. However as we were letting staff go, Tony ended up being responsible for a lot more and this proved to be a little too much for him to cope with. Gary supported him where possible but the job had now changed. Tony decided to leave so again we were looking for a new commercial manager. Before this person could be found however we were pre-occupied with the final disposal of the club as time was running out.

The whole commercial department experience was extremely trying and frustrating. As long term fans Denis and Gary's view was that in the past this would have been their dream job, but it had declined somewhat since the days of Dave Nicholls, and it would take longer than 18 months to turn it around. Gary did mention in his programme notes that we were looking for a Dave Nicholls type person, and within a week, he called from Cyprus to say that he would help in any way he could. Unfortunately,

Denis Coleman (right) and Gary Hall at Brentford. The game was a 1-1 draw.

shortly afterwards Dave died suddenly at home in Cyprus. He was a Miller through and through and would be sadly missed.

Gary said the hardest part of his role was trying to make money in the Tivoli suite. He tried everything from poker nights, sporting dinners, boxing nights and even clairvoyants. He always made us laugh when he said, "what chance do we stand when the clairvoyant couldn't even foresee there would have been a better turn out?". It was so hard to get people through the door. For example we had an evening with Gordon Banks; a local hero that we thought would bring in the punters. We advertised it extensively, we used excellent caterers, we made it affordable, but we sold just 10 tickets. The evening only went ahead because Gary, Gavin and Redtooth, the shirt sponsors, sold 100 tickets to people they knew.

Again with the Tivoli, we went through three bar and function managers who all left or were pushed for different reasons. I am sure you are now thinking well "Gary appears to be the common denominator here." The reality was that Gary's past performance in recruitment and staff retention over the years was impressive; we just couldn't find the right people for these roles. He did make progress in improving the sponsorship facilities at Millmoor. He influenced the discounts for kids on family days and help create some excellent partnerships that are still strong now, with the likes of Redtooth and Parkgate. Gary admits that in all honestly this had been the hardest sales job ever and this comes from a man who looked after 79 bank and estate branches with over 2000 staff.

If Gary had known what was on the horizon with the credit crunch he probably would not have got involved with the club as much as he did in the 18 months he spent on the board. This period came just as his company was expanding. The Company had grown from nothing to a several million pound turnover business within 2 years of start up. Unfortunately by October 2007 his business was starting to feel the crunch and part of the reason was because of his involvement with the club 24 hours a day 7 days a week. If he wasn't at Millmoor or talking to one of the other directors on the phone he was thinking about the club and how we could generate income. His business had been neglected somewhat because of his commitment to the club. To quote Gary though "Don't get me wrong the passion for the club is stronger than ever and I loved every second of the challenge. My company is now ok again and my time now is spent looking after the business, but I miss being involved with the club so much".

HOME GAMES

Gary always said that Saturday afternoon, at 3.00pm, once a fortnight, used to be the most enjoyable time of the week for him. The Millers' home game, a couple of beers a Pukka pie and then let the team decide if he was to have a good weekend or not. This of course all changed as soon as he was on the board. Saturday afternoons became work, work and more work. He recalls that one of the first matches he went to he was walking into the Tivoli to meet Denis for a pre-match drink and a man in his 60s met him at the door. 'Are you the new director?' Gary said 'Yes; how can I help?' He then let him have it with both barrels as they had run out of nuts in the suite. This would be the norm for a home match from now on.

Gary said he used to think the result meant a lot when he was a fan, but as a director the result meant income and in the end survival of the club. He still enjoyed the games win, lose or draw it was still the best place to be on a Saturday afternoon, but that extra enjoyment was now coupled to whether the club's sales team had a good or bad week. He felt there were some fantastic staff on match days at Millmoor and it was a pleasure to work with them and has to admit he misses the buzz being around the place. A big regret was that after all that work and sacrifice he never had time to say goodbye.

AWAY GAMES

Gary so much looked forward to the away games it was the only time he could wind down for a few hours. Yes, the result was important but he could have a relaxing day and the away clubs would look after him for a change. He had some great days out like at Carlisle United, which was his first with the board. Carlisle made everyone very welcome and he remembers it was about 4.00am the next morning when he got back. His fondest memory was when we beat Chesterfield on the Tuesday night away. It was a great night when we all felt as though we were turning the corner. Mark Robins and John Breckin were over the moon and so were the board; it was a great night.

He recalls there were some bad days though. The one that stands out for him was a 3-0 drubbing at Northampton. Denis had to leave early to get to a meeting in London. Gary was left to go back into the boardroom on his own. We had been poor that day and he suddenly found himself being the only representative of RUFC. He found it a little weird as his supporter's head was telling him to go home and have a rubbish night but the professional side of him had to go and say well done you played well. Sometimes that is hard to do but it is football etiquette at this level.

SPECIAL EVENTS

There were many events that Gary felt lucky enough to have been invited on. One close to his heart was involving Corus. We were invited for a trip round the steel works and, as all Gary's family had worked there in the past, he found it extremely interesting. Corus were very proud of what they did and if we had still been at the helm were confident that Gary would have forged strong links with the company and with many Millers that worked there. (Tony take note).

CHAIRMAN'S CONFERENCE

This was held annually in Portugal and, since David and I were predisposed, Gary volunteered to step in. It was attended by the Football Leagues chairmen, co directors, wives and girlfriends. Their respective partners were subsequently referred to as DWAGs...try saying that one, Jonathan Ross.

Joking apart, a lot of wheeling and dealing was done there. While there the guests would share their off the field troubles, as they were not competing against each other. It was in Portugal that Gary picked up the idea of having under 8s free season tickets. This had been initiated by none other than Leicester City, and proved to be very popular, and a way of getting future fans hooked.

Gary asked me to say on his behalf that "in all he made some mistakes during his 18 months on the board but he brought some changes that will stay with the club. He enjoyed every second of it, but looking back spent far too much time at the ground at the expense of his own business. But do you know what? He said he would probably do it all again."

Gary gave the club a lot and it was great to work alongside him.

Chapter – 16 (G.H.B.)

Possession Hearing

As December 2006 approached, we knew the cash flow would be tight. It was becoming a regular problem ensuring that funds were available to settle the rent on the 1st of each month. We knew that, although we might be late paying December's rent, with a few decent home games coming up we just needed three or four weeks grace. I asked Paul to let C F Booth Limited know, which he did by letter. With this renewed activity regarding the lease DLA Piper (C F Booth Limited's lawyers) whilst reviewing their files suddenly realised they had never collected their fees from the previous summer regarding the lease assignment. I must state we had never received an invoice previously. It may have been sent to our lawyers but we certainly hadn't seen it. Under the terms and conditions of the lease, RUFC was responsible for paying all of C F Booth Limited's legal costs. The downside of this was that as we were paying a third parties legal expenses, we were unable to claim the VAT back because the legal services were not carried out on our behalf. DLA Piper were now starting to pile on the pressure to remedy this oversight as a separate issue.

The current month's rent should have been paid on 1 December 2006 in the sum of £13.000. On 5 December 2006, DLA Piper wrote to the club confirming they were acting for the landlords and were left with no option but to inform us that we were in breach of the lease and we should send by telegraphic transfer £12,970.37 to their client's account within seven days of the letter as a remedy for the breach. They also reminded us that we were responsible for their legal costs. The letter concluded by saying that they had been asked to stress their client's reluctance to take action but to reiterate that their clients will take action if they have no other option to secure payment of monies or property due to them. The speed at which they were prepared to act was, in my book, unreasonable and aggressive, particularly after we had approached them previously to forewarn them of the problem with a payment plan. It was only a cash flow issue nothing more nothing less. If they were reluctant to carry out this action then why bother incurring further costs, one must ask.

The rest of December trickled on with business as usual. The 9th December saw us at home again playing Bristol City where we drew 1-1 in front of a crowd of 4862. DLA Piper then wrote again over the Christmas period. On the 28th December 2006, they sent a letter to the club confirming that they were taking county court proceedings for repossession of Millmoor and the Hooton Lodge training ground, the case would be listed as early as the 18th January 2007. This was followed by a further letter on the 2nd January 2007, confirming that they now had a hearing date for 5 February 2007 at 10.00am. The initial hearing date had now been vacated.

As we promised in our original payment proposal, we had sent them a cheque for £7850 between Christmas and the New Year. This was acknowledged in their letter but they were advising their client not to cash the cheque at present. The letter went on to remind us that now they were also looking for nearly £8,000 in addition to cover their legal costs. The letter also went on to say that their clients would consent to any application for relief from forfeiture on the following terms: -

> payment of rent due 1 December 2006 - £4583.33 for the ground
> payment of £416.67 being rent due on the training ground
> payment of £2600 for rent due on the Tivoli Suite
> payment of £250 for rent due 1 December 2006 on the changing rooms at Hooton Roberts.

In addition to the above, we had to pay daily interest and also, the January rent was added to the claim. All in all, considering the cheque they already had off us of £7850, they required another £37793.43. I penned the following press release in haste and eventually decided not to send it, but you can sense the pent up frustration I was ready to unleash to the public.

PRESS STATEMENT OF G H BREARLEY F.C.M.A.
FINANCE DIRECTOR OF ROTHERHAM UNITED FOOTBALL CLUB

What We Are Up Against

You have to admire the tireless efforts of certain individuals in helping us with the task of taking the club forward.

November was a difficult month as there was only one home match. The cash flow tightened up and special skills were applied to get us through until the New Year. December was just the opposite as four home games reversed the cash issues. The Board asked Chief Executive, Paul Douglas, to approach the stadium owners at the end of November to inform them we would struggle making the December payment on time but we would be in a position to rectify the matter after the December games. Unfortunately, the stadium owners resorted to legal proceedings and had their lawyers serve the club with a Breach Notice and claimed the respective legal costs associated, demanding all payments in full within seven days. The club made further approaches to the owners to reconfirm the situation during December.

They obviously have little regard for their tenant, as the response was to, over Christmas, serve notice of a hearing to "Repossess the Ground". This is set for the 18th January 2007 and guess who would also be looked upon to pick that tab up. – Rotherham United.

This is after Rotherham United Football Club had paid to date every bit due on the lease and the other attached liabilities despite the club having no income for the first few months of it's operation. We also spent near on £200,000 in putting the owners stadium back into a state of repair that the football league would find acceptable. I wonder where the owners imagine that money came from! Why didn't they offer to assist, one has to question?

The situation with regard to the stadium continues to rock on! The club has been talking to various investors in the wings but many are deterred by the ground situation and aggressive attitude of the stadium's owners.

There has been so much positive work done at the club, with hope being generated for the future, it is a shame not all appreciate the situation. The club has instructed it's own lawyers and will address the situation head on as January 2007 gets into gear.

It is actions like these that do drive you on to continue the search for a new stadium away from the whims of a few. This will obviously be put back at the top of the board's agenda.

Press Release -END

At every board meeting we had discussed the whole issues of the demon lease. The aggression shown in December 2007 really pushed us over the edge. We decided that we would "head them off at the pass" and commence our own legal action for the formal annulment of the lease.

On 29 January 2007 to cover the amount of rent, legal fees etc owed, the sum of £65,000 was lodged into our lawyers' client account in readiness as well as a writ presented at Leeds High Court challenging the validity of the lease.

C F Booth Limited (claimant) and Rotherham United FC Limited (defendant) case sprung into action before District Judge Hill on 5 February 2007 (case number 6R504765).

The judge was reluctant to make a decision on the whole issue whilst ever our court action for annulment of the lease was hanging over the proceedings. It was ordered that, commencing on 1 April 2007, we paid £13,220.37 into the court as an act of good faith and that we should also pay the interest pursuant to the licence fee, direct to C F Booth Limited on 1 April, 1 July, 1 October and 1 January.

We wanted to suspend the Hospitality agreement and we wrote to C F Booth Limited on the following lines: -

Dear Sirs,

> Agreement Dated 7 June 2006 between Changing Finish Limited and C F Booth Limited.
>
> We write in relation to the above agreement. As you are aware, we have taken legal advice as to the transactions that took place in December 2004 and as a result, have issued a claim in the High Court in Leeds against you to set aside certain transactions, which took place at this time. Our claim is to set aside leases between us and equally the hospitality agreement. Therefore, at this time, the club's board of directors inform you that the benefits afforded to you under the agreement will no longer be provided until such time as the court decides on whether what took place in December 2004 was lawful and proper. We would be obliged if you would acknowledge receipt of this letter."

Yours faithfully
The Board of Directors RUFC

That letter really upset them and we were again threatened with legal action. One of our concerns regarding this was the safety of Ken Booth Senior. As the publicity got out, there were some ugly things being said on the terraces and in internet chat rooms. We didn't want to be spending more money on legal fees fighting something that was less important in that it would not really gain us anything, better to keep funds for the bigger fight. We all agreed not to enforce the ban.

Paul contacted C F Booth Limited and said that we agreed to allow the hospitality package to continue and in the circumstances that we would ensure that security in the ground was made available for Ken Booth senior's personal protection but that they should make their own arrangements regarding safety outside the ground. Feelings of some fans were running high.

Ken senior really was the casualty in all this ill feeling. On 9 May 2007, we received notification that they were taking up their options to review the rent on the Tivoli suite and this was to rise from £2,600 to £3,033.33 per month, i.e., from £31,200 to £36,400 per annum. We continued paying funds into court, ensuring that we were never late.

My own view on all of this in essence is that business is business. Because a football club is a passion and close to your heart, it should not make it an exception in business. However, under the normal course of business, one would be unlikely to plough on into legal proceedings so quickly because a tenant informs you they will be missing a payment but remedying it the month after.

C F Booth Limited was paid everything it was entitled to under the lease so far. The substantial legal costs incurred were nothing really to do with the Booths'. What was to do with them however was a significant omission from their own vocabulary of "compassion and understanding".

The judge at the first County Court hearing in Rotherham seemed to show some great sympathy for the club's situation, particularly considering the payments made to date.

CHAPTER 17 (G.H.B.)

ALAN KNILL

Alan Richard Knill first joined Rotherham United in 1997, when he was signed as a central defender. He remained a player with the Millers until 2001 making 77 appearances and scoring 6 goals along the way. After a spell as youth team manager he emerged once more in January 2005 when appointed caretaker manager following the sacking of Ronnie Moore. This lasted until April 2005 when Mick Harford was handed the permanent manager's role. In December 2005 the board of directors sacked Harford after a series of heavy defeats, which left them staring in the face of relegation. Alan again emerged in the caretaker role, which was eventually made permanent by the incoming chairman Denis Coleman in March 2006. He subsequently managed to avoid relegation by a single point on the last day of the season.

His football career started back in 1982 with the following playing record:

Years	Club	App (Gls)*
1982–1984	Southampton	0 (0)
1984–1987	Halifax Town	118 (6)
1987–1989	Swansea City	89 (3)
1989–1993	Bury	144 (8)
1993	Cardiff City (loan)	4 (0)
1993–1997	Scunthorpe United	130 (8)
1997–2001	Rotherham United	77 (6)

Alan also made an International appearance playing for Wales in 1988.

I personally liked Alan and admired him for his politeness and professionalism.

He took the news of the 10 point deduction for 2006/07 season very well. It was mentioned in an article in the Guardian that Alan Knill even managed to make the prospect of starting with a negative points tally sound appealing.

"There's something about the 10-point penalty I like," said the manager who has transformed the club's fortunes after taking charge in December.

In another paper he was quoted;

> "It sets a challenge and I like a challenge. I've spoken to the players and they are not too bothered because they all thought we could have easily got 10 more points [this season]. Our improvement has not been rocket science, just belief."

The Team budget for 2006/2007 season was about £1,500,000, which was too high, but there were ongoing contracts that made it difficult to reduce overnight. At one of our first board meetings to which Alan was invited to do a presentation, he did tell us that he was warming to Eugene Bopp and his improved performances and that he was to start interim talks with Lee Williamson and his agent to try and secure him for a further contract period.

Alan took his job very seriously and if a team member felt pain then so did he. He didn't suffer fools gladly though and would put foolhardiness into its place.

One of my first jobs involving Alan was trying to convince him that his players would from hereon have to buy their own sandwiches at the Training ground. We were monitoring all costs, when a bill landed across my desk for nearly £2,000 from a local supplier in Rotherham for a month's compliment of snacks including sandwiches, sausage rolls soft drinks etc,. "What the bloody hell is this for?" I remember asking Paul in amazement. Paul being such a diplomat went on to brief me as to how this practice had always taken place and I had to be careful not to upset the apple cart without giving matters their full consideration.

This in reality was a players' matter. I raised the subject at the next board meeting so Denis being responsible for all playing and coaching staff could air his views. I proposed a resolution for an immediate termination of this arrangement. Denis being realistic agreed that this was an unnecessary cost. "How many people go out to work and have to buy their own sandwiches – the majority." he said. It was unanimously agreed that particularly with the level of salaries being enjoyed by the playing staff the practice would end forthwith.

I was on my way to Robin Hood's Bay when my car phone rang. It was the hotline from the training ground. "Are you serious" the first team coach Nick Daws enquired? I then had a 5-minute lecture that this was seen as an erosion of one of the very few privileges Millers players had. "Okay, How many years has this gone on for" I enquired.

"Ever since I can remember" came the reply.

"The Inland Revenue will love this." I said and went on to explain that the provision of regular lunches was another way of being paid in reality and so a P11D benefit in kind form should have been completed for everyone involved, tax assessments would have to be raised for this year and of course their will also be assessments for prior years.

The caller suddenly changed tack and said, "Well if it's for the good of the club then I suppose its okay". Oh the powers of Her Majesty.

Alan would regularly fetch matters to the boardroom for discussion. One matter always sticks in my memory, when he raised concerns over a female member of staff regularly walking into the changing rooms when the lads were coming out of the showers. After several minutes of really hilarious banter Paul was given the task of letting the staff member know she had been "Exposed" and it had to stop.

During 2006 Alan was hunting for new blood and we signed a young full back on loan from Derby, who had recently been on loan at Doncaster. Denis asked him "If he was any good ?" and his reply was "Don' t know. Den I've never seen him play"

So Denis quite astounded asked "What made you sign him then?" and Alan replied "Someone had told him he might be worth a punt" this did leave us all gob smacked.

Whenever he wanted to sign someone and was asked about the player's ability Alan always replied, " he can head it and he can kick it and that's what we need" It always made us smile. Alan liked to keep his office private and if he was not in his office he kept it locked. He would not even let his assistant Nick Daws have access so Dawsy had to do his paperwork in the car. One potentially good signing he made was Martin Woods from Sunderland but he was well outside our budget. Alan had to talk Denis round to agree to sign him and promised Den he would make the club some money.

Alan Knill signing autographs for the young fans.

Unfortunately this did not materialise as while Denis was away on holiday the deal was completed in his absence allowing Wood's to have an escape clause in his contract stating that he could leave on a free transfer if the club was relegated.

Alan had made other high profile signings in addition to Woods during the pre-season to bolster the squad including: former Liverpool and Sheffield Wednesday winger Richie Partridge and ex-Premiership players Delroy Facey and former Bayern Munich and Notts Forest star Eugen Bopp to name but a few.

Alan and his famous "Knilly Coat" became known as a bit of a fashion icon. I don't know where he got it from but he certainly had his money's worth out of it. He strutted up and down the touchline as if he was on the catwalk. Unbelievably some fans were asking if we were selling these coats in the club shop as they wanted to buy one.

By the 16th September after three wins and two draws from the first nine games, Rotherham had wiped out their points' deficit and the club was looking to catch up with the teams just above them in the league. Although beaten 4-2 by Norwich in the Carling Cup game at home we were deemed to have been the better side and unlucky on the night. Alan gathered his players together in the centre of the pitch at the end of this game as the

Norwich players limped off. He did it to show there was a togetherness and he wanted the players to relish the applause they deserved. As a board we were dissapointed with the attendance at just over 4000 fans, particularly as we had been beating the drum to "Come on down." Denis gave a heart felt statement out to the press "we need the town to get behind us".

With Cup worries out of the way for now Alan concentrated on the forthcoming league games, and by the 14th October we had moved off the bottom of the table. After a further run of three successive victories we finally moved out of the relegation zone, which was a magnificent achievement. This was after after a 5-1 win against Crewe Alexander on the 28th October 2006. After winning every league game in October, Knill was awarded the Manager of the Month (which is often referred to as the kiss of death) and also the Yorkshire TV Manager of the Year award. What a coup! We bought Alan a large bottle of Dom Perignon champagne as a gesture from the Board for his success.

From the second week in November things started to go wrong for Alan. The 10-point deduction for the club had been a bitter pill to swallow. Many people felt that this huge hurdle gave Alan an almost impossible task, but he worked hard all pre-season to give the club a fighting chance of survival in League One and the fans were right behind him.

Then the black clouds circled

We were playing Peterborough in the F.A. Cup on Saturday the 11th November. It was a funny old game right from the start. In this match both Lee Williamson and Michael Keane were injured, depleting the squad. Peterborough won the game comfortably 3-0. By the time Williamson was fit and ready to rejoin the squad we were selling him on to Watford and his absence for over 6 weeks did coincide with our dip in form.

The poor run of games without a win weighed heavily on Alan Knill's shoulders. The sale of Hoskins and Williamson was often blamed. It was obvious that losing our two best players would undoubtedly take its toll but we as a Board lived in hope. The gloom continued as we sunk back to the bottom of the table after winning only one match in over three months. As March arrived we were 13 point adrift of safety and the fans were becoming very irritated. A great apathy had spread across the club and all confidences were knocked for six. The Millers Mad web site back in February had some early threads saying Alan should go. As the results continued to be unfavourable the threads gained more support. Probably acting in his own defence Alan started making comments to the media about the club and the board, being quite critical of the lack of funds made available to him from the so called Watford deals. The problem was that we had a backlog of creditors to bring up to date and I, in particular, wanted to keep funds in the War Chest for the future fight. I did not want to simply plough it back into the players' budget with no guarantees. After all Alan had picked many of the players in his existing squad and in my view ought to have been whipping them into shape. They had ability but seemed to lack motivation.

Since receiving the Watford cash everyone was jumping on the band wagon, theoretically spending the money on just about everything. One of the players who was our biggest overhead who hadn't played all season through an alleged injury even asked Alan for a pay rise now that the bank account was flush. I could not believe the man's cheek. Alan put a lot of pressure on Denis for us to spend some of the transfer money. Denis admitted he erred by letting Alan convince him that Craig Fleming an experienced player from Norwich would keep us up. This proved to be so misguided in fact his performance was only average to say the least. Denis felt that by not doing his homework Alan cost us the best part of £70,000. The deal made him our most expensive player even though Denis knocked him down £500 a week from what Alan had initially promised him.

At times there was disharmony with players as Alan had a job to do. One time Michael Keane went to see Denis after Alan had dropped him from the first team. He was fuming and wanted Denis to overrule him. Denis told him he couldn't do that. If Alan had known about this incident he would rightly have been furious. Another of the squad members came to borrow some money, £6000 as he had debt problems he did not want to reveal. We told him to discuss it first with Alan but he didn't wish to. He said he couldn't face him. We loaned him the money and he did duly pay it back. We got no thanks though. As I was always the gatekeeper of the cash purse new signings had to be justified to me. I was not easily convinced and my accountants head often clashed with team management strategy. We did authorise the signing of Chris O Grady from Leicester City for £60,000 who was another player on Alan's wish list.

Alan's position was discussed at a few board meetings and sacking him was a very hard decision to make. The problem now was not only the lack of team performance but the unrest among the fans was becoming unbearable. For weeks on Radio Sheffield's Football Heaven it had become routine for Alan to apologise frequently criticising his team's commitment, He confirmed that things had been getting tough between himself and Denis in one of his final interviews. Just before Alan's departure he started asking Denis to go into the changing rooms and give the lads a pep talk. Denis recalled, "The players must have thought both of us had lost the plot."

I think Alan had just run out of ideas.

The final game under Alan Knill was a 2-1 defeat against Swansea at Millmoor on the Tuesday night. Denis had a talk with Alan and then a special emergency meeting of the board was held on the 7th March 2007 at our lawyer's office in Leeds at which the decision was finally made to sack him.

PRESS ARTICLES

'Unanimous decision'

So why has Knill been sacked? Denis Coleman had this to say:

"We met as a board yesterday [Wednesday] and we've had meetings with Alan over the last week or so.

"We just thought it was the best thing for the club at the moment. We had to make a very hard decision and do a lot of soul-searching yesterday and that was the conclusion we came to."

This press release was not entirely correct in that I actually abstained in the final boardroom vote.

Mark Thomas of Rust said when interviewed by Radio Sheffield:

"Over the last three games it's been evident that perhaps some of the players haven't been playing for him.

"Certainly some of those players in that dressing room should be feeling guilty because I think that ultimately the players have got him the sack. They've put the directors in a very difficult position.

"As supporters we're entitled to expect better from the players - they've not all been doing a full shift in the last few games and they needed to."

Mark Thomas of R.U.S.T. also had every sympathy with Knill: "You've got to say that fate's dealt him a horrendous hand this season.

"He's had to work with a handicap of minus 10; he lost four key players at Peterborough, nine games before Christmas (which is when I believe the rot really set in) and then he lost his leading striker and midfielder on January 1st. He's had a difficult hand to play with."

MANAGER REPLACEMENT

Coleman told BBC Radio Sheffield that the club will fill their managers position before the end of the season and have already received 40 applications for the job.

He stands by his decision to sack Alan Knill, believing it was the right time to make a change:

> "If we had have waited 'till the end of the season all the players would have disappeared. Then you've got to find a man to come in and rebuild the squad.
>
> "We've got time on our hands now, everybody thinks we're down anyway, maybe that's not true, maybe we can still do it, if we don't we've got time to build for next season."

In the end Alan could have made things more awkward for the club. You do not break a contract without any repercussions and issues to settle. For the record, Alan's compromise agreement was also where some more of the Watford money went.

I did think though that Alan later let himself down when we played Chesterfield away on the 5th December 2007. It was an evening match, freezing cold in a ground worse than Rotherham's. The match had been good for Rotherham in that we won despite the high-spirited fracas that occurred on the pitch. The team took a few knocks along the way with Ryan Taylor off injured. Peter Holmes came on and did a great job along with Pablo who was going from strength to strength. It was a great result with a 2-0 win. At the end of the game I watched Alan with a view of perhaps saying "Hello" again. The opportunity did not arise. Instead of shaking hands with Mark Robins as is expected he totally snubbed him, which I thought to be very unprofessional. He was obviously seething at losing to his old club Rotherham United, now managed by his once youth team assistant coach.

When we played Yeovil away on the 21st April 2007 the Director of Yeovil told Denis and Mark Robins that Alan had been on the phone to them discussing the club and players. The Director said he thought it was bad sportsmanship. He did not want to tell us prior to the game in case it revved the players up even more. We lost the game 1-0 from a first half injury time goal so maybe they gleaned something from his little pep talk with the manager after all. Alan left Chesterfield as assistant manager and joined his old club Bury as first team manager on the 4th February 2008. He was very popular there as a player and he was welcomed back like a long lost son. When the Millers played Bury at Gigg Lane the following month we were soundly beaten 3 – 0. It was a shocking game and comments were made that the die-hard fans that had made the Tuesday evening journey over the Pennines deserved better. This time though at the end of the game Alan couldn't get over to Mark Robins quickly enough to shake his hand. But, he let himself down once more by turning towards the Rotherham directors and giving us all the two fingers.

Ah well that's football for you.

CHAPTER – 18 (G.H.B.)

THE COUNCIL MEN COMETH

Before my involvement with Rotherham United, I knew very little of Roger Stone, leader of Rotherham Borough Council. He turned up once on our Swinton Heritage 'Kilnhurst History Tour' a few years earlier in 2000. But since then only briefly through contact with my good friend, Councillor Ken Wyatt. Roger had been a serving Councillor since 1988 holding many positions before finally becoming leader of the Council in 2003.

When I met Roger in the directors' lounge, at Rotherham's home games, he always volunteered to tell me "I paid for the ticket myself, you know". It was as if he expected me, even as a relative stranger, to jump straight down his throat, demanding to know if this was a grace and favour attendance or had he paid his way. I was surprised to find out he was in fact a Derby County supporter. He explained that it was for his grandson's sake but as the season unfolded I think Roger became quite fond of the Millers.

As Christmas of 2006 was looming, the scant number of approaching home matches meant the cash flow would need stage-managing. The Council had given massive financial assistance to Rotherham Rugby Club previously so perhaps they could help us out a little now. We knew they had in the past, been in support of the 'Try line' centre based at the rugby club and in recognition of the work undertaken by their players acting as mentors in schools and organising school holiday training etc.

We felt that we were a deserving case in comparison because of all the hard work done through 'Football in the Community' and the work with the youth of the town and many schools.

We sent a request to Roger to see if he could try and support us.

If we could only get the rates' bill quashed for this year or at least, get the rates' department to stop the threatening reminders and phone calls. Within three days, we got an answer. Paul phoned me at the office for his daily bad news bulletin to tell me he had a bailiff present wanting to distrain on the Club's assets. I told Paul that as he was doing such a good job he was an asset to the club so perhaps he could get distrained upon himself. As this had to be dealt with immediately, I had to terminate my meeting with Darren Marshall, a NatWest manager and massive Rotherham fan.

After discussions with the bailiff, I managed to broker a deal with him acceptable to all. He was in fairness quite sympathetic; although a Wednesday, fan he did have some feelings for the club.

That was another crisis resolved. I can well imagine the hierarchy in the rates' department saying "Step up the action. If the business community know we have gone soft on Rotherham United, we will struggle with collecting any business rates this year".

Setting this incident aside, which was laughable, Roger was generally supportive of the club and would do anything he could to promote it along the way, although a problem was that this was not the view of some of his fellow councillors. He always did say he wanted league football in Rotherham and I believe he meant every word. There was a lot of negotiating with the Booth's and the Council re the possibility of purchasing back the land at Millmoor and redeveloping the stadium with private investors. This moved slowly at first but then gained pace except for one sticking point the Hospitality package, which was non-negotiable as far as C F Booth's

Yes, that's the man concerned. Darren Marshall (Commercial Manager Nat West Bank) being entertained by a club representative at Notts Forest. Darren had gone as a guest of club director Giles Brearley. A lifelong fan: this was a big day for him.

Roger Stone (leader of Rotherham Council) not looking too happy, catches a minute at half time at Millmoor.

The Liberty stadium at Swansea. They hosted a visit from the club and Rotherham Council to pass on knowledge as to how they brokered their new stadium deal.

Doncaster's new stadium gave us some hope, it could be done.

Inside Doncaster's new Stadium. The match day of 16th September 2006 was a little marred when some Rotherham fans were ejected from the ground by over zealous Stewarding. The game was a 0-0 draw.

were concerned. The overall price that was negotiated was at a level far higher than that indicated on the club's balance sheet. The balance sheet value was also used for the court case? The new selling price was more than the Council really wanted to pay. Independent valuers were instructed but it came to nothing and the Council finally pulled out when our subsequent court battle with the Booths' ensued. Unfortunate as it was, I still maintain we did not start this war. It was a shame in some respects as Millmoor could have been re-modernised with new facilities introduced, almost as good as a new stadium with the correct funding made available.

The new community stadium situation was not a new creation in our stewardship but had been seriously banded about back in 2001. The Council then cited that the recent promotion to Division 1 in particular necessitated better ground facilities, the same also applied to the Rugby Club.

Cost estimates then were between £5 million if Millmoor could be bought and refurbished to £20 million for a brand new Stadium. Sites considered for a New Stadium included the Training ground at Hooton Roberts. Herringthorpe Playing fields and a site owned by Stadium Developments Ltd at Aldwarke. (The site proposed now) and a site owned by Ron Hull Junior Ltd off Rotherham Road, Parkgate. Sites in the Templeborough / Canklow area had been dismissed as unsuitable.

Swansea F.C had achieved the ultimate dream of most clubs and built a brand new stadium in partnership with the local council and Doncaster Rovers were virtually ready to move in to the brand new Keep Moat Stadium built on a similar arrangement. Following on from a contact of R.M.B.C Chief Executive Mike Cuff's, a delegation from Rotherham went down to Swansea and received the grand tour and held discussions as to how they had financed it. Dave, Dino, Paul, Mike Cuff and Roger Stone were all present. They came back with glowing reports. The Stadium was a 20,000 capacity all seater and was a credit to the town. As Denis missed the first opportunity to view the Stadium he took advantage of his own personal tour when we played them on New Years' day 2007.

It was built by Interserve for a cost of around £27m, Interserve were quite interested in talking to us about tendering for Rotherham's new stadium. Swansea's stadium was just completed in time for the first game in July 2005. Although somewhat conservative in design, the stadium is very impressive to look at. It is completely enclosed with all four corners filled with seating. Each of the four stands are two tiered and three of the Stands are of the same height. The West Stand at one side of the pitch being slightly taller as it had a row of 28 corporate hospitality boxes, situated above the upper tier. This was deemed crucial towards making commercial success. The Club's offices are also located behind this stand. A revolutionary feature is the incorporation of transparent roofing towards the South End of the stadium. This allows natural light into this area whilst still giving the crowd that "Stadium Effect". Both the home and away ends have individual electric scoreboards situated on the front of their roofs; the scoreboard at the North End is larger than the one at the South End. This gave the opportunity of having two score board sponsors for the same game. The stadium was shared with Neath-Swansea Ospreys Rugby Union Club.

This was of great interest to us. How did the ground share work and was it successful? They indicated it worked well. There was some inconvenience but these were greatly outweighed by the advantages. One disappointment for Swansea was that the crowds did increase but they struggled to get above 13,000. A further visit was organised to the new Hull City ground by Mike Cuff.

Denis and David were given the grand tour in October 2006 by the Hull City F.C Chief Executive. The Kingston Communications Stadium (commonly referred to as the KC Stadium) was opened in December 2002. It had cost far more than Swansea's at almost £44m. It was built by Birse Construction and like Swansea is home to both the Football & Rugby Clubs.

The Stadium is situated in a parkland setting and can be seen for miles around.

Its design is excellent. Credit due to the Architects.

The stadium is also totally enclosed, with the West Stand being double the size of the other three sides. The roof rises up and curves around the West Stand, giving the stadium an interesting vista.

Inside, the curves continue as each of the stands bow around the playing areas drawing them all in together in one sweep. Each of the stands is single tiered, that is apart from the two-tiered West Stand. Here there is also housed a row of executive boxes running right across the middle. There is an electric scoreboard at the North End of the stadium, where the Police Control Box is also situated. The pitch has under soil heating installed. The sound system within the stadium is very impressive. Everyone thought this Stadium would not look out of place in the Premiership not realising that within two years this would be the case. Now that Hull have bought our young rising star goalkeeper for a bargain price a piece of Rotherham United will hopefully be represented there. When the Advertiser later wrote an article comparing Martin Winter's achievements as the elected Mayor of Doncaster to Rotherham Councils track record, Roger was really upset. The article quoted how in Martin's time there had been the Lakeside development, a new airport, a new town centre development, the railway station upgraded oh, and a new sporting stadium. Ouch – that hurt! I suppose in fairness the criticism was justified, Rotherham's renaissance plan is to be somewhat revolutionary but was someway behind Doncaster in its implementation.

Roger did keep his ear to the ground and would three or four times a week ring David Costin and meet with him on his way into the office on a Friday morning. David would tell him our news and would keep him updated. They struck up a good rapport and David even went to some Derby games with Roger.

At a board meeting, under any other business, Paul raised a confidential memo from the Council. There was to be a meeting regarding a new stadium but it was to be a secret meeting. No one was to know. It was agreed that Denis and I would attend and report back. The meeting was timed to be after 5.00pm in the Eric Mann's building after the staff had gone. As confidentiality was stressed with such vigour as a pre-condition, Denis and I parked well away from the building. As we approached the building we cautiously looked up and down the street ensuring we were not in the wakeful gaze of someone in the surrounding office blocks. We paused for a moment outside the Eric Mann's building confident there was no one looking we slid inside with great stealth. In the Reception a young lady was just making her way out. "Hello" she said, "Are you hear about the meeting for the new stadium? It's down there. The rugby lads are already here" So much for secrets!

After that first meeting, we went over to Wetherspoons with the rugby lads for a beer. We liked the idea of a new stadium. "Could it happen?" was our thought. We'd had talks before with Martin and his co directors about the possibility of the football and rugby club sharing Millmoor, developing it privately so both clubs owned the ground. We talked through all the logistics. Martin indicated that the rugby club could pull up some funds to make it happen. One thing I did like about the new stadium meetings was having the opportunity to meet Mike Cuff. He seemed to portray a "Yes Prime Minister" role. He was a very knowledgeable, professional and had delivered a stadium before whilst with another Local Authority so he seemed to be the right man for the job.

As for the confidentiality issue, it was all blown out of the water when detailed references to the stadium started to appear in the press. For the record, that leak did not come from us! The press leak was in such detail it does lead one to ask the question "Does the Council have a mole"?

There were some who thought that Roger adopted a bit of a cavalier approach in his furthering of the New Stadium. Some of his fellow Councillors believed there should be more open consultation on matters. I can understand Roger's viewpoint in that he probably wants to deliver a complete package for consideration rather than a concept. There is no guarantee that all the Councillors will be in favour. Hopefully they will.

As late as January 2008 quotes from Councillors on the proposed site showed matters were still in the very early stages as far as the Council was concerned:

> "As a council we have not discussed the option of deciding on a community stadium yet. The council in its year ahead statement stated it would investigate the possibility of a community stadium. Speaking personally I think a community stadium would be a good idea, however we need to look at other key factors such as capital and revenue costs, income streams, whether we have support for the stadium by the people of Rotherham, will major sporting clubs of Rotherham play there.
>
> The campaign run by Rotherham United on saturday, which I attended, under the banner 'United Rotherham' was very successful and well supported by the local people of Rotherham and the Rotherham Advertiser.
>
> In addition, I do want to make sure that sporting provision around the borough are maintained and enhanced. The proposed enhancements to Herringthorpe stadium will definitely improve the services there. A new 500 seater stand, new changing rooms, new 5 a side football pitches with the latest all weather turf and an

indoor warm up area will bring the athletics sporting facilities up to a modern standard. All the existing 11 a side football pitches and cricket pitches on the playing fields will be relaid and drainage problems due to flooding will be sorted out to ensure they are of the highest quality to play on.

These proposed enhancements have the support of the local athletics club and players.

I hope this information helps, if you have any further questions please let me know."

All the best.
Councillor Mahroof Hussain

December 2007 (Mike Cuff)

"The Council are fully supporting plans for a new Community Stadium."

Roger showed his devoted support for the Millers in that he was very influential in securing the new syndicate purchasers for the club. Strangely enough, when we approached the same people the year before, they were not interested. Perhaps Roger Stone's negotiating skills are far superior to ours? Our only hope is that the downturn in the economy does not deter the development of the new stadium. Congratulations to Roger and his team for the concept of realism applied to sorting this problem out. If the funds had to come from borrowed money it would not work and the new Stadium would become a liability for the ratepayers. Even with prudent management, care has to be taken, Doncaster have already run into some controversy over the Stadium's self financing.

The £700,000 bond that the League has insisted the Club deposit with them in order to play in the interim at the Don Valley Stadium in Sheffield has been a real tester. This bond was levied on the club because of the outstanding issues with the Football Foundation Stadia Improvement Fund who were trying to reclaim the £1.7m grant monies provided to Millers 05 when building the new main stand at Millmoor. The bond will be repaid if Rotherham United do move to a purpose built stadium within 4 years. The Council have covered the bulk of this deposit which more than emphasises their commitment to the New Stadium. It also gives us a feeling of regret that they did not do more for us at the time. Especially considering the previous comments regarding the Rugby Club. I wonder how the other Councillors and ratepayers feel about all this.

A recent press release stated:

> "Rotherham Borough Council agreed on Wednesday to put forward to the full council, a recommendation of £500,000 commitment towards the bond for the football foundation trust.
>
> The bond would only come in to force if substantial progress has not been made towards the building of a new stadium within four years time."

In a further statement issued to the Advertiser Roger Stone said:

> "The local authority had sent a letter of commitment but the football foundation were looking for a greater deal of reassurance. Following on Mr Stone added... Rotherham Borough Council has made no secret that it supports the idea of a community stadium but we hope the offer of this bond is concrete proof of our commitment to see a 15,000 all seater stadium built in the town that will provide both sporting and community facilities for the people of Rotherham".

Obviously, there are no guarantees the Stadium will be built. That is the risk the authority will have to take and I am sure it will be carefully monitored. I personally feel that there should have been more pressure exerted via the local M.P John Healey. The sporting grant system was originally set up by the Government and although allowed to operate independently should not be allowed to prevent progress for unconnected parties. Why should a debt from Millers 05 have had a precedent over us and also why should Tony Stewart and his syndicate of new owners be affected when they are not even playing at Millmoor and never have. It is an absurd situation and the Government should have become involved to find a sensible remedy to this.

CHAPTER - 19 (G.H.B.)

STAMPING ON OUR RIGHTS

Not wanting to sound repetitive, the original lease for Millmoor and the training ground was issued on 31 December 2004 during the Millers 05 takeover. On 7 June 2006, a license to assign the lease was entered into between C F Booth Limited and our company Changing Finish Limited. As part of the overall terms, as the assignee of the lease, we had to agree to pay C F Booth Limited £600,000. A covenant was entered into to pay a single payment of £20,000 and thereafter, 108 consecutive monthly payments of £5370.37 .We also had to undertake to pay interest on this outstanding balance, which was initially around £2700 per month. All this carried over from Millers 05.

Confusion seemed to arise as to the position regarding Stamp Duty and if the deal constituted a chargeable event. The lease was actually assigned for a nominal amount of £1 and initial views were that because the transaction did not exceed £120,000 SDLT would be chargeable at the 0% rate. The issue was around whether the giving of consent to an assignment of the lease constituted a disposal and acquisition of the chargeable interest in land within the scope of Section 43(1) Finance Act 2003.

Correspondence had apparently been going back and forth between our lawyers and the Manchester Stamp Taxes Office for some time. On Friday, 3 November 2006, a phone call from our lawyers gave Paul his daily fix of bad news that he so welcomed before calling our office for advice.

Gavin initially took the call and jumped into gear on Rotherham's behalf.The lease they originally issued in December 2004 contained a clause preventing Rotherham United from assigning the lease. H M Revenue & Customs view was that the lease did not contain any provision giving the landlord the right to make a charge beyond his legal costs for the giving of a licence to assign. Thus the basis of the charge made of £600,000 was, in their opinion, "imposed". They viewed it as part of the deal and so they belatedly wanted their stamp duty. From my point of view it certainly was imposed

This out of the blue decision now left the club with a bill of

£24,000 plus interest and penalties. Talk about wanting your pound of flesh and eating it! and for what? To simply burden Rotherham United with another thumping great bill from the Revenue. If it was tax generated from income received, like the sale of an asset at, least there would be funds to pay it from. But this is just a cost addition for the Treasuries benefit that is non-negotiable. This was certainly rubbing salt into our wounds.

Stamp duty was first levied in the UK in 1694 to pay for the war with France. Although initially only planned for four years, it proved to be such a good earner for the government that it was never repealed. The tax's range was extended during the 18th and 19th century to cover a range of goods, including insurance policies, gold and silver plate and even hair powder The tax was duly extended to cover property sales in 1808. In 1891, today's main legal basis for stamp duty was introduced in the Stamp Duties Management Act and the Stamp Duties Act. In 2003, Stamp Duty Land Tax was established in its own right; the basis for the tax now is the transaction rather than the documents that underpin the transaction.

I did write to try and slow things down in view of the fact we were finding cash flow tight:

7 March 2007
H M Revenue and Customs
Excise and Stamp Duty Taxes
Manchester Stamp Office
Upper 5th Floor, Royal Exchange
Exchange Street
MANCHESTER
M2 7EB
Dear Sir

Ref: MAN/06/24989/PAL – Rotherham United FC Ltd formerly Changing Finish Ltd

Further to your letter of 26 February 2007 to the Chief Executive of Rotherham United, we have been asked to write on the Club's behalf.

You may well be aware that the Club is currently in litigation with C F Booth Ltd over the legitimacy of the lease. The Club is seeking High Court action to have the lease overturned on the basis of a sham. The Court has ordered the Club to stop making any payments on the lease direct and sums are being paid into Court.

We therefore wish to apply for a hold over of any Stamp Duty until the Court case is settled? As far as Rotherham United are concerned, the lease is not proper and does not bind them.

We appreciate these are unusual circumstances but the Club are fiercely fighting this issue.

We look forward to hearing from you in the near future.

Yours faithfully
G H BREARLEY
Brearley & Co Accountants Limited

We were granted a lifeline in fairness as they seemed to leave us alone. We initially thought until our litigation with C F Booth Limited was over, but it continued long after. Talking afterwards to a Revenue

Officer he said that this was only because our file was lost during the transfer of records to the new Birmingham Stamp Duty Office following the closure of the old Manchester office. As far as he was concerned it was payable until evidenced otherwise and we should have been bludgeoned (or similar) until we paid.

Rotherham United certainly created unusual situations! I thought that HMRC were very understanding of our plight when in reality we benefited only from their clerical errors.

After the court case finished and the publicity machine relayed the bad news to the world, I suspected they would be in touch, but we heard nothing. After hearing of our plight, a friend of Tobin's agreed that if the shove came, he would discharge the liability on the club's behalf.

What a star! I would though rather have used that lifeline on something more benefiting the club's needs.

Chapter 20 (G.H.B.)

The Crumbling Foundations of the Football Stadium Crisis.

One March morning in 2007 I was in my office, opening the posts, which in the main were copies of clients' tax statements. I was placing these into meaningful piles: Can pay tax but won't; Will pay the tax; Can't pay now but will do; Please bear with me I am trying to pay; HMRC correspondence direct; junk mail and the cheque pile, which if I remember rightly looked a bit sad that day.

Leanne rang up from reception to politely announce Mr Douglas was on the phone. I thought this will be Paul with his usual bad news fix for me. I guessed he had just been opening the club's post and I was right.

"You will never believe what's come in the post today" he said.

"Let me guess" I replied, "A cheque for £100,000 from the League or confirmation Sky TV want to film us again."

"They only want £1.7million off of us." Paul said disdainfully.

"Who does" I enquired.

"That lot who gave Millers 05 a boat load of money to build the Stand. They are saying because its not finished we are in breach and we have to pay it back." Paul spluttered out before the phone then went silent.

I had the document faxed to me so I could have a proper read.

The grant was originally awarded by the Football Foundation Stadia Improvement Fund. They are the UK's largest sports charity. They are funded by the Premier League, The Football Association, Sport England and the Government, who each invest £15 million per annum. They claim their mission is to "improve facilities, create opportunities and build communities throughout England".

They are the country's largest provider of funds to grass roots football. In the past the Foundation has delivered thousands of Ground facility and community projects, as well as smaller support with free kit and safe goalposts. It commenced operations in July 2000.

Back in may 2005 the Millers 05 board secured the financial assistance of £1,712,178 towards the building of the new main stand. Part of the terms of the grant gave a timescale for which the building works had to be complete. The London lawyers who were writing on their client's behalf claimed this was a "football debt "and as such was inherited by us as an ongoing liability. It seemed so unfair. The letter went on to say that their client considered that the Club had breached its obligation to provide the balance of funding in respect of the Main Stand Development and to so use the Stand for the purpose for which the grant was given in the first place.

They reiterated it was with some regret that this action had to be taken but that their client had to answer to their regulator and must be seen to be adhering to the conditions, rules and terms to which the grant was offered. It also said that if we could give re-assurances that we would finish the stand they would stave off any immediate actions.

There was a Board meeting the following week so I decided to leave everything on hold until then but I would speak to our Lawyers in the meantime. I travelled through to Leeds and sat with David Hinchcliffe, both of us re-examining the documentation. David confirmed that indeed their claim of this being a football debt was correct and it was technically collectable under the rules prevailing. We both thought however that stepping outside the world of football and into civil law they would be unable to enforce it. The present club was not a contractual party to the original agreement, did not own the grant assisted asset and could side step any claim ...great news.

The downer though was that if we told them to "go forth and multiply" we would be in breach of the League's rules on football debts and be expelled from the League altogether. So again Rotherham's future was being threatened. I told the Board the news regarding the claim and like Paul they couldn't believe it either. Following on from my discussions with David, we constructed a letter to be sent back, pointing out the Club's current situation. We outlined how we were in dispute with our Landlords and going to litigation for recovery and if successful would hope to secure funding to finish the development. We wrote back to them on the 2nd April 2007.

Denis and David organised one of the big 6 construction

companies to get us an estimate for completion of everything on the part built Stand. This was a whopping £4 million. We all felt that we could make large savings on this, if it ever came to fruition.

By the 25th April 2007 the solicitors in London wrote back They had consulted with their client and taken further instructions. Whilst they understood our predicament they felt that the real prospects of a short term solution were negligible. The letter left the door open though by asking for some further clarifications from our lawyers. They wanted them to confirm as to when the legal dispute was likely to reach trial in court and what advice as to the merits of the case had been given and what R.U.F.C's likely position was. They wanted a reply by the 2nd May 2007.

Any lawyer would be very uncomfortable at releasing detailed information about an ongoing case and ours was no exception. After a series of telephone calls and a meeting in London they agreed that subject to us providing acceptable copies of past accounts and our forward projections they would sit in the wings to await the outcome of the court case. This done and approved, we put the matter on the back burner.

The court case came and went, and all was quiet.

We didn't let things rest though. I personally felt that there should be more compassion and sympathy shown. We needed to demonstrate to the sponsors of the Football Foundation the injustice it brought to clubs like Rotherham United.

I mentioned it to local M.P. John Healey, who I have always found to be very supportive and helpful. I believe he spoke briefly to the Minister of Sport about the matter but needed more information. I was to arrange a meeting at the Millmoor Ground with John when his diary permitted. I think John agreed with us and thought it was grossly unfair. I was convinced that with more prompting and support from the local community and from the football fraternity in general we could have done something more to suppress this unnecessary action.

Chapter - 21 (G.J.M.)

The Football League Awards

Following the 2-1 home defeat to Swansea City on a cold miserable Tuesday evening on 27 February 2007, Alan Knill was sacked as team manager of Rotherham United Football Club. In the interim, Mark Robins, head of the youth academy, was asked to take control as caretaker manager until a permanent appointment could be made. The following Saturday, an emphatic 4-1 home win against fellow strugglers, Bradford City, had given the club a much needed shot in the arm as this was our first win since Saturday, 2 December 2006 when we beat Yeovil Town 3-2 at home.

During the weeks leading up to Alan Knill's dismissal, the club had booked a table at the Grosvenor House Hotel in London for the Football League awards to be held on Sunday 4th March 2007. The idea of this award ceremony was to acknowledge the thankless work that goes on behind the scenes in promoting, marketing and organising the running of a football league club. We were given the nod it may be a good idea to attend. These unsung heroes are very often overlooked when the season finishes and the event is an attempt by the league to show their appreciation. The guest list for the RUFC table were Denis Coleman, Dave Costin, Giles Brearley, Gary Hall, Paul Douglas, Gavin Mackinder, Tony Jones, Ian Herbert, Ron Hull and Trevor Smallwood. There were nine guests travelling down from South Yorkshire on the train from Sheffield Midland Station whilst Trevor travelled up from Bristol and met us at our hotel later that afternoon.

During the train journey down, we contemplated whether or not Rotherham United were nominated for any awards but as we had not heard anything further from the League, as is often the case with these types of awards, then we had not set our hopes too highly.

It was however, a good opportunity to chat to Ron Hull, a local self made business man, of the type of calibre we all hoped one day would step forward and take over the club. I sensed that in Ron's case, the family ties with the previous owners and current landlords excluded him somewhat from this scenario. However,

Directors and guests at Sheffield Station setting off for the Football League awards in London.

Trevor Smallwood (left) and Ron Hull in deep discussion at the football league awards dinner, London. They both went as our guests.

Rotherham's directors at the Football league awards dinner London consoling themselves the club did not pick up any awards....

David Costin and Ian Herbert (Herbie) savour a moment. The cigarettes on the table date the scene.

it didn't hurt to have someone like him still showing his support for the club both financially and in spirit.

The awards ceremony itself was hosted by Jeff Stelling a self confessed Hartlepool fan who presents Gillette Soccer Saturday on Sky Sports News. There were awards for categories such as Fan of the Year, Best Away Ground, Good Sport Award, Young Apprentice Award, Best Club Sponsorship, Best Community Initiative, etc, etc. We all agreed that the dinner itself was pretty average if you can appreciate ten ravenous Yorkshire men having to make do with a delicately presented half portion of chicken with a few fancy potatoes and vegetables, then you probably get my drift. We did manage to network somewhat with the other clubs in attendance and a few old faces came to our table to say hello, including Richard Finney (ex Rotherham player), John Duncan (ex Chesterfield manager) and Dennis Leman (ex Sheffield Wednesday and Manchester City player). I suppose even though we only had eleven games left until the end of the season, we were still hopeful that we could just avoid relegation by the skin of our teeth so despite the lousy food and slightly boring ceremony, we were determined to make the most of this rare outing representing Rotherham United Football Club in the presence of our peers.

I myself was especially keen to speak to Tad Detko who was the main finance director at the Football League. I had raised a point several weeks earlier when chatting with the financial representative of Brentford Football Club. The hypothetical situation I suggested was that all seventy two members of the Football League get their heads together and agree to boycott the FA Cup. The thought process behind this was to show the powers that be in television and the media that we could operate autonomously without the "big boys". I put forward the idea that the Football League could have its own knock out cup competition without the Premier League clubs and felt this could be just as exciting and rewarding as the FA Cup and marketable too. If this was successful then I suggested removing promotion and relegation to and from the Premiership and making our Championship the Premier League. I think the reason for my very forthright approach was brought about after hours and hours of painstaking budgeting and planning the ongoing cash flow of the club, living hand to mouth from day to day, knowing that there were only twenty football clubs in the Premiership, who were creaming in the income from television and media all over the world and keeping it for themselves. The smaller League One and Two clubs were all struggling week in, week out, to make ends meet and going through various forms of administration from one season to the next. Incurring point's deductions, which only made their plight even harder when, as we all know, success in football is based on results. We ourselves at Rotherham had started the season with a ten-point deduction and it was looking more likely that this in itself could send us down to League Two next season.

Tad didn't seem too impressed with my maverick approach and like most of the suits within the Football League, seemed quite happy to sit back and let the FA and Premier League walk all over them. Their members are treated as the poor relations of football and when the going gets tough, they reward them with point deductions which, nine times out of ten, forces the clubs into certain relegation. I believe that football at this level is on the decline and the average supporter who wants to follow their local team will eventually be sat at home on a Saturday afternoon twiddling their thumbs or with their other half in the dreaded shopping malls up and down the country. Strangely enough just before the start of the 2007/2008 season the FA Premier League released a series of what they called "Solidarity Payments" to all Football League clubs from the Championship down to League Two. There was somewhere in the region of £32 million in total paid out of which we got about £70K. I wonder if Tad Detko knew this was in the pipeline during our conversation?

Nevertheless, its quite obvious that the whispers and rumblings throughout English football concerning the great divide in incomes may be starting to sink in but for me the solidarity payments are only a drop in the ocean compared to the money that passes through the Premier League coffers each season and the Football League in my opinion just seem to be thankful for small mercies.

What a shame!

CHAPTER 22 (G.J.M.)

FISH, CHIPS & MUSHY FEES

Towards the end of March 2007, barring a miracle, Rotherham United looked doomed for relegation to League Two. Since the halcyon days between August and November 2006, Alan Knill's team had gone into freefall i.e. played 15, won 1, drawn 4 and lost 10 in the three months from December 2006 to February 2007.

Giles Brearley, Denis Coleman and I had arranged a meeting at Brearley & Co's offices to commence the difficult process of setting the budget for next season on the basis that we would ultimately be relegated. Since January, the average home attendance had plummeted to well below 4,000, which was over 1,000 per game less than in the first half of the season. This loss of income was eating into the cash reserves of the club, generated mainly from the Hoskins and Williamson transfer deals at a rate of £20,000 per home game. We also had to take into account that May, June and July were the three months of the year where, except for season ticket sales, virtually no other significant amounts of income would be coming into the club. It was important the club did not depend on the season ticket income during the summer months as this was mostly needed to kick start the cash flow for the new football season, commencing in August.

I laid before the chairman and finance director, the previous year's budget and actual figures, highlighting the various income streams and the costs attributed to these. One of the most difficult things for the fans to appreciate is that following relegation, whilst income falls dramatically from gate receipts and the Football League Basic Award, etc, the match day costs, staff salaries and majority of the player's remaining contracts, do not fall at the same level. In fact, certain areas, including fees for policing, health and safety etc were anticipated to increase and it's at times like this when you realise you have got a real fight on your hands.

Denis believed that our only hope of survival next season was to set the budget with the intention of bouncing straight back into League One. His belief was that if the team could make a good start and remain in the top five up to Christmas 2007, then our home attendances would be in excess of 4,500 fans. I must admit that I was not as optimistic as Denis. However, I did understand his thought process and as he had been a Miller for over 30 years, I felt less qualified than him to dismiss his theories outright. As an accountant of 30 years standing however, I had to put forward the argument that whilst Denis was hoping for the best case scenario, there was a worst case, which had to be considered and in my opinion, home attendances below 3,500 could be a reality if the team made a bad start to the new season.

We needed to set a players' budget that would allow Mark Robins to bring new players into the club, strengthen the team and hopefully make a challenge for promotion but on paper, trying to balance this budget was becoming a virtual impossibility. If I can explain further, a £1 million players' budget would rely upon a fantastic start to the season with home attendances being in excess of 4,500. On the other hand a £700k players budget most likely would be unable to compete for a promotion place and would cause home attendances to fall well below 3,500 fans. The nightmare scenario would be to set the players' budget at the highest possible level with the intention of bouncing straight back into League One only to see home attendances fall below 4,000 fans irrespective of the performances on the field and that in effect is what happened.

Once these various scenarios were put to Denis and Giles and latterly, the board of directors, I can tell you there were quite a few sleepless nights and much soul searching during the next few weeks.

On a lighter note, you are probably wondering what prompted the title of this chapter. Well, after about four or five hours of trawling through the budget figures, contemplating the various different scenarios and permutations for the future of the club, Denis looked up at the clock on the wall, now showing 1.30pm, standing up he said "That's it; I'm starving. Does anyone fancy some fish and chips?" at which point myself and Giles burst into tears of laughter, threw down our pens and promptly replied, "Yeah, what a good idea!". It just goes to show we are all human and even in the face of adversity and with the weight of responsibility on our shoulders, we still found a moment to eat, drink and be merry.

CHAPTER - 23 (JOINT)

OUR CREDIT CARD CRUNCH

As the start of the 2007/2008 season was almost upon us the clubs cash flow kicked into gear mainly from the sale of season tickets which despite the clubs relegation seemed to be on target with our budget of approx 2000 tickets. Unfortunately, as was becoming the norm the cash engine began to splutter and virtually stalled as it seemed we had run out of gas.

Paul Douglas called me at my office with the opening line "Guess what Barclay's have done?" "Doubled their share price?" I joked with him. There was no joking in Paul. "They have only pulled the plug on the club's credit card. How are we going to operate now?" Paul asked. Barclay's had been reviewing their exposure within the football sector particularly the League One and Two clubs and had decided to mitigate their risk profile by withholding the funds from credit card sales of season tickets and they planned to only release them to the club on a month by month basis until the end of the season. The Football League were aware of the problems this created and started lobbying to establish new credit card facilities for its members. Barclay's concern was that if they accept payment of a season ticket and a club goes under, they would be liable for repaying the debt balance back to the supporter for games not played.

We could live with finding another replacement credit card provider but the letter to Paul had a sting in the tail. They wanted to hold onto the £50,000 of transactions already received from season ticket holders, which would wreak havoc with the clubs cash flow. Paul faxed the letter and I immediately rang the number. The young lady who answered was quite abrupt standing her ground and was very matter of fact. I asked for her unavailable manager to ring me back. This was at 11.00am and by 1.30pm; I had still not received a call. I rang back and was promised he would ring me by 2.15pm. The young man who rang back seemed very cool, calm and collected in comparison and there was an inference that RUFC had been a little devious when completing the application form in the first instance.

"In what respect?" I asked.

"Well, it doesn't mention you want us to finance season ticket sales" he told me. Dino had filled in the original form and I had a copy.

"Don't be ridiculous" I said.

"Look at the projected turnover for the season." Clare had provided the figures perfectly for Dino to complete the application. There was nothing wrong with the form.

"Oh, we didn't realise" he said, changing tack. "You were advised of this by your bank manager when he took you on and also when he did his review" he finished off.

I duly looked at bank manager Matthew Chenery's letter of engagement and guess what? There was no mention of season tickets. I faxed him a copy and awaited his response. He phoned back thirty minutes later.

"I have spoken to Matthew and he says he did mention it but didn't put it in the letter" he said.

"Rubbish" I shouted, now losing my cool. One must bear in mind the club never had any overdraft facilities with the bank. They always stayed in the black.

"Look, I have had a word at the top and I can begin drip feeding this money back to you, OK?" he said as if making a massive concession.

"No, it is not OK. I want to know the name of the director in charge of this."

"It will do no good. I am your relationship manager on this so please think about what I have offered."

He ended the conversation. Using our mole in the banking fraternity, I got to know who the director in charge was in that section. Low and behold it turned out to be the person I spoke to.

I sent him a note saying that the withholding of funds due to the club would impact seriously on the cash flow and affect its ability to pay creditors. If there were any insolvency problems as a result of this, we would appoint lawyers immediately to instigate legal action against Barclay's.

Next morning I got a call saying all our funds would be released immediately and that there would be a mutual ending of our relationship. We had a fortnight to find another credit card service provider! Fantastic but it had taken me almost two days on the phone and although we were getting the funds released, we had to find a new provider and start form filling again. This did take a few weeks but could have been worse. Fortunately Gavin had made contact with a Chris Marshall from HBOS First Data Corp who had done a presentation at the previous League Finance Committee meeting on the same subject of credit card facilities for season ticket sales. The club would have to pay a slightly higher interest rate to insure the risk but HBOS were heavily promoting this. It took Gavin about a fortnight to get the new card machines up and running and in the meantime we were only taking cash and cheques for season tickets. If anyone wanted to pay by card then names and contact details were taken so we could let them know when the facilities were back online and also so they would still qualify for the discounted ticket price, in the event that the deadline had expired.

In honesty, banks and football clubs never cease to amaze me. In the higher leagues, there are some overdraft and loan facilities in existence that normal businesses would not be granted even with the right collateral. However, in the lower leagues, life was really tough. If it weren't for the support of directors and shareholders, banks would pull the plug. There were occasions when Denis and David were loaning £40,000 at a month end to ensure the wages were met. Nonetheless, our own particular problem with the banks was that we were a shocking proposition for them. No freehold assets for security, taking over a club which had run up £1.5 million past debts and a ground lease of a cancerous nature hardly inspires, does it.

CHAPTER – 24 (G.J.M.)

ROBO - THE QUIET MAN

Mark Gordon Robins started his football career in the Manchester United youth side. In 1990, he scored one of the most important goals in Manchester United's recent history when he scored the winning goal in an FA Cup tie against Nottingham Forest. It was at the time when manager Alex Ferguson's job was reputedly in the balance. Now with his job secure again, Ferguson's side went on to win the F.A Cup that same year (Robins scored the winner in the semi-final replay against Oldham Athletic at Maine Road). Ferguson subsequently went on to attain much success. Mark would eventually score 17 goals during his Manchester United career.

Robins left Old Trafford for Norwich City for a fee of £800,000. Once there he became instrumental in lifting morale and team performance and shared in some of the club's greatest historical successes. In Mark's first game he scored two first class goals to deliver the shock result of the season when Norwich defeated the mighty Arsenal at Highbury on the opening day of the first ever Premier League.

Mark helped them qualify for the UEFA Cup at the end of the 1992-93 season. Norwich finished the competition in third place. During 1993-94 a serious injury prevented Mark fulfilling his potential from the previous season. He was sorely missed by his team mates and his absence from the squad coincided with a slump in the team's performance on the pitch. Norwich finished that season in 12th position after having spent most of the first half in the Premier League's top five.

During the 1994-95 season, after a disagreement with the then Norwich manager John Deehan, he was sold to Leicester City. They were having a poor season but even Mark was unable to prevent them from being relegated to Division One along with former club Norwich.

Mark found form with the Foxes and did help them to win back promotion into the Premier League via the play offs in 1995-96. He was with Leicester when they won the Coca-Cola Cup in 1996-97. They also looked a lot healthier finishing a respectable ninth in the Premier League.

After Mark left Leicester he played for a whole variety of clubs including;

F.C. Copenhagen, Reading F.C., CD Orense, Panionios, Manchester City, Walsall, , Bristol City, Sheffield Wednesday, Burton Albion and Rotherham United.

He joined Rotherham United in June 2000 as a player and was subsequently appointed as youth team coach. Mark got a taste of Club Management when he enjoyed a brief spell as joint caretaker manager with Alan Knill the then youth team manager. Alan Knill was 12 months later offered the permanent manager's job after Mick Harford was sacked in January 2006. However Alan's reign only lasted until the end of February 2007, the Millers sat 13 points adrift of safety, making the threat of relegation almost inevitable. This resulted in Knill being sacked on March 1.

During the selection process for a new manager after Alan Knill's exit, Mark was asked to take over team affairs temporarily although I expected that he would be applying himself and staking his own claim for the permanent post. He immediately made an impact with a stunning 4 – 1 home win against Bradford City followed by an equally amazing 5-1 away defeat 7 days later at Port Vale. Further victories against Brentford and Blackpool during his 6 match reign convinced the board that he was the right man for the very difficult job in hand. After a spell of three wins in six games whilst in temporary charge and moving the club off the bottom of League One, Robins' position was made permanent on 6 April

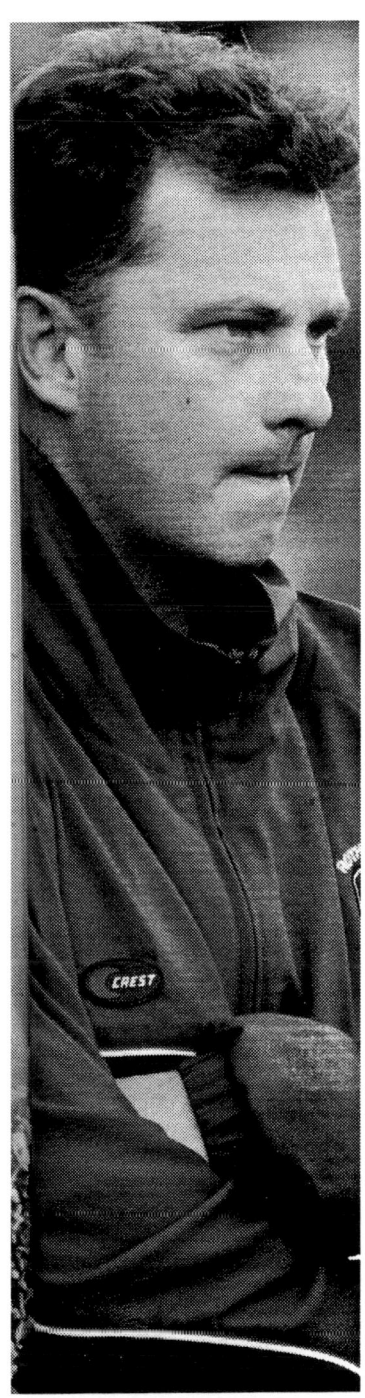

Team Manager Mark Robins
"Deep in thought"

2007. Unfortunately it was too big a hill to climb for the Millers and despite all Marks efforts the club was eventually relegated at the end of that season.

As Mark was an existing employee at the club before his appointment as manager our paths had crossed several times, reviewing budgets and arranging club funding via Clare Yeardley for the "Centre of Excellence". He was always quietly spoken, but was a dedicated employee, a good team player who took his responsibilities and the clubs future very seriously. I found him very easy to get on with but just wished he would "smile" a little sometimes. You never knew what he was thinking, was he ecstatic? or disappointed ? But that was his make up and probably what made him a successful career pro.

Ryan Taylor heads up against Barnet F.C at home.

Mark had indicated that he needed an experienced assistant manager who had toughed it out before and whilst discussions were in progress the name John Breckin came into the equation. John as we all know was the right hand man of Ronnie Moore the fans hero who had taken the Millers from Division Three to Division One (renamed The Championship) in successive seasons from 1999-2000 to 2000-2001. John and Ronnie had both played for Rotherham United during the 1970's and 1980's and were still together now as the management team at Tranmere Rovers.

John was often seen at Millmoor watching the midweek home games, when he could, and obviously still had an affinity for his home town club. We were getting signals that John would love the opportunity to come back to Rotherham despite his loyalty to Ronnie. They were very close friends but I think Ronnie respected John's desire to come back home. I recall there were a few wrangling's over this with the lady chairperson at Tranmere. She was very frustrated at John's wish to leave her club and break up a successful managing partnership.

As we all got excited at the prospect of John returning things were arranged a little hastily. The planned press conference scheduled to confirm Johns appointment had to be postponed leaving the media and photographers scratching their heads in the car park at Millmoor. We didn't want to breach any Football League rules or put John's position in jeopardy but finally he was allowed to leave Tranmere and to some extent sneaked into Millmoor via the back door.

During the close season before the commencement of the 2007/2008 season Mark and John worked tirelessly with Denis and the board to reduce the player's budget and bring in some new talent at a more affordable level now that we were in League Two. Some of the contracts of the existing players were unsustainable so Colin Murdock, David Worrel, Michael Keane, Richie Partridge, Delroy Facey, Martin Woods , Eugen Bopp and Neil Cutler all had to go.

These were all first team regulars subject to injuries and most were in the high earners bracket at the club. Pablo Mills was another player who may have been released but despite a few difference of opinions over his fitness Mark and John must have thought he could do a job at Rotherham but needed to get his attitude right. He was obviously a talented player who seemed to have lost his way a little. He was eventually sent out on loan to Crawley Town for three months the

Raising a smile: Jamie Yates' goal celebrations at Mansfield.

Mark Robins "Manager of the Month" November 2007.

events of which are covered in another chapter in the book.

The incoming players were Andy Warrington, Dale Tonge, Danny Harrison, Graham Coughlan, Andy Todd, Peter Holmes, Derek Holmes, Mark Hudson, Marc Joseph and Tom Cahill. Some of these players were very experienced and would hopefully bring a new zest into the side which would hopefully help us bounce back into League One at the first attempt. To add to this we also had several youth team players who had just or were about to break into the squad ie the likes of Stephen Brogan, Ryan Taylor, Liam King, Sam Duncum, Mark Newsham, Jamie Yates and of course Ian Sharps along with the old stalwart Paul Hurst who was about to break the all time appearance record if he could get a few more games under his belt.

Between them Denis and Mark had managed to reduce the player's budget by approx £300k but ideally we needed to wipe a further £200k off the budget to fall in with our projections and make them viable. This final task was a real tough one as we didn't want to leave Mark too thin with the squad being quite a small one already. We agreed to monitor the situation and trusted Mark would adhere to our requests, which he started to address, with the further releases of Craig Fleming and the loaning out of Pablo Mills.

The 2007/2008 season got off to a pretty good start with 6 wins 6 draws and only 2 defeats by the end of October. Mark had been asked to attend one or two of the board meetings and one had to applaud his approach and professionalism when facing the board. He always prepared himself with reports or notes on the various points he needed to discuss with us. He was totally aware of the club's position regarding finances, so never made any ridiculous requests to fund his squad.

He knew to the pound exactly what the player's budget allocation was, including the employers national insurance often overlooked but which adds a further 13% to the wages bill. Except in emergencies brought about by injuries Mark would always try to balance the books every time he wanted to bring in a loan player. He would arrange to let another player go out on loan so minimizing the cost. That's a good manager. I often listen to the post match comments of the managers on local radio and you can always tell when they are trying to paper over the cracks and make excuses for the poor game etc. On the contrary in Mark's case I always sense he is more sincere and transparent about his feelings towards the players and their performances, without ridiculing them in public, but letting them know in no uncertain terms that he will not tolerate it.

Giles recently bumped into Mark and John Breckin at a Sportsman's Charity Dinner in Mexborough. They exchanged a few pleasantries and when asked if he had any regrets during his time as manager under our control, Mark did say that "his only real moan was that we had not included him more in the board meetings as he felt his input may have been useful to us when planning the clubs financial strategy for the 2007/2008 season." Which just shows the level of his commitment? In my opinion he is a genuine, down to earth, hard working and determined young manager who I think will go on to better things hopefully with the Millers but if not, like many of his old team mates at Man United such as Steve Bruce, Mark Hughes, Bryan Robson and recently Paul Ince, maybe one day managing at the highest level in the Premiership of English Football.

CHAPTER 25 (G.H.B.)

YOU CAN TELL NEIL WARNOCK'S GONE

It had become a bit of a tradition since Neil Warnock took charge at Sheffield United, that "a little bit of extra help" was available to the Millers, if they needed it. As an ex-Rotherham player, some of his sympathy lay with the club and its problems. Neil played for Rotherham United from 1969 to 1971, making fifty-two appearances and scoring five goals. He was a midfield player who although not a star, certainly made his contribution to the action on the field. He had his own regular "after match" routine. He always was curious as to what the journalists in the press box thought of his performances on Rotherham's turf. After getting changed, he would ensure they had his own opinions made known to them before they left offering quotes on his performance for them to use.

Later on during his managerial career he had given the Millers players on loan, standing the wages costs, charged nominal expenses on benefit matches, provided signed shirts, etc for our fund raising and he was always at the end of the phone if the Rotherham manager wanted to ask his advice on something. I would just like to say we have also had support from Sheffield Wednesday, Barnsley and Doncaster but not to the same level. Right at the outset when the board took over, Stephen Quinn and Jonathan Forte were on loan to the Millers with their wages being paid by Sheffield United.

Denis recalled, an incident just after the chairman had taken over. Alan Cartledge had arranged a sportsman's dinner promoted as "An evening with Neil Warnock". At the end of the evening the person who had organised the event, a Mr John Green stood up in front of the audience and announced he would like the Rotherham United F.C party to come forward with the money to pay for their tickets now as he knew how skint the club was. Obviously he didn't book a comedian thinking he himself was quite funny. Most of the guests in attendance that night were disgusted by this including Neil Warnock who was very upset by what he said.

Denis told him to come to the club office to collect a cheque the next day. When he did he was told in no uncertain terms he was not welcome at Millmoor again. Interestingly when Dino and Alan Cartledge were later vying for a takeover of the club 2 years later they used the back up of none other than Mr John Green. How strange?

One of Neil's last public engagements, at the end of the 2006/2007 season, was at the Marriott Hotel, Sheffield. My son Alex and myself were invited to the event courtesy of the Royal Bank of Scotland/Natwest Bank. The evening ended in a question and answer session. My question centred on which of the players he encountered, whilst playing for Rotherham United, did he most rate? His answer was "Dave Watson and Neil Hague". Someone else asked him if he was looking forward to the last game of the season on Sunday against Wigan Athletic to which he shook his head said a most definite "No". He knew deep down, hand on heart, if things didn't go well for the Blades on Sunday, his departure from the club may well be imminent. That fateful day finally arrived and ended in defeat, and due to the unprecedented results involving the clubs around them, Sheffield United were ultimately relegated, leaving Neil Warnock eventually out of a job.

When Rotherham played the traditional pre-season friendly against Sheffield United at the start of the 2007/2008 season, you could certainly tell there was a change in attitude towards the club. Whilst we were grateful for the opportunity to raise money for our much needed funds, we were a little insulted that on the night of the match, I was pulled aside by the Sheffield United FC executive and asked if we could arrange for the 50% share of the net monies to be made available that evening to take away with them. "Unbelievable!" I thought, "I know we've been relegated and its no secret things are going to be tight but that's taking it a little bit far". I told him that no way could this happen and that I would not receive certain invoices for services performed on the night until a couple of days time and until I had all the paperwork in place, no proper accountability could be given. They reluctantly accepted this.

Following the sale of Billy Sharp from Scunthorpe United back to Sheffield United, we were owed £47,500 from sell on clauses. Getting this money into the club's account was like getting blood out of a stone. Phone call after phone call was made; every obstacle you could imagine was put in front of us for reasons as to why this was not paid. In the end, Paul Douglas had to involve the Football League and use their influence. We eventually received the funds in September 2007.

Ian Ross was generously loaned to us in December 2007 as an inducement to see if we would sign him in the January 2008 window, clearly he wasn't fitting into the Blades future plans. The sell on clause wanted by them was however 40%, hardly a gift! When one considers that Sheffield United allegedly had in the region of £30 million through their coffers in the previous season compared to our trivial league payments, it certainly wasn't cricket. We will certainly miss Neil Warnock

CHAPTER - 26 (G.H.B.)

THE ENSUING COURT CASE

For some time, we had been stewing over the events that had occurred previously regarding the removal of the club's assets from its balance sheet. There was, in our opinion a large question mark over whether matters had been handled correctly at arms length, as the law dictates.

Back in the Autumn of 2006, we had been in deep discussion with our legal advisors regarding the whole issue. It appeared there were a few options open to us as a strategy. Our first consideration was, should we pursue a claim against former chairman Mr Ken Booth personally or against the C.F. Booth Group instead. The other alternative was to appeal to the court that it was "a sham of an agreement" and that it should be set aside. If this could be achieved, Millmoor would be returned back to the club where, in our view, it should rightly be. This would not be without cost as some payments would have to be reimbursed to C F Booth Limited in settlement of their original liability. Considering the rentals they had received on our behalf and the counter claims against it, it was felt this would be tolerable for the club.

As part of the CVA, we had all the rights of the old club assigned to us so were in a position to be able to take legal actions. In April 2004 there was correspondence flying around saying that Millmoor and the whole of its site and the Training Ground was up for sale at a price of £4.75 million with a further £0.5 million for the Hooton Lodge giving an overall indicative price of £5.25 million for the lot. A well respected local firm carried out a valuation for the prospective purchaser, Neil Freeman, dated 29 April 2004. This valued the Millmoor ground, Tivoli nightclub, training ground and the Hooton Lodge farm and land at £3,650,000. This value did not include the car park land at Millmoor where the New Stand now sits. This pushed the value up to £4,450,000. (This land was not owned by the Club but by C.F Booth Group).

The Hooton Lodge farm was not part of Rotherham's current lease package and its value would have to be deducted to establish a like for like comparison when drawing up our claim.

No separate valuation of Hooton Lodge farm was unfortunately enclosed within the report. The report does go on to say the valuation assumes no contaminated ground and does not include a business valuation of the Football league club and squad. All league clubs have an intrinsic value due to the fact it is virtually a closed shop with only 92 members. A race track bookmaker who has a bad spell and wants out still has a value for his pitch at the racetrack as there is a long waiting list for places.

The proposed purchase by Neil Freeman never completed as publicised at the time. By October 2004 there were further talks re the purchase of the club even to the point where BBC Sport were reporting the club had been bought by Shirt sponsor, Earth Mortgages Limited. Company directors Darren Millington and Mike Worthington were bombarded by the press and a news conference was called. Purely coincidentally I was at their offices at Hellaby with a client who had some business to conduct with them when this all broke out. They were constantly side lined with the national Press. Just why this manifested is strange as again nothing ever came of it and the club remained unsold.

Then along came Millers 05. As they had little funds a new perspective had to be applied in order to broker a deal. Background paperwork indicated that a valuation had been commissioned by C F Booth Limited on 20 December 2004 with another large firm. Their market valuation of the three properties; Millmoor football ground, the Training ground and the Tivoli nightclub, gave an unbelievable total of only £1,050,000. The chairman of Millers 05 apparently never even saw this valuation. Building land alone at this time was going for around £500,000 an acre. Something certainly looked amiss somewhere.

With the aggressive attitude shown during the December 2006 rent fiasco, we decided to show our hand early and file the papers just before the County Court hearing for repossession of the ground. The particulars of the claim were:-

a)   A declaration that an agreement, dated 23 December 2004 made between C F Booth Limited and a company called Miller 05 Limited, was a transaction defrauding creditors within the meaning of Section 423 Insolvency Act 1986 alternatively meaning that the Miller 05 Limited agreement was a 'sham' and that in the event, it should be set aside. The document went on to state that in the event of this, various leases entered into between the

Rotherham United FC Limited and the defendant and Hooton Lodge Limited, be set aside as they were entered into consequent upon or could not have been entered into but for the Miller 05 agreement.

b) Under Millers 05 agreement of 23 December 2004, the seller was C F Booth Limited and the buyer was Millers 05 Limited. Under this, C F Booth Limited agreed to sell its shareholding for £1 to Millers 05 upon conditions that the property transactions and inter-company transactions shall be completed prior to completion to the satisfaction of the buyer.

The club under the control of Ken Booth Sr had run up an overdraft of £3,025,804 with the Natwest Bank. C F Booth Limited were guarantors and had to take responsibility for settlement of the debt. In return, C F Booth Limited took all the freehold premises and a value of £1,800,000 was attached to them. In addition, they attached the value of £100,000 to the family package and £250,000 worth of tax losses they owed the club so, in summary they claim to have received the benefit from all this

The Directors of Rotherham United pose outside Walker Morris's offices at Leeds in readiness for the court case re the ground. (left to right David Costin, Giles Brearley, Gary Hall, Denis Coleman.

of £2,150,000 when they were entitled to £3,025,000 and as a goodwill gesture to complete the deal Booth's agreed to write the shortfall off. However, It was our contention that the money owed back to the old club for tax losses enjoyed by the C.F. Booth Group alone was nearly £750,000.

I understand that C F Booth Limited and their advisors were fuming at our late hijacking of their repossession hearing. But it wasn't us that started it. We would have preferred to wait until later in the Spring. We knew they wouldn't just take it on the chin and they would have to do something. They applied to Leeds High Court with a striking out claim which effectively meant they were telling the court it should strike out our potential High Court action on the grounds it had no basis. We received notice that this application was to be heard on 21st May 2007. Our barrister, Louis Doyle, hoped that this would be treated as it was, ie, a hearing to discuss validity of a claim and he did not want it to be mirroring the actual impending trial.

On the morning of 21st May, we four directors caught the early morning train to Leeds, thinking we would have a quick breakfast and discussion before we went to the offices of Walker Morris to meet up with our legal team.. We found the procuring of a breakfast in Leeds a little more complicated than envisaged and in the end, had to settle for bacon butties. We had a quick meeting at Walker Morris's offices then made our way to the High Court. The Booths and their legal team were already there. Denis had to point out James and Ken Booth to me as I had never seen or met them before. It is always a strange moment in the time just before a court case commences, when both sides are standing near each other, not wanting to be seen observing each other but clearly are.

While we were there, Mark Thomas, Steve Exley and Lee Rowbotham from RUST turned up – always good company to have around you. Apparently, there had been a request for the hearing to be held in private (not from us) but we and RUST both felt it important that RUST were aware of everything that was happening. To this end, Mark Thomas spoke to the clerk of the court to ask the judge for permission to sit in the hearing and submitted a letter to the judge asking for such permission. District Judge Saffman had no issue with this or with a further request from the journalists who had gathered who wished to sit in the press section. With all this sorted, we trundled into Court Room 12 to start case number 7LS30115.

Louis Doyle's wishes that this be a short, sharp fact based hearing with skeleton arguments was unfortunately not to be. There had been one day allocated to the case, which turned out to be farcical. Miss Leah was the barrister acting for C F Booth Group. She had travelled from London and stayed in a nearby hotel. She had probably been reading the papers intensely. She had certainly not come for skeleton arguments.

ROTHERHAM UNITED FC LIMITED V C F BOOTH LIMITED

Summary of Representations Made at the Hearing on 21 May 2007 at Leeds High Court

Throughout this summary, so far as possible, the parties have been described using the descriptions given to them at Court by the Barristers, as follows:-

Rotherham United FC Limited:	Old Co (i.e. Rotherham United up to the point where Mr Coleman and Mr Maccio became the owners of the Club)
C. F. Booth Limited:	Booth

SUMMARY OF REPRESENTATIONS MADE BY THE DEFENDANT'S BARRISTER

(I.E. The Booths' Barrister)

This is the Booths' Application for:-

1. The Statement of Case to be struck out.
2. And/or for Summary Judgment to be entered in favour of Booth.
3. For an Order for Security for Costs.

BACKGROUND

Until 31 December 2004 Booth held 86% shareholding in RUFC Limited (Old Co). Booth guaranteed the overdraft facility with National Westminster Bank which was in excess of £3 million at the end of 2004. For many years Booth wanted to sell its shares.

On 24 November 2004 Millers 05 Limited was incorporated. In 2004 Booth was approached by Millers 05 who wanted to purchase his shares. On 23 December 2004 the Millers 05 Agreement was entered into between Booth and Millers 05 Limited whereby Millers 05 agreed to buy the Booth shares for £1, Booth would discharge the overdraft and in return old co would transfer the club's long term freehold properties to Booth.

Properties:-
1. Millmoor Ground.
2. Training Ground.
3. Tivoli Nightclub.
4. Changing Room facilities at Hooton Lodge.

As the Car Park was already owned by Booth and Hooton Lodge was owned by Hooton Lodge Limited, a 100% subsidiary of Booth's, these properties were excluded from the sale agreement. Booth then entered into a £660,000.00 loan facility agreement to provide short-term funding of Old Co.

Mr Ken Booth Senior was Chairman of Old Co and on 30 December 2004 he resigned. On 31 December 2004 all the Directors of Millers 05 were appointed Directors of Old Co.

On 31 December 2004 Old Co held a Board Meeting to decide whether to enter into the transactions. At that Board Meeting all the Old Co transactions were approved as follows: the transfer of Booth shares to Millers 05, the repayment by Booth of the overdraft debt on 4 January 2005, the transfer of the Old Co properties from Old Co to Booth, the Lease back arrangements of those properties from Booth to Old Co and the loan facility agreement.

Old Co did not prosper and on 22 March 2006 Mr Denis Coleman and Mr Dino Maccio took over Old Co.

On 31 March 2006 the Claimant was incorporated as Changing Finish Limited and Mr Coleman and Mr Maccio became Directors of Old Co on that date. Old Co was insolvent and a CVA followed under which there was a sale of business and assets of Old Co to the Claimant. Booth agreed to licence the assignment of the Leases to the Claimant at a premium and to support the CVA. On 9 May 2006 the CVA was approved and all Leases, including the changing room lease were assigned with Booth's consent. The Claimant then paid rent plus premium instalments charged as consideration for the assignment of the leases.

On or around October 2006 Booth was approached by the Claimant for a Rent Holiday. Booth declined. Claimant failed to pay the 30 November rent instalment and also failed to pay the 1 December premium instalment. On 28 December 2006 Booth commenced Possession Proceedings seeking Orders for Possession in relation to the Tivoli, Millmoor Ground, Training Ground and Changing Room facilities. These Proceedings were returnable before the Court on Monday 5 February 2007. On Friday 2 February 2007 without warning Booth was served with the current proceedings. The Booth Barrister commented that she thought it curious that these Proceedings were started on Friday 2 February 2007 when the Possession Proceedings were due in Court on Monday 5 February 2007.

ROTHERHAM UNITED'S CASE

The Booth Barrister said that the Club's case is as follows:-

1.   That the Millers 05 Agreement is a transaction defrauding creditors within the meaning of Section 423 of the Insolvency Act 1986 in that the Millers 05 Agreement was a transaction at an undervalue [in other words the transfers of the freehold properties – Millmoor Ground, Tivoli Nightclub, Training Ground – from the Club (Old Co) to Booth and the Family Package Agreement in favour of Booth in return for Booth paying off the overdraft and transferring his shares amounted to a transaction at an undervalue i.e. Booth allegedly paid less to the Club for these transfers and Family Package than should have been the case] or

2.   That it is a sham agreement – and that under the inherent jurisdiction of the Court it should be set aside.

The Claimant says that all the leases entered into and all the assignments of those leases should be set aside and that the Millmoor Ground should be re-vested in the Claimant.

The Booth Barrister then referred to the following valuations:-

GVA GRIMLEY VALUATION FOR BOOTH – 20 DECEMBER 2004

A market valuation of the three properties – Millmoor Football Ground, the Training Ground and the Tivoli Nightclub was prepared for Booth on 20 December 2004 and gave a total valuation of these properties of **£1,050,000.00** (One million and fifty thousand pounds).

BROWNILL VICKERS AND PLATTS VALUATION FOR NEIL FREEMAN DATED 29 APRIL 2004

This was a market valuation prepared for Neil Freeman and it valued the Millmoor Ground, Tivoli Nightclub, the Training Ground and Hooton Lodge Farm at **£3,650,000.00** (three million six hundred and fifty thousand pounds).

With the car park at Millmoor Ground included, the Brownill Vickers valuation was **£4,450,000.00** (four million four hundred and fifty thousand pounds).

There is no separate valuation of Hooton Lodge farm to assist us. It is therefore not possible to say how much of the £3,650,000.00 is comprised of the value of Hooton Lodge Farm. For insurance purposes Merryweathers reported to C F Booth that Hooton Lodge as a whole should be insured for reinstatement purposes for £600,000.00. This is the best we can do to show you that Hooton Lodge is a very substantial premise.

[By way of summary the GVA Grimley valuation at £1,050,000.00 did not include the value of Hooton Lodge Farm. The Brownill Vickers and Platts valuation of £3,650,000.00 did include the value of Hooton Lodge Farm. There is no separate valuation of Hooton Lodge Farm.]

MILLERS 05 AGREEMENT – 23 DECEMBER 2004

Under this agreement the seller was C F Booth Limited and the buyer was Millers 05 Limited. Under paragraph 3.2 the consideration for the purchase of the shares was £1.00. There were Conditions Precedent – "the seller shall procure that the property transactions and inter-company transactions shall be completed prior to completion to the reasonable satisfaction of the buyer". The Club will say that Booth was required to procure Old Co into the property transactions. Booth will say that procure can only mean that Booth would try to do its best to enter into the transactions and cannot possibly mean that Booth would procure Old Co to do something.

Booth gave Old Co £3.025 million by paying off the NatWest debt. In return, Old Co transferred to Booth the Old Co properties for £1.8 million. This was a considerable set off against the debt due to Booth from Old Co because Booth paid the NatWest overdraft. Booth will say that they also wanted £250,000.00 worth of tax losses and tickets to matches: "the Family Package": valued at £100,000.00. Therefore in total Old Co is to give Booth £2,150,000.00 (made up of £1.8 million for the Old Co properties, £250,000.00 tax losses and £100,000.00 family package). Booth will say they decided to write off the shortfall between £3.025 million and £2.15 million.

The Booth Barrister said that the Club will say that the family package is worth in excess of £2 million. (The Supporters Trust understands that the family package is for 79 years. It is part of the Club's case that the family package was substantially undervalued).

BOARD MEETING OF OLD CO ON 31 DECEMBER 2004

The Booth Barrister referred to the Board Minutes of the meeting held on 31 December 2004 and said that the Board of Old Co were obviously satisfied after proper consideration and that they passed Resolutions approving of all the property transfers, the loan agreement of £660,000.00 from Booth, the Family Package. The Board of Old Co recorded in the Minutes that £1.8 million consideration for the property transfers was to be offset against the overdraft and that the properties were to be leased back to Old Co by Booth.

The Family Package Agreement was dated 31 December 2004 and made between Old Co, Booth and Millers 05. This was described by the Booth Barrister as a long and complicated agreement. [Details of the contents of the Family Package Agreement were not given and the Club Barrister has not yet made representations on the Family Package Agreement].

Booth provided a six months interest free loan by way of five instalments of £132,000.00 to Old Co. The Booth Barrister said that without Booth the CVA would have failed.

THE BOOTH'S CASE AS TO WHY IT BELIEVES THAT THE CLUB'S CASE SHOULD BE STRUCK OUT

1. The Booth Barrister said that the Claimant i.e. the Club, does not have the standing i.e. does not have the legal right, to bring these Proceedings. The Booth case on this point is that the right to make a Claim has not been effectively assigned (i.e. passed from Old Co to New Co) or is incapable of being assigned as a matter of law.

2. Booth believes there is a fundamental flaw in the Club's case. : The Club is asking the Court for a Declaration that the Millers 05 Agreement is a transaction defrauding creditors or that it is a sham. Consequent on those Declarations the Club is asking the Court for an Order setting aside the Millers 05 Agreement. Booth believes that the Club's case is flawed because Booth says that the Old Co properties were not transferred pursuant to the Millers 05 Agreement.

3. Booth says that the Club's Section 423 Claim is entirely misconceived.

4. Booth says that the sham case is misconceived as it is based on a misapprehension as to what the law is.

The Booth Barrister then made reference to the provisions in section 423 Insolvency Act 1986 which enable the Court, where a person has entered into a transaction at an undervalue with the purpose of putting assets beyond the reach or claims of creditors or of prejudicing victims of the transaction, to make orders restoring the status quo.

The Booth Barrister then made detailed technical legal submissions to the Judge as to her view of the meaning and interpretation of the wording of this section and related provisions. (The Club Barrister made it clear that he will also be making legal submissions on the interpretation of the Law)

THE BOOTH BARRISTER THEN SAID THAT:-

It is the Claimant's (Club's) case that the victim of the Millers 05 Agreement was Old Co because Old Co gave to Booth its freehold properties for no consideration or insufficient consideration. [i.e. Booth effectively (allegedly) got the freehold properties for nothing or did not pay enough for them]

The Booth Barrister said that the Section 423 Claim is misconceived because on her interpretation of the law Old Co cannot be regarded as a victim (of the alleged transaction at an undervalue i.e. the Millers 05 Agreement) and cannot establish that Old Co had the requisite purpose of putting assets beyond reach. She also said that the Old Co transactions were approved by Millers 05 who stood to suffer most if the Old Co properties were transferred at an undervalue to an unconnected third party – Booth.

The Booth Barrister said that Old Co's auditors, Ernst & Young, said that the Old Co transactions [i.e. the transfer by Old Co to Booth of its freehold properties and the payment of the NatWest overdraft by Booth] would return Old Co to balance sheet solvency and that the transactions would therefore be in the best interests of Old Co. At this stage the Club Barrister objected and said that the Booth Barrister was in no position to say that the transactions were in the best interests of Old Co. He said that all she was able to say was precisely what Ernst & Young said which was simply that the transactions would return Old Co to balance sheet solvency. The Booth Barrister accepted the objection.

The Booth Barrister said that if Old Co was regarded as a victim under Section 423 it would be difficult to see how RUFC would benefit because the Section 423 Claim would be treated as a Class Action on behalf of every victim i.e. all the Creditors under the CVA. She said that if the Court sets aside the Millers 05 Agreement an indemnity is then due from Old Co to Booth in relation to the sum paid by Booth in settlement of the NatWest overdraft. [The Club's case is that it would benefit from the Orders it seeks. The Club Barrister is yet to make his representations on this point].

SUMMARY OF REPRESENTATIONS MADE BY THE CLAIMANT'S BARRISTER (I.E. The Club's Barrister)

- The Club Barrister referred the Judge to the Threshold Hurdle for a Strikeout Application and said that for the Judge to strike the Club's Application out he would have to be satisfied that there are no reasonable grounds for allowing the Claim to proceed.

- The Club Barrister said that the two contractors under the Millers 05 Agreement were Booth and Millers 05. He said that the substance of the Millers 05 Agreement necessarily involved Old Co itself. He said that in fact all that Old Co amounts to at the time of the Millers 05 Agreement is a puppet for either Booth and / or Millers 05.

- The Club Barrister said that there was a restricted value in the open market for the three properties (Millmoor Ground, Training Ground, Tivoli Nightclub) but that Booth was in a very different position because of the adjacent land owned. The Club Barrister said that what Booth was acquiring was worth an awful lot more than £1,050,000.00. He said that the land to the South East is occupied by Booth Scrap Metal Merchants. He said that the Ground and Training Ground might have a more significant value to Booths than an open market purchaser who would have to purchase subject to the existence of adjoining owners. He said that Booth was not in the same position as any prospective purchaser because Booth owns the adjoining land. He referred to the development potential of the ground and the adjoining land.

- The Club Barrister said that there was an issue of fact which could not possibly be resolved at this stage – as to whether £1.8 million is significantly less than the real value of the properties.

- The Club Barrister said that in the Millers 05 Agreement £1.8 million is put in as the value of the properties.

- The Club Barrister stressed that his representations were being made in response to a Strikeout Application and he urged the Judge not to be drawn into the trap of approaching the matter like a Trial. He pointed out that the Booth Barrister had opened the matter at length and that although a lot of the background information she had given was very helpful she had opened as though her Application was a Trial.

- The Club Barrister said that the Club does have the legal right to take these Proceedings because under the Asset Sale Agreement (made between Old Co and New Co i.e. Mr Coleman and Mr Maccio as Changing Finish Limited which later changed its name to Rotherham United FC Limited) Old Co's rights of legal action passed to New Co and Booth was aware of this right.

- The Club Barrister said that in late December 2004 the Company was in severe financial difficulties and that putting it in the black [by Booth paying off the NatWest overdraft and the Club transferring the properties to Booth] does not mean that it is in the best interests of the Company.

- The Club Barrister suggested that the Directors either did not understand the Millers 05 Agreement or they were under a misapprehension.

THE SHAM CASE

The Booth Barrister made technical legal representations on the meaning of Sham.

The Club Barrister has yet to make his representations on this point.

[The Club Barrister will continue his representations at the next Hearing. He made it clear that he will develop various aspects of the Club's case at the next Hearing. The Club's case is that the Club would certainly benefit from the Orders it seeks]

THE JUDGE indicated at about 4.15pm that it was an appropriate time to adjourn the case. At this stage the Booth Barrister asked the Judge if he would deal with Booth's Application for Security for Costs. She said that as there was to be a further Hearing there would be exposure to further costs and that already her Client was exposed to costs of £40,000.00. [It was not clear whether this was an estimate of the Booth's costs so far or an estimate of the total costs of both parties so far.] The Judge said that he did not think it appropriate to deal with Security for Costs at this stage because that issue involves consideration of the merits of the case and at this stage the Judge had not heard full representations from both parties.

We all left the court buildings at 4-30 pm. We did not rush as we decided to let the Leeds city rush hour go and get a later train. We toured a few of the local hostelries up the Headrow and got back into Swinton about 9pm that evening.

The court hearing recommenced in Leeds on 5 July 2007, commencing at 12 noon. I was not very happy about such a long delay before our Barrister could effectively put up our case as I felt this slowed down the momentum of the case and blurred facts. There is nothing like everything being hot off the press. Louis Doyle took to the stand promptly and began his presentation. After giving a brief presentation, he explained that the Grimley valuation of the old company's assets of £1.05 million was the value attributed for the purpose of the deal and that Brownhill Vickers' valuation suggested (he can do no more than suggest) at best, that old company properties were worth considerably more.

He argued that the value of the land to the defendants was worth considerably more than £1.8 million. He pointed out that the old company properties completed a jigsaw for the defendant since they fall in the middle of properties owned by the defendant to the east, west and south. This would inevitably makes them worth more to the defendants than it would to anyone else.

It soon became apparent that one of the problems we had was that some of the defence we were dealing with was, in reality, developing areas of law. He went on to argue that there was a puppet-master relationship between Millers 05 and the old company. With the debtor and victim argument, Louis Doyle argued that if the debtor and victim had to be the same party, this would lead to absurd results that Parliament surely could not have intended. He gave the example of where a company under the control of say X divests itself of assets to Y for no consideration, which is also under the same control but then control of X is passed to other parties then whilst creditors and liquidators would be able to make claims on behalf of the company, the company itself would be unable to claim. The point seemed to be laboured long and hard.

Louis then went on to confirm that the value of the tax losses was £727000 and that the family package had a value of some £2 million, demonstrating how the mathematics of this deal done were not balancing out.

As the proceedings came to a close, there had been that much discussed, my head was swimming with no real feeling of how things had gone. The judge had appeared critical to both parties at various times. It was announced that the judgement would be handed down on 16 August 2007.

In the ensuing period, Denis and David Costin did have a couple of brief conversations with Ken Booth Junior who suggested we should stop spending all this money on lawyers and sit down and sort something out properly. Denis met Ken junior at the Red Lion, Todwick for secret talks. Denis had a further lunch meeting at The Brecks with Dave Costin and both Ken senior and junior to try and strike a deal. This was mentioned at one of our board meetings in early August. We agreed anything was worth exploring and asked David, to follow it up, when he finally made contact with them and tried to arrange another meeting, their tone had changed and he was rebuffed as if the previous conversations had never taken place and told "perhaps they should wait for the outcome". What did they know that we didn't?

Things were very busy at the club with the new season underway. It was decided that Gary Hall and I should attend the Handing down of the Verdict hearing on 16 August 2007. Don't ask me why but we both seemed to accept, in our hearts, that things were not going to go well for us, we just sensed it.

When we got to court, we were joined by a lady who we had never met before from our lawyers and we all went in to court together. The R.U.S.T members and the press were also there.

As the judge started to hand down his long deliberation, we did not get a feel for which way it was going in that he found against us on certain points and found for us on others. Then, as he got near to the end, he went on to state he could only work with the information he had got and that he felt we had provided insufficient evidence as to the correct valuation of the assets and the hospitality package and as such, they were really cast out from his thoughts. With these taken out, there is no real case to consider in my book. The problem that arose here was that we were fully intending to have full valuations for the court hearing but as this was supposed to be a look at skeleton arguments, it wasn't felt necessary to have full weight in evidence thrown into the ring.

With reference to the valuation of benefits, I had written to the Institute in London for their opinion as well as to another firm who specialised in benefit package valuations and costings. Again, we could have had the reports addressed to the court for consideration, had we known that this was crucial at this point and we were directed to do so by our Lawyers. The judge at the end said that he was aware this decision to recommend a strike out would come as a profound disappointment to the claimant and the club's supporters. He said that he regarded the power given to the court to strike out on a summary basis as being not just a power that benefits the winning party but which also benefits the losing party. It seemed to him that it was far better for a losing party to learn at an early stage before tens of thousands of pounds of costs are incurred. He said he felt that the sense of disappointment would be greater had he allowed the case to go to a final hearing where defeat would have meant both sides suffering greatly enhanced costs.

As everyone stood to rise and started to mingle, I was near the court door. I put my thumb up to Mark Thomas to try and gain his attention to see what the RUST contingent thought. I think James Booth thought I was gesturing towards him as he questioned, "Does Brearley think that they have won the case! As disappointing as the verdict was it was not in reality, the end of the world; there was always "Plan B". Right at the outset, we were told, Plan B, would be the easiest legal claim for us but were reluctant to implement it at the time. Now we had an option to use it if we wanted. The strike out was only relevant for Louis Doyle's initial arguments used.

We had a further meeting with our lawyers and barrister and must admit, we all felt cheated. Credit due to Miss Leah, she had done her job for her clients magnificently. I wondered what the outcome would have been, had we managed to present the detailed various valuations addressed to the court.

We were being pressured by the newspapers for our reaction and what our plans were. We did indicate that we did have Plan B which could be implemented and we were thinking about it. The reality was that we would have to wait to amass some more funds before we could realistically consider it

I asked Tobin if, through his contacts, he thought he may be able to help start a "legal fighting fund" but he had been warned by his lawyer about a case precedent, whereby third party funders of legal cases could be made parties to the action if a case was lost for costs, etc. This problem wasn't insurmountable however as donations could simply be made to the club who could then take up the action again but it clouded the issue a little.

The case was very hard to put behind us as inside, we were all somewhat eaten away with the genuine belief that the club should never have lost its assets. It was the future for the club. If it had Millmoor back it could have looked for partners to help develop the stadium and overall facilities. Millmoor had been the home to the Millers for over 100 years and they should still be there. If you have freehold property to offer as security you can get all sorts of funding deals. It was a gamble and we lost. If we had more funds we could have returned to the court arena and we still believe we could have won. We knew that it would be very hard for the future with a landlord who insisted on applying the strict terms of the lease with very little compassion for the club. The decision to do what we did was not taken lightly or frivolously we needed to make a stand to try and shape the long-term future.

Chapter - 27 (G.H.B.)

The Insurance Claim – Making A Crisis Out Of A Drama

One could argue that God was kind to us by having the flood disaster during the close season.

If it had happened half way through, it could have been a far worse situation trying to find an alternative ground as well. I was on holiday in Dubrovnik at the time it all occurred. I was watching Sky News in my room on the Monday evening getting ready to go out when I saw Millmoor flash on the screen. Then I saw more film taken from a Helicopter hovering over Retail World at Parkgate showing it being awash. It was unbelievable. I phoned our camera man Ron James of Kilnhurst and asked him to film the events as they unfolded. He did not disappoint me.

At first I thought yes here am I basking in the sun, when back home, it's a washout. But as the pictures continued through the evening, my thoughts turned to a sickening horror as I realised the mayhem and problems I would eventually be returning home to. June the 25th or "Monsoon Monday" as it became known, when 80mm of rain fell in 18 hours, was the start of the biggest Civil Emergency for South Yorkshire since The Second World War. The damage was widespread particularly down the valleys carved out by our rivers; Don, Dearne and Rother. There was a real concern that the reservoir at Ulley would burst its banks and recreate the 1867 'Sheffield Flood' when Dale Dyke reservoir did just that. The police closed both carriageways of the M1 between junctions 32 and 34, because of the risk posed by the creaking dam. Rotherham's own fire brigade worked tirelessly for hours with thirteen high-powered pumps to remove some of the water and lessen the pressures exerted on the dam wall. Eventually they were able to lower the water level by several feet and reduce the immediate danger.

At 11-00am that morning Chief Inspector Whitehouse of the South Yorkshire Police over at Doncaster put "Silver Command" into operation. This brought together Crisis Management Teams to start working in the communities. As water from the surrounding hills started to drain away the streams became torrents, the rivers huge open waterways, bringing the County to a standstill. It had taken Gavin 7 hours to travel home from Swinton to Sheffield that Monday evening due to the roads being gridlocked for hours. It was quite unbelievable. Only when the water had finally subsided, (almost two weeks later in some areas of Doncaster) did the massive clean up and repair operation start to fully enfold. Emergency relief donation funds were quickly set up. Hilary Benn appeared on the scene to confirm the Governments commitment to help. There were 30,000 homes affected and some 7,000 businesses halted. It was estimated the damage stood at over £1 Billion.

Following the floods there was a panic and urgency that set in around South Yorkshire as people tried to get back to a normal way of life again. It soon became obvious that resources were stretched and delays in the essential repairs began to cause unrest among the worst affected. It was not only the hundreds of families who found themselves without a home, there was also the wheels of industry that needed to start turning again as soon as possible. It was unlucky for Rotherham United that we ended up being hit with a double dose. Not only a flooded Millmoor but also a decimated training ground to contend with, as the River Don cut out its new escape route.

The effects of the June 2007 Flood can be seen here.

The job of getting things back to something like normality had already started before I returned back to the U.K. Denis and David were to take charge amidst complete turmoil in the community.

The Harris Claim Group of Leeds were appointed as our agents for the claim. The principal was Howard Armstrong who I knew, but had not seen for many years. The last time was in London at an Insurance Claim settlement meeting. I was there to be cross-examined as I had done all the calculations for business losses and it was complex. As the meeting unfolded I had to restrain the claimant as he tried to thump the director of the Guardian Insurance Company when adverse criticism was made of his business skills. The meeting was temporarily adjourned. The incident was so unforgettable, that when we spoke again 12 years later, I wasn't surprised when Howard asked me "Whatever happened to Mr F? Do you still hear from him?"

As is often the case, with large claims, you need plenty of documentary evidence, lots of photographs and the constitution of a lion. Despite the hype it is a stressful time. You want to get

The seats in the Railway end had to be replaced due to the contamination left behind from the flood water.

everything back to normal and the loss adjusters want to clip back their clients financial exposure. The insurance company in fairness were very good in that they promptly sent out their assessor who, on the face of it, seemed very happy with the way things were being handled. Denis and Dave used their influence and contacts to get quotations for works to be done and had many meetings with those concerned to get the repair works underway.

The overall claim was broken down as follows:

    Flooding and contamination of the Training Ground pitches and cabins
    Flooding and contamination of the Millmoor Pitch
    Damage to the Gymnasium floor
    Contamination of seating in three tiers of the Railway End and other associated areas
    Cancellation of private functions causing loss of profits.
    Costs incurred in hiring temporary training facilities
    Costs incurred in replacing training equipment.

The River Don ebbs its way across the Training Ground and access road.

The problem with contamination from the flooded River Don was that it had been abused badly with pollutants since the Industrial revolution. The smell it left was awful and god knows what could be infested in the turf. The pitches had to be re-laid both at Millmoor and at the Training Ground.

At Millmoor we couldn't just relay half a pitch, the whole lot had to be done, as well as the shale perimeter. This ended up costing some £130,000 alone. The full claim ran into hundreds of thousands of pounds. There was no miracle cure. We had to battle on to get ready for the start of the season and could not afford any delays.

One of the problems encountered with such a catastrophe of this magnitude was the void between supply and demand of available tradesmen in the area, which increases costs dramatically. This, in time, works against you as the whole basis of a settlement is on the insured risk covered. At the inception of the policy it was probably valued with normal replacement costs. But when claiming in a disaster, these costs escalate and you could end up under insured. There were also contentious areas to negotiate. For example, if the Gordon Banks sporting dinner had gone ahead as normal, How much would have been taken over the bar? How many staff would be required? What profit was lost in the memorabilia auction? What income would the raffle tickets have raised? What would the food bill have cost? How much would the clean up be the following day? Need I go on? There were many aspects to be considered and agreed upon in order to finalise the losses.

The implications of this claim took up a lot of boardroom time and my office was in overdrive. We were very grateful to companies like Sheffield Site Services Ltd who dropped everything to help our cause. We also had to hire a professional Quantity Surveyor to cost out building works and keep control of the expenditure. The jokes were doing the rounds on the texts:

> "Following the extensive Flood damage at Millmoor assessors reckon it has improved the property value by approximately £500,000."

> "Millmoor was at long last subjected to an extensive clean up, it took a crisis to bring it on."

> "One supporter said it made a change for water to be coming in at ground level instead of through the roof."

The upshot of all this was that it would eventually leave the club (after the insurance claims were settled) approximately £200,000 short to rectify the problems. With excesses and rising costs it was a struggle .The Professional representation cost £44,000 alone. Some aspects ended up being paid for by the Directors personally by way of donations. We also received some other generous help from supporting parties. There was a lot of sympathy with our plight and the Council and H.M.R.C let us divert resources into paying restoration bills rather than themselves in the short term. Our own local M.P John Healey was appointed National Floods Minister and offered what comfort he could. When the fans came for the first game of the season everything looked normal. Little did they know the finishing touches were such that the paint had only just dried earlier that day.

Despite all of this, the final parts of the claim were still being ironed out as late as November 2007 The delay in receiving the final pay out set us back months with our cash flow projections. Creditors who had been very patient including HMRC were now starting to apply pressure. We could only tell them that the final settlement was imminent, and this went on for weeks.

In December 2007 the insurance company made the club an offer to settle the lion's share of the claim. It was considerably less than the original claim but we were so drained of cash at this point, we had hardly any energy or fight left in us. To try and appeal the offer would only subject the club to another lengthy delay, which held no guarantee of a substantial increase anyway. It was at this point that the pressure of it all was starting to tell on the board of directors. The number of phone calls, meetings, negotiations etc was just relentless. We also knew that in the next few months this shortfall of cash was going to make life very difficult for us and leave the club in serious financial hardship.

CHAPTER - 28 (G.H.B.)

CREEPY "CRAWLEY" OR THE PABLO MILLS AFFAIR

Pablo Mills often edged on some controversy or other. He was a central defender who had joined Derby County as a trainee at the age of 14. Whilst there he made 62 appearances for the first team both in league and cup matches. In the early stages of his career Pablo attracted interest from the likes of Barcelona, Arsenal and Manchester United but remained at Derby. He played for England at youth levels and was seen as a solid and valuable member of any squad he played in. After loan spells to M. K Dons and Walsall he moved on a free transfer to Rotherham United joining in 2006.

There was some bad publicity in the press following allegations he had broken into the flat of his former girlfriend and mother of his child Zoe Newman. Apparently this was after receiving a text to tell him she was with someone else. He kicked in the door and smashed some panelling on an airing cupboard. As the news broke the Press were onto the Club in no time at all. He was news and could help sell the papers but this publicity would be no good to us. Paul had the task of seeing Pablo, after all, anything he did in his personal time still impacted on the Club. He was very remorseful and promised Paul he would keep his head down. Clearly he had flipped and reacted in haste as probably most of us would. Pablo came in for some criticism from Alan Knill after the Christmas/New Year of 2006/07 because of his then overall body weight .He had been gradually putting on the pounds and after Christmas there was real concern it would impact onto his match fitness. His contract was such that it could cost him financially if he did not get his body mass index or BMI ratio right. He was days away from being sacked.

There were further concerns with Pablo after Mark Robins took over. Pablo's performances on the football field were mixed. Following my request to Mark via Denis to make what savings we could on the player's budget. Mark Robins told us of the arrangement he had organised for Pablo which would be his last chance and it would assist the budget. For an unspecified period he had arranged for Pablo to go on loan to Crawley Town FC, with them paying his wages. That was music to my ears as the cash saving it gave would be very welcome. Apparently, Mark had a contact at Crawley and the deal was swiftly done. It was also partly as a wake-up call for Pablo, he had great talent and needed a kick up the backside. The 24th August 2007 saw his departure.Crawley was a long established club being formed back in 1896. They were playing in the Conference League and like Rotherham United had recently experienced financial troubles, suffered a 10 point deduction and applied to enter into a C.V.A. The previous season with veteran footballer John Hollins as team manager they had managed to avoid relegation. On the 14th September Crawley apparently contacted us as they really appreciated Pablo's contribution and it was agreed to extend his loan for a further month.

I was not aware at the start how this deal had been set up. It was agreed however, that we continue to pay Pablo's wages and recharge them via an invoice. I did question this, knowing of their track record. A credit reference taken by me listed them as very high risk. If I had known sooner the deal would have been put on hold. It soon materialised that my fears were not confounded as Crawley did not pay any of the bills sent to them. They initially asked for more time to pay. It predictably ended up as a debt collectors' nightmare. Phone call after phone call was made. In true "bill dodging" style no-one was ever there. When we did get someone we were told "The chairman will ring you back himself" but never did. It was one excuse after another. As they were a non-league outfit, we couldn't use the Football League to exert their influence. After much threatening they wrote us a ridiculous letter, begging us not to carry out our proposed action of a winding up petition and to keep the faith with them. As you can imagine, it was referred to in the minutes of every board meeting. I was always droning on about cash and was very unhappy about it all. I think Paul was at the end of his tether.

Mark Robbins announced to the board meeting in October 2007 that he desperately needed a midfield player to strengthen the side. Matches were being lost with poor midfield performances.

Pablo Mills

Gary Hall recalls:

"GILES THE TACTICIAN"

We were struggling to find a fit midfielder and Mark was asking if he could bring one in on loan. We had our defender Pablo Mills who was out on loan at Crawley Town. Giles said can't we bring Pablo back and play him in midfield. Giles took a bit of ribbing in this meeting and was told that if our goalie was injured we could just stick a striker in there then could we. As you will now know Mark did bring back Pablo and he, in accord with Giles's view played him in midfield and he ended up winning the player of the season. Why "Fabio Cappello" when we have "Gilespi Brearleyoni".

Pablo's first game back saw him playing against Sheffield Wednesday Reserves at Millmoor on the 24th October 2007 winning the game 1-0 with Liam King scoring our goal.

So there you go – Accountants often do know best!

Pablo had played 14 games for Crawley, getting them a goal along the way. The consensus of everyone was that his time at Crawley had been well spent as Pablo came back a different more mature character. The debt from Crawley was still outstanding as we entered into Administration. Pressure was maintained in collecting this debt. It was needed to fund the Administration. We all continued to get nowhere with them. A winding up petition was duly served on them on Rotherham United's behalf by Walker Morris which meant cough up or your gone. A cheque was received at the Solicitors just before the set hearing date to save their bacon... so Crawley live on to fight another day. As for Mark Robin's theory of Crawley doing Pablo some good, it most certainly did.

As Gary Hall mentioned from hereon in he was magnificent, working for the team, creating chances and he scored his first goal of the season for us during the home game against Shrewsbury on the 8th March 2008. The match ended up a 1-1 draw as they equalised before half time. This was the first goal from Pablo since playing against Scunthorpe in August 2006. After the game he said, "It was nice to get my own goal and not have someone try and take it off me this time."

CHAPTER – 29 (G.H.B.)

I DIDN'T THINK RAY WOULD MAKE IT

Saturday, 25 August 2007 was the kind of summer's day when the weather wasn't letting us down. We were playing Stockport County away from home and I was really looking forward to the game. Unfortunately, some very urgent shopping business had cropped up again at Meadowhall, which meant that my wife Ruth had to attend to this for most of the afternoon so she obviously wouldn't be going to the match. Although only at short notice, I decided to ring Ray Dawson, the landlord of the Ring O Bells at Swinton, a lifelong Miller's fan.

When the club got into trouble in 2006, Ray rallied to the cause. He along with fellow regulars were very active in the "Save the Millers campaign" raising hundreds of pounds.. His pub is like a shrine to the Millers' cause. The Swinton branch of the supporter's club is based at the pub, they are good fund raisers which they re-invest back into the club. To quote Ray, "The Ring O Bells is a shrine to Yorkshire's finest!"

The phone rang about seven times before Ray answered. I asked him if he was going to the game today. He said it was a bit of a sore subject as although he would really like to, he had tried to coerce some of his staff into providing extra cover so he could get away but no-one was forthcoming. I told him this was a great shame as I would like to take him to Stockport County as my guest in the directors' lounge. "Stop right there!" shouted Ray down the phone. "Give me twenty minutes" he said. Within ten minutes he called back "Mission complete! I couldn't pull it off using my own staff but I've managed it by using somebody else's! It's cost me some favours but it's worth it." I pulled outside the Ring O Bells at 12.45pm in my XKR. Ray was waiting outside, in he jumped and away we went.

The sun continued to shine and as we got towards the end of the Stocksbridge bypass, I said to Ray, "Let's have the benefit of some proper fresh air". I pulled the car into a lay-by and down came the car's roof. Unfortunately, this was something of a misjudgement. The traffic over the Woodhead Pass was wicked. As we set off, we became locked into a slow moving convoy that edged its way along, kissing Yorkshire goodbye for its re-

The Ring O Bells Swinton – HQ of the Swinton branch of the supporters club.

Paul Chuckle sat engrossed at the Stockport County away game 25th August 2007.

Goal mouth action at Stockport County 25th August 2007. We drew 2-2 in the end.

Ray Dawson landlord of the Ring O Bells Swinton and lifelong Miller.

emergence in Lancashire. Unfortunately, as we got to the top, some low cloud had appeared, the temperature had dropped several notches and Ray and I inched our way across looking like we were sat in a mobile sauna only being frozen to death. There was nowhere to stop. As we got down towards Tintwistle fortunately, there was a lay-by where we could pull in and put the roof back on and crank the heating up. The heavy traffic continued and it was not until 2.15pm that we got to Stockport.

I personally think the Edgeley Park ground Stockport share with the Sale Sharks rugby club is excellent. The facilities under the Cheadle end stand are second to none. After parking up in front of the offices we were whisked through into one of the large function rooms where a lot of supporters were all sat down dining together. The directors had their own table where we sat. It was a charged atmosphere with all the executive members sat around you and some light entertainment thrown in to boot. As we were a little late we attacked lunch as if it was our last.

Paul Chuckle, our patron, had come along for the game and a lot of the Stockport fans instantly recognised him. The club's chief executive coerced Paul onto the mini stage to say a hello to everyone. Paul explained how pleased he was to be there and he apologised for his brother, Barry's absence, explaining that he couldn't make it as he was having to play for the Rotherham Reserves this very afternoon. Paul and Barry Chuckle were great supporters of Rotherham and did their bit whenever they could.

I always took the opportunity of talking to the home directors. You could often get some good ideas as well as pick up some football scandal. One question I always asked them was the state of their club's finances? On asking this question, you were often directed to "go and talk to him over there". You often found with directors that the finance part of board meetings was always the dreaded part. Discussions about players and acquisition were fun but discussions about cash flows and adverse stocktaker's reports clearly were not. The finance directors would always give you a frank discussion and answer your questions. Like most clubs, everything at Stockport was hand to mouth. There was never quite enough cash to do everything needed. Like Rotherham, they had been involved in a few roller coaster seasons, having had two relegations in four years with Jim Gannon pulling the rabbit out of the hat in 2005/06 to keep them in league football. I was told they would like to take control of their ground back completely so no longer having a ground share arrangement. Whilst it worked, it was at a price and at times quite inconvenient. You had problems with the wear and tear of the pitch, advertising boards being swapped about, event clashes and the lack of personalisation opportunities for rooms and reception etc. A large banner was unfurled and rolled out the full length of one stand but had to be taken down after every game and stored away.

I wondered how all this might impact on Rotherham with a new shared stadium. They would need to work hard to get it right.

Rotherham took nigh on one thousand fans to the game that afternoon, pushing the attendance figure up to 5764, which was good for them.

There was one change to our team as that day Danny Harrison was called off to the hospital as his wife was about to give birth so Stephen Brogan returned back to the first team squad.

Rotherham nearly turned a first minute free kick into an opening goal when Derek Holmes got a header in on goal. Stockport quickly replied with Dickinson nearly scoring . It was only last ditch defending that saved the day. In the tenth minute though we let them in and Elding rose unmarked to head a fine ball into the net following a cross from Poole. The Stockport supporters were giving full chant to their team and it was working. We were under siege for about 20 minutes then gradually we started to get a feel for them and started closing them down a bit. We desperately needed a goal before half time but it wasn't to be , O Grady nearly equalised for us with a 20 yard shot at goal and Derek Holmes's header went just wide giving us some optimism that we would compete better in the second half.

I would imagine the changing room banter from Mark Robins was along the line "you can beat these, do not let the crowd phase you, keep your heads down and just get out there and do the job "

In the second half someone must have listened as we now had the lions share of possession. We all went hysterical when after a few tussles we equalised with a fine header from Sharps' . The joy turned to despair though when the referee disallowed the goal for an earlier push highlighted by the linesman, which none of us watching in the directors box saw or could believe. Ray's vocal protest and waving of his arms was so intense I think he would have throttled the referee if he had got his hands on him. The Millers' supporters also felt the same way about the referee, considering their later vocals. Not to be outdone in the 56th minute Stephen Brogan took a free kick which was headed superbly by Sharps past the keeper and the scores were justly level. Stockport players and their manager protested that the whistle was blown after the kick had been taken. The referee would have none of it and the goal stood. Stockport manager Jim Gannon continued to protest and was promptly dismissed to the stands!

Rotherham filled with enthusiasm were pushing forward time after time. Bad luck struck in the 67th minute when a run into our half forced a corner, which was headed home by Griffin who had been left unmarked at the far post. So Stockport County now led 2-1. Mark Robins went into vocal mode urging his team on. One advantage being in the Directors seats is that you are positioned so that you can often hear the team manager's instructions .We put the pressure back on and in a goalmouth flurry filled with panic we equalised once again following a strange own goal, headed home by McNeil. Marcus Bean could have won us the game with a shot, which went just wide and Eldon's header caught out Andy Warrington but luckily deflected off the post .The final result of a 2-2 draw was probably a fair result. I wanted Ray to see a good game and by god he did. He could hardly speak for 20 minutes whilst his hoarse vocals steadied themselves down.

On the way back over the Pennines, Ray explained to me how he had followed the Millers since being a boy. He started watching Rotherham in 1958 going with his friend Colin Dawson (no relation). Ray was hard put to say which was his most memorable game but the match against Manchester United at which Rotherham United lost 1-0 is very high up on his list. At the last Luton game Ray identified none other than the referee of that game Jack Taylor in the crowd. Ray referred to the game in conversation with him and he replied "A lot of people said I made a wrong decision that day. Even Sir Matt Busby after the match told him "we have been very lucky today"."

Ray also remembers the inaugural League Cup Final back in 1960/61 when Second Division Rotherham United came runners up to Aston Villa. They beat them 2-1 on the home game in front of a crowd of 12226 (Webster and Kirkman scoring) but then lost 3-0 in the away game in front of 31202 spectators so losing on aggregate. He was a great fan and it was nice to be able to offer him something back, as small a gesture as it was. As we pulled up at the pub, Ray said how much he'd enjoyed the day. "I will let the staff get off back to their proper jobs now" he chuckled.

CHAPTER - 30 (G.H.B.)

I THINK HE THINKS HE'S DON CORLEONE

There was plenty of speculation in the press as to what we were going to do now following the court case decision. Our "Plan B" had been quoted as a possible course of action despite no detailed information ever being made available of what exactly Plan B was for obvious legal reasons.

A very good friend of mine, called to see me one day to say that he had been contacted by a well-known Rotherham businessman and asked to pass on a message. The message stated that he was a good friend of the Booth's and he may well be able to broker a deal between the club and our landlords, which may mean a satisfactory outcome for everyone. I decided that I would most certainly call this person, as anything that could assist the club was worthy of pursuit. I thought it strange however that he had not contacted me directly as we had met in the past and our office number is in all the phone books and directories. Very strange indeed.

I rang him on the number I was given on the following Monday evening, when I can usually get five minutes to myself in the peace of my Library. I have to say that the conversation that followed was not what I expected. He initially explained that he was a good friend of the Booth's and had been following the events in the paper quite closely. I explained to him that we were finding the rent and repairs unsustainable at the levels they were at and that we had been very disappointed to date with the attitude of the landlords towards us.

He listened patiently to what I had to say then he asked me "So what are you going to do next?"

I wasn't too comfortable about talking in depth about the case to a third party but I was honest with him. "Well" I said, "there is an option for us to go back to court but I stressed that this was something we did not particularly wish to do, we were all unanimous on that point. Even the lawyers were a little reluctant to pursue this initially. He stopped me short, suddenly raising his voice he said. "If the board were planning to pursue an action against an 85 year old man then there would be no-one in

Rotherham prepared to speak to any of you again. Do you realise that you would be the scourge of society." I told him to calm down and interjected and repeated" that we didn't particularly want to do this in any case, if we had, we would have already gone ahead."

He continued, "Do you realise how strong feelings are in the town about this affair" "Well I suspect from the fans point of view very much so" was my reply. "Come on" he said "Don't you think it's about time to let sleeping dogs lie otherwise you are going to open a real can of worms". He paused then said "You know what I mean" trying to take on what could be deemed as a menacing tone. I noticed my briefcase was only a feet away and I outstretched my leg and shuffled down the chair trying not to alert him to my movements. Inside the briefcase was my dictation machine. This could be useful I thought.

"No I don't know what you mean" was my delayed reply "I'm not phased by the fact we lost the last battle, its just part of my job to try and resolve this in the best interest of the club. I always take situations as I find them after all we are mere human beings aren't we?" I managed to get the machine out and press the record button. He went on "Listen, the last thing you and the club needs is another battle on your hands especially with the Booth's" he said " Well that's nice, so do we just sit back then and let them walk all over us ?" I said. The red record light on the tape flashed merrily away. I went on "It sounds like these are veiled threats then are they?" He told me he was speaking to me off his own back and it was just what he thought. Then the conversation finished.

This was certainly very sinister. Why did the man go through my friend to speak to me – why didn't he just come to me direct? He clearly had no intention whatsoever of trying to assist the club and I bet he certainly wasn't speaking like this with the Booth's authority. If he had something to say then say it to me face to face, not hiding behind others and a telephone. What a waste of my time. I have not really had any close contact with him in the past to pass judgement, but I can certainly formulate an opinion of him now.

I reported the incident, in full, to the South Yorkshire Police to place these events firmly in their records. They surprisingly took it very seriously and were to do some discrete background

Ken Booth (senior) caught deep in thought in the Directors' Marquee at Millmoor.

digging. They checked the telephone records and confirmed the existence of my call. If I heard from him again I was to report straight back to them. I did not reveal to them that I was holding a tape containing part of the conversation. When I returned to the office the next day, I dictated a letter to the gentleman concerned. The letter simply said, "I think the role you are trying to play is that of Mountjoy in Shakespeare's Henry V". I never heard anything further from him.

I mentioned these events at the next Board Meeting and there was astonishment that he would wish to carry on in this manner. No one was impressed by it. Why doesn't he come here to see us all if he feels that strongly about matters and try and do something positive instead? I reported the incident to Tobin who just laughed about it. Tobin always in the know said, with your evidence gained under duress you could bring about a prosecution under the Telecommunications abuse law. "A very silly man, using the telephone like that, in this day and age". I always sorted my own "problems" over the years, no-one better than oneself to meat out ones own justice. Tobin knew the man reasonably well by association and thought that he was probably trying to gain a few "brownie points" with his mates. He did not believe that he would have phoned me with their blessing.

"I think he thinks he is Don Corleone" he quipped.

Ah well, nothing surprises me any more especially when it involves football.

CHAPTER – 31 (G.H.B.)

HOAX INHERITANCE

During the first week of October 2007, Paul rang me at the office to tell me that for once the club seemed to have had some unbelievable luck. As I wasn't used to hearing these words, I slumped back in my chair and listened with awe. Paul explained he had just had a phone call from a Mr Peter Anderson from Norfolk who was acting as executor on his late father's will. He explained his father originated from Rotherham and had moved to the Swaffham area as a teenager. Over the years, he had done very well in Norfolk. He set up his own business, finally selling his company for several million pounds and retiring. The caller said his father wished to leave the club a sum of £500,000 as a thank you for the many happy childhood memories he had of attending the Millers' games with his father. Peter went on to reiterate how his father was well travelled but always checked the football results no matter where he was in the world. He explained that his father had been a good friend of Gladstone Guest who had played for Rotherham United in the late 1930,s just before the war. They both had previously played football as lads for a Rawmarsh team. The conversation ended by Peter asking for the club's professional advisors to get in touch with him direct. Paul wrote down the contact number, which he then passed on to me.

I whizzed round in my swivel chair thinking, "I don't believe this!" I dashed into Gavin's office not realising he had a client in for a meeting and my bursting through the door made the both of them jump. After humbly apologising for the interruption, I told Gavin I would touch base with him later. About an hour later, Gavin came into my office and I told him the news. He commented, "It seems too good to be true". I was going to telephone Walker Morris in Leeds to pass on the information but we had second thoughts. We decided to get Mr Anderson on the speaker phone and get him to reiterate all of this. Gavin dialled the number. The room was then filled with that annoying deafening beep tone whenever you hit a wrong number. Gavin apologised and said "Read it again". This time, he punched in the numbers most precisely and again, the same thing happened. We rang Paul back to double check the number he had given us but the number was correct. "Paul" I said, "We may have a hoaxer, that number doesn't exist". Paul was extremely gutted as he had spent a good half hour talking to this individual who had seemed so plausible. Paul said to leave it with him while he went back to the notes he had made to see if there were any other clues of this guy's identity. He dialled numbers around the number he had written down to see if he had perhaps entered a digit incorrectly, all to no avail.

The next day a search was made of the residential phone book from British Telecom covering the Norfolk area, which revealed a possible 33 Andersons all in that location. A phone trawl through them that afternoon proved negative. There was something clearly not right here and we were starting to smell a rat. After further discussions, we asked Paul to get in touch with the telephone company to learn the identity of the caller. This was not as easy as it should have been as we had changed telephone provider to one of the "all singing, all dancing" alternative companies that unfortunately, do not sing and dance when you want something.

I decided that perhaps I would try a new line of enquiry.

Paul Douglas (Chief Executive Rotherham United).

One of my clients was well versed with football in and around the Rawmarsh area having been involved with two different teams for many years. His dad "Old Jock" who he always described for the last 10 years as being "still barely alive" was also very active in the football scene in his younger days. I wondered if Jock could perhaps put any knowledge together as to who this Anderson fellow could be. The reply came back "Best I can think of young un is that he would have most certainly played for Rawmarsh Welfare. They were a good team then everyone wanted to play for them". I toyed with the idea of asking Swinton Heritage researcher Ron (the Ferret) James to look up the old Advertiser papers of the day and see if he could find his name in a team report or something. It was a long shot though and as I already had my doubts I couldn't get enthused.

It was not until the 30th October 2007 that Paul managed to get the information, confirming the telephone number of the caller. I was attending the ground that afternoon and Paul agreed he would wait until I arrived to call the number. As I stood in Pauls office I said "OK let's see if it's a deal or no deal. Paul then dialled the Norfolk number to be greeted by a person who appeared to be very elderly, a little deaf and thought we were someone phoning from the Local Council. She certainly knew nothing of Rotherham United so as suspected, it was too good to be true .It could have been a workman or anyone who had used the old lady's phone without her knowing for a joke. Either way our lottery type windfall was not to be. Could we really expect that someone up there liked us?

If so then surely we shouldn't be in this predicament in the first instance... Should we?

CHAPTER – 32 (G.J.M.)

DON VALLEY OR BUST

After the bitter disappointment of relegation from League One and the court decision which barred us from pursuing any further claims against CF Booth Limited regarding the terms of the lease. The summer of 2007 was one of discontent to say the least.

At a board meeting in early September 2007 discussions were mainly surrounding the future of the Millers continuing to operate from Millmoor especially with the ongoing maintenance costs and poor facilities for the fans, players and staff at the club. The courts had restricted any further claims against the landlord but there was still the option of suing Ken Booth Senior personally under his fiduciary duty as chairman of the club during the Millers 05 takeover which allowed the transfer of the ground to settle old debts and the creation of the onerous lease. At the meeting it was decided that whatever legal options were still open to us an alternative venue needed to be considered if Rotherham United was going to survive the next few seasons.

Director David Costin at the M.K Stadium.

We had a landlord who wasn't prepared to help our plight and after the court case was unlikely to change. Match day costs were increasing season by season and because of the poor facilities ,revenue streams from sponsorships, corporate hospitality and refreshment bars were diminishing rapidly.

The board decided that whilst a move may seem extreme something had to be done quickly and Denis and Gary were sent on a mercy mission to the owners of Don Valley Stadium in Sheffield to enquire about the possibility of moving there. The Stadium staff treated the enquiry very positively and they were given a full tour of the ground and its facilities and also estimates of the costs which would be incurred on a match by match basis. When this was reported back to us at the next board meeting, Giles and myself were asked to prepare cash flows based on a move to Don Valley from say November 2007 until the end of the season and another report showing the effect if we had moved to Sheffield from the beginning of this season in order to get a comparison over a full 12 month period.

The whole scenario did, however, hinge on the fact that since the court case with CF Booth Limited it had been an order of the court that the landlord could and would issue repossession proceedings against the club if there were any more problems regarding the payment of rent. We took legal advice on our position if this happened and as to whether or not the club would be responsible for any future unpaid rents and dilapidations at the ground. Dave Costin had been worried for months about the unfinished main stand and the pile of rubble behind it. The timing of a move would have to be critical and top secret so as not to alert the landlords at any point until everything was in place. The other main issue would be the fans response at moving to Sheffield including transportation, local rivalries and the nostalgia problem that has often held football clubs back, when trying to improve its facilities.

Our report was presented to the board and revealed a significant saving of approx £150K if we were to move mid season and a full 12 months comparison revealed savings of up to £300k. There were certain assumptions including home attendances averaging 2500 and reductions in match day stewarding and policing costs etc. However, we had to be very conservative with our projections so as not to exaggerate the benefits when, in our experience, theory can often be flawed by the practicalities later on. We knew there would be many issues and matters to overcome, the likes of which cannot be easily measured and set out on paper.

Eyebrows were raised when the possibility of moving looked more realistic now the figures seemed to support the argument, but I could sense there had been some sleepless nights among the die hard supporters in the boardroom who were paranoid about the fans reaction to all this if it were to become a reality. Paul Douglas was strongly opposed to the move and Denis was also beginning to get cold feet. I suppose it was easier for myself and Giles who as accountants could hide behind the figures and detach ourselves from the passion and feeling that consumes fans when their clubs long history and tradition is being tampered with. But the cold hard facts were that the clubs future survival was at stake and not the 100 years residency at Millmoor.

The other consideration was that Don Valley would only be a temporary venue whilst the possibility of a purpose built stadium was still being championed by Denis and the board with the help from members of Rotherham Council. Denis had recently met representatives from a company called Stadium Developments Limited who owned a large piece of land at the rear of Parkgate Retail World. Although talks were in the very early stages it had been suggested that the owners and developers may consider building a purpose built community stadium for the town and Denis had managed to persuade them to contribute up to 50% of the capital cost if and when they obtained planning permission to extend the Parkgate Retail site. We understand in the past there had been objections to this further development of the site and it was obviously a very delicate subject especially from the council's point of view. Sometimes it was so frustrating when we were trying our best to be proactive and move the club forward only to be held back constantly by politics and red tape. We needed decisive action on this potential site so we could generate interest and excitement among the bankers, financiers, fans and future investors who eventually would be called upon to fund the remaining 50% build cost. The Parkgate site would appear now to have been set aside following the Rotherham Titans Rugby Club's announcement that they were planning to secure their own facilities elsewhere.

It seems ironic that less than a year later Rotherham United has now moved to Don Valley Stadium and is averaging home attendances of 4000 supporters. Based on our own projections this would have put us back into profit and at the same time strengthening our cash flow without a doubt. Hindsight is a wonderful thing and although in itself the exodus from Millmoor was not the answer to all our problems one often thinks this may have been the foundation stone to start rebuilding the football club and allow us the time to plan, negotiate and hopefully deliver the dream of a Community Stadium for the fans and people of Rotherham. As it turned out, time was not on our side and the legal team could not fully guarantee that even if we allowed the landlords to take possession of the ground that law suites would not be forthcoming for default and breaching the terms of the lease. The board had a heavy responsibility to act in the best interests of Rotherham United F.C. Limited and after a bloody and expensive court battle with the Booth's still ringing in our ears we were not prepared to jeopardise anymore of the clubs dwindling funds despite the potential long term benefits it might bring.

CHAPTER - 33 (G.H.B.)

SHARES, BLOODY SHARES AND THE 99

The question of the club issuing shares to investors, to raise vital funds needed for the fight to secure financial stability at Millmoor was often discussed at board meetings. It was something that Denis was keen to explore but was very problematic. First we needed to get the company into much better shape so that it appealed to investors. Considerations had to be given to: -

> What return could be offered to potential investors?
> What share price should we set?
> Would the share price be paid up front or in stages?
> What voting rights would be attached?
> Which market would we sell them in?
> How many shares would we be likely to sell?
> What perks were we able to offer?
> What about declaration of the lease and its imposition in the future?

Another apparent problem was the definite hangover from fans let down by the Millers 05 "Buy a Brick" scheme. People contributed to this in good faith and felt cheated with the outcome. This created an air of mistrust and the "Would you buy a Car from this man" scenario.

I recall Denis excitedly saying to me in mid October 2007 "Giles, there is a non-league club who have sold £390,000 worth of shares via the internet to get it out of the mire. Why can't we do the same?" I explained it wasn't as simple as that. I was very familiar with share issues from clients' dealings in the past but this was a new situation and I agreed I would look into it and report back at the next board meeting. My initial enquiries confirmed my thoughts. The club in question 'Ebbsfleet United' had changed its entity to an Industrial and Provident Society with a trust in perpetuity set up for its shares and so no-one ever really owned the club. This would not suit Rotherham's situation for the future and may not be approved by the Football League.

Looking at a new issue of shares I contacted the Financial Services Authority at Canary Wharf in London and asked them for their guidance. They were very helpful, confirming what I already knew but giving me an idea. If we were to offer shares in Rotherham United to the public, we had to appoint an agent, prepare a prospectus, have it approved by the FSA and only then could we go to the market. The cost of this would be at least £30,000, and the application fee was £6,000. with no guarantee of the shares being taken up. There was an alternative however where we could get leave to appeal to up to ninety nine investors and invite them to buy shares with none of the public company restrictions previously stated. One problem though was if any of the ninety-nine we approached backed off, we could not then approach someone else. It would be a one-time offer only campaign and the selection process for invitations to potential investors would be critical.

The F.S.A also insisted that each investor had to sign a statement that they earned more than a £100,000 in the previous 12 months or held net assets of at least £250,000 over the same period.

The next board meeting at our offices was proving difficult for me due to a sensitive meeting with HMRC and a client overrunning its time slot. I skipped the normal protocol of apologies for absence and the previous minutes and went straight onto the share situation. I explained to my co directors the alternatives and that we would also have to appoint an Independent Financial Advisor to oversee it all. Gary Hall said he could sort that out quite easily, he had many contacts in that field. I then gave them all a note pad and said "Right, while I just nip back into the Revenue meeting, jot down the hit list – Who is going to be in the 99?"

For their discussions I proposed a couple of alternatives for consideration;

> a) The first was for 99 blocks of 4,141 shares to be sold, each block costing £25,000 in total.
>
> Payment would be £5000 now and then a further £5000 on each of the next four anniversaries.
>
> This would realise some £2,475,000, which would help move the club forward.
>
> b) As a lesser alternative I proposed to issue 99 blocks of 2,070 shares at a cost of £12,420 for each block with stage payments of £2500 now, followed by 48 monthly payments of £208.33.

This would raise £1,229,580 although further investment may be required later.

We were to offer other incentives like a half-yearly meeting with the Board, 2 free seats in the main stand for the next 4 seasons and other incentives.

I eventually returned to the board meeting a short while later "Well, how many have we got?" I enquired. Denis looked very perplexed. Their lists for both options had only a few names on them. To make this work, we needed a one hundred per cent uptake and that was no mean feat. Hours of discussions on the 99 took place over the next few weeks. It was not as easy as first thought. We did start having talks with one or two potential investors but the ground ownership issues kept coming back to haunt us.

As another alternative Denis and Gary went to London to meet with "Investing in Sport" (based in Southampton) as in an earlier meeting, they intimated they could help us with the share issue. Unfortunately, like the others we approached, they wanted a good lump up front. Why I thought if everyone is so confident of raising funds for the club in an alternative market listing, do they always need such a large lump up front? We were to pay them a non-refundable fee of £30,000 and a final settlement fee of between 3.5 and 5.0% of the total transaction value. If they successfully obtained investors of £2 million, including the up front payment we would pay them a total amount of somewhere between £100,000 and £130,000. I personally am not a big fan of commissions, as they do not reflect payment for actual work done. If a man wants to invest say £3 million instead of £2 million what extra work has actually been undertaken? Unfortunately it is the way of the financial World.

As an organisation they were there to identify and develop business opportunities in sport nationally. They were chaired by Ken Bruce and called on contributions from the ex England manager Graham Taylor to help inject that bit of expertise. Graham Taylor was to examine R.U.F.C from the pitch side of the business. They were to plan how we could be in a mid table position in League One within five years. If they could get us the cash we so desperately needed I suppose what does it matter what their final bill is. The body blow for us was that they needed at least 6 months to deliver the goods. They did have some interesting ideas though, by generating new income from loyalty schemes, which were tried and tested with other clubs. This was very attractive for consideration for the next season as they estimated that we would create extra income of £263,000 a year for every 5000 regular attending fans.

The sale of shares had worked for some football league clubs. Brentford managed it very successfully, so did Port Vale. I was told by one of the directors that Robbie Williams had purchased £250,000 worth. He had not been to a game for years but apparently, had a recording of every home game sent to him. He makes sure he doesn't know the results beforehand so that he enjoys the game as much as if he was watching it live. After writing this book, I can foresee mischievous people bombarding his website with Port Vale scores to ruin his enjoyment.

We were also conscious of the fact that the new share issues may cause boardroom rifts. This was particularly evident at Notts County where there seemed to be two boards – the original board and the " fans" board representatives who clearly did not get on. At Brentford, it was the fans appointed directors who wanted Terry Butcher removed and orchestrated his departure. The chief executive of Brentford resigned in protest at this and then moved to the MK Dons.

I got talking to a club chairman at one of our away games knowing they had a recent share issue, thinking he could give us some good advice. I was shocked when he told me he didn't bother with all that regulatory fuss. When they needed some cash, they simply contacted the local newspaper, made some shares available and just flogged them! "Bloody marvellous" I thought. "Flouts every regulation and just gets away with it. "Knowing Rotherham's past luck, if we did that, the FSA would keel haul us in the South Yorkshire Navigation Cut"

CHAPTER – 34 (G.J.M.)

ACCRINGTON STANLEY?... WHO ARE THEY?? ...EXACTLY !!!

For me, the TV advert from the 1980's, must be the club's biggest claim to fame in recent times.

"Ian Rush says if I don't drink lots of milk, when I grow up I'll only be good enough to play for Accrington Stanley!"

In the early days of association football, Accrington F.C. were one of the football leagues founder members back in 1888. When that club disbanded 5 years later the other local team Stanley Villa adopted the town name and became Accrington Stanley. In 2006, the club had gained promotion from the Conference League and became fully fledged members of the Football League once more. So following Rotherham United's relegation from League One, and the fixtures being released in June, this was one away game I was determined to attend.

Redtooth Director Martin Green presenting the new away kit. The kit is being worn by Danny Harrison and Marie Hitchens.

It was Saturday, 17 November 2007. The Millers were in a decent vain of form especially away from home. In fact, it had been pointed out earlier in the day by my guest, Martin Green of Redtooth (our shirt sponsors), that so far, we were unbeaten in the yellow away strip. En route, I also picked up Paul Douglas, who only lives down the road from me and all three of us set off across the Pennines for Accrington.

None of us had ever been there before and probably, never had the need to so Paul brought his portable Sat Nav, typed in the postcode, slapped it on my windscreen and off we went.

The journey took just over an hour and a half. As we were approaching the outskirts of the town, Giles Brearley and his guest, Ralph Milner, went tearing past us in his Jaguar waving and grinning like some boy racer with his co pilot trying to prove a point. Apparently it is quite a common fault with some of these Sat Nav systems, entering the postcode only didn't exactly take us to the ground as we expected so we had to drive around for a short while until we found "The Fraser Eagle Stadium".

As we turned down Livingstone Road towards the ground, Denis, Gary, Herbie and Pedro were walking up the road towards us so we stopped and asked where they were going and they said they were off to find a pub as there were a couple of hours to go before kick off and they would meet us later. We drove into the club's car park and our first thoughts were "Small, quaint, non-league club". The facilities were very basic. Turning right into the reception, we had to walk through the sponsor's lounge into the directors' boardroom where light refreshments were available. Giles and Ralph, despite overtaking us at least half an hour ago, eventually turned up fifteen minutes later. Obviously, they'd been on a magical mystery tour themselves and had taken a wrong turning at some point, ending up on the outskirts of Bury. "Mmmn Less haste more speed" I thought.

Despite being delayed Giles did manage to speak to their finance director which he made it his job to do so at every game where possible. He established that the club had benefited greatly from windfalls of transfer cash via sell on clauses when their ex players had moved on to bigger and better things as we had done from the sale of Billy Sharp from Scunthorpe back to Sheffield Utd.

The match attendances were very average with stiff competition in the local area from the two Manchester clubs, Blackburn and Burnley as well as Rochdale and Bury who were also in League Two. One unusual income stream had been nailed down by issuing membership cards to the far east for an annual fee where a Chinese branch of supporters had been formed following the successful milk advert overseas. Apparently it showed a bit of class when a Hong Kong businessman let the card fall from his wallet in front of his dinner guests. Rumour has it that the membership card has now become a must have fashion item.

Like many football clubs, often, the board of directors are split and refuse to speak to each other. This causes an atmosphere when introducing the away team's directors and their guests. Accrington Stanley was no exception. The chairman was not there to greet us; he was apparently going to be late for the game and would be joining us nearer half time. We finished our drinks and were escorted to our seats in the main stand. There were three covered stands and one uncovered, which typically, was allocated to the away fans so it was fortunate for the travelling Millers that other than the cold breeze, it was a dry afternoon. Now

Gavin Mackinder (Right) in the Accrington Stanley boardroom with friend and client, Martin Green Director of Redtooth, who are Rotherham's away shirt sponsors.

when I said main stand earlier in fact, there was nothing main about it. I would go as far as to say that it was smaller than any one of the four sides at Millmoor and had no more than twenty rows of seats from top to bottom. It looked as though it had been built, along with other areas of the ground, in breeze blocks probably by local volunteers from the community. Yes, there was nothing classy about this joint, even the boardroom was a tastefully decorated portakabin.

The away end was filling up nicely; we must have brought near on a thousand fans with us and immediately there was a good omen when the teams ran out and the Millers were wearing the yellow away strip. We spotted Dave Costin on the far side of the uncovered section behind the goal, he had travelled up with his family and wanted to stand with the fans and take in the atmosphere. As I pointed him out, Giles smirked as he had also spotted Tobin standing about 6 feet away from Dave

For the first five minutes, Accrington came out with all guns blazing so we had to soak up the initial pressure. However, once we started to pass the ball with regular accuracy we seemed to

A good crowd of Rotherham fans brave the elements at Accrington Stanley 17th November 2007. We won 1-0.

take control, the half finished with us looking the stronger side even though the score was still 0-0. During the half time interval the Accrington Stanley's chairman who had just arrived came over to speak to Denis. When Denis relayed the story to us he was grinning all over his face. Apparently, their chairman apologised for being late but he'd been on a do the night before and had a massive hangover that made him so ill at one point, he was contemplating not going to the game. It was a night on the tiles with a price attached. Well, at least we couldn't fault him for his honesty.

Rotherham United dominated the second half but only managed to score one goal (Mark Hudson) despite creating four or five guilt edged opportunities to bury the Stanley. As you might imagine, the last few minutes were a little nerve racking, holding onto a 1-0 lead when the home team, desperate to equalise are pumping long balls into the box for all they were worth. Eventually, the final whistle came and we had earned another three points away from home and another unbeaten outing in the yellow strip. Martin was pleased with the win and the airing of his company logo again.

Whilst the directors and guests were having drinks and refreshments with their post match analysis, I decided to walk outside and congratulate the players as they were climbing back on the team bus. It was good to see the first team players mucking in with the clearing up and kit loading operations. In particular, the younger professionals like Stephen Brogan and Jamie Yates, who were still learning their trade, but hadn't lost sight of the other duties they were expected to do.

Denis Coleman had also come outside to congratulate the lads and chuckled to himself when I offered to help load some of the gear onto the coach. Dave Costin and his family appeared alongside us outside. David said he had really enjoyed the experience standing along side the Millers fans, joining in with the banter and celebrating yet another away win with them.

When Giles appeared he asked David if he had clocked Tobin. "Tobin who" was David's reply.

CHAPTER - 35 (G.H.B.)

THE 50/50 TURNS INTO 3 TO 1 AS "BAH HUMBUG" SETS IN

Some people tell me I should loosen up more and chill out a bit but at times I can't help myself if I feel something is not right.

Immediately after the Wrexham game on 22nd December 2007, it was the Rotherham United's staff party. The result of the day should have lifted everyone's spirits as we had won 3-0 with Derek Holmes scoring a brace in the 40th and 72nd minute and Marc Newsham bagging a third in the 82nd minute. The Welshmen were down to 10 men after 14 minutes when Crowell made a two footed tackle on Ian Ross. It was an easy game for the Millers and we could have scored another 5 or 6. The attendance was poor though, only 3,773. Perhaps the rest were out Christmas shopping.

As often happens at this time of the year, one becomes inundated with invitations for Christmas merriment and sometimes these obligations can turn into a punishing timetable.

The staff party kicked off early after the mopping up had finished from the game that afternoon. It had been a good afternoon for me personally in that I had won the top prize of £500 in the 50/50 draw. As we Directors always permed our tickets on home games this was an unexpected windfall for us all. It was agreed, after discussion in the marquee that the funds would go straight back into the company Bank account for the club's cash flow.

By the time Ruth and I got to the party, it was 9.00pm and in full swing. Of the players, only Chris O'Grady, his wife and child remained and they were just ready to leave. I looked round and knew a few but in all honesty, not many. I wondered who they all were. I went up to the bar and asked for a pint of Stella (as I do when real ale is not available) and a glass of red wine. Will, the barman delivered the drinks and then walked off. I stood and paused full of thought recalling what we had agreed at the our meeting earlier. A rather sumptuous buffet had been paid for by the club and we agreed that everyone would have a free drink on us at the bar on entry. We thought about making it two or even three drinks but it would be too hard to control.

I then observed others going up to the bar, getting drinks and not paying who clearly had been here for a while. I shouted Will over, "Will, Why haven't you charged them for their drinks?"

"Well earlier, it was announced that directors had won the 50/50 draw and you were putting it over the bar tonight for everyone." he told me.

Gary Hall was standing nearby, so I shouted him over "Gary, what on earth is going on with this £500?"

"Well, we thought it would be a gesture to put it over the bar for everyone as a Christmas thank you. We didn't think you'd mind", he said.

I then shouted David over. "I would never agree to this", I said. They looked on in some disbelief as I took on the mantle of Scrooge. Then a gentleman pushed past us with a tray rammed full of After Shocks.

"Alright" I said, "who is that person?" David confirmed he believed he was a family member of one of the ground staff.

"Point proven" I stated. "It is all just being pissed in the wind by people who don't even work for the club." I told them the £500 would be banked on Monday and they had better work out what they were going to do with the bar bill. I told Will "Start running the till forthwith."

Denis got involved but I stood my ground. I had not been consulted and it was not unanimous and I was sorry but it was not going to happen. I put the clubs cash flow as more important a priority. Sorry Father Christmas fans but that is how I saw it. An emergency meeting of the three other directors was then speedily called at the edge of the dance floor. Denis said they had all agreed to continue with the free bar and they would stand the cost personally between the three of them. I told them they were crackers. We left the party at about 10.00pm to show our faces at another Christmas bash we had been invited to.

Mike and Christine Lee who owned Constant Security Services Ltd had spent some considerable time trying to help us by looking to negotiate a reduction in our policing costs. Mike certainly knew Millmoor well, as a young Constable he regularly policed the Ground. He was a client and a very good friend whose party I wasn't going to miss.

True to my word, after the weekend, I passed the cash over to Paul to arrange for banking. Just before the board meeting later that week, I was reviewing the debtors list. "What's this?" I asked David Ness. "I don't owe any money to the club." David explained it was his estimate of the missing bar sales from the party split between the four directors, which Denis had told him to do.

"You can re-estimate that right away" I told him "And split it three ways". I brought the matter up at the board meeting and was met with frosty stares. Their hangover from the weekend was now continuing and it was going to cost about £700 each for the books to balance.

No-one protested at my remonstrating.

In fairness, I was probably being a little harsh. We had been under some strain, rushing here, there and everywhere of late but good business principles had to apply. This was in honesty a very rare disagreement for me on Rotherham United business but was accepted in good faith by all.

CHAPTER - 36 (G.H.B.)

THE DARLINGTON AWAY STADIUM EXPERIENCE

I was quite looking forward to the away game on 26 December 2007 as I had not previously been to Darlington. It was the Christmas break and I thought I would extend the trip to kill three birds with one stone, see the game, stay overnight in Darlington and then call at Scarborough on the way home to see my mother. I had phoned the club the month before and the receptionist recommended a local coaching inn that she knew which served "real ales". This was crucial for a staunch C.A.M.R.A member.

I left home at about 11am, accompanied by my good lady, Ruth, my daughter, Amy and my future son-in-law, George Legg. As we headed North up the A1, we noticed quite a lot of cars with RUFC stickers and scarves in their windows and thought this is definitely going to be a well attended game. As we got near to Darlington's ground, my Satellite Navigation system diverted me away for about ten minutes to the village of Croft on Tees where we checked in at the Croft Hotel. After relaxing and taking in some light refreshments, it was time to make our way to the ground.

Everything had so far gone very smoothly but I had a feeling something had to go wrong.

It's still debatable as to whose fault it was but when we arrived at Darlington FC, the security man on the gate said my car wasn't on his list and he'd never heard of me. I gave him sufficient reassurances that I was a genuine director of the club and he waved me in, suggesting that we report to the office straight away. At the office, I met a similar frosty reception as I did at the gate. "I'm sorry, you are definitely not on our list and the numbers have clearly been phoned in by Rotherham" the eagle-eyed receptionist informed me. I was just about to protest louder when in walked Denis, accompanied by his wife, Helen and some of his family. I explained to Denis the predicament and he immediately reassured the lady that I was indeed a director of Rotherham and the mistake must have been made at their end. "What's your name?" she enquired "Denis Coleman, chairman of Rotherham United Football Club" came Denis's reply. "Well, you're not on the list either" she said Denis wasn't best pleased by this announcement and neither was I. The chief executive was sent for. He explained that he took the call from Rotherham himself and a lady had phoned giving the numbers of people attending and we were definitely not included. He arranged for us to be issued with directors' box tickets and taken up to meet the rest of the Darlington brethren. Unfortunately, this did not extend to Amy and George and they had to make do with being accommodated in the press sandwich room, which I think had originally been built as a gun store with thick walls and no natural light from windows.

Once in the boardroom, I must say we were made extremely welcome. A nice sit-down meal awaited us, which we only picked at as we had arranged to go into Darlington to dine that evening and I especially didn't want to spoil my Adonis-like figure with any middle age paunch. I had read up a little about Darlington Football Club and its history before I came and was keen to extend this knowledge with the people there. Darlington Football Club, known as "Darlo" if you live in Darlington or "the Quakers" if you are a member of the press and you wish to make a point. The nickname "the Quakers" was in fact a reference to the religious movement that flourished in the town in its past. The club was founded back in 1883, turned professional in 1908 when joining the North Eastern League. They became the league champions in 1919-1920, which gave them automatic entry into the newly formed football league's third division. Their first season in the third division saw them as runners up.

The club has had what one could call a roller-coaster ride on and off the pitch through the years. They had remained in the bottom tier of league two since 1992, making them the league's second longest inhabitant after Rochdale. From 1883 until 2003, Darlington had played at Feethams, which has since been demolished. I was interested in the club mainly from the 1999-2000 season onwards when the ambitious new chairman, George Reynolds, took over. Darlington incidentally that year, were the first team to lose an FA Cup tie and still qualify for the next round. Manchester United's involvement in the FIFA Club World Championship meant that they were unable to enter the third round of the FA Cup. To decide who took their place, a "lucky losers" draw was held containing the twenty teams knocked out in the second round. Darlington was drawn out, giving them their second bite of the cherry. Unfortunately, they lost the tie, 2-1, to Aston Villa at Villa Park.

Club Chairman George Reynolds was apparently a charismatic character. Press reports stated how he had built Whitton Hall as his main residence. Some of his extravagant purchases in the past had included jets, helicopters, swimming pools, a London property (next door to the Spice Girls), a yacht, a Spanish Villa and a fleet of top of the range cars. He wanted to take Darlington forward and bring Premiership football to the town not flinching at what the cost might be. George Reynolds (born 1937) was previously jailed in the 1960's for smuggling watches. It was also stated that he had been in and out of prison for safe cracking and burglary. He went into business and established a series of companies including, latterly, a £25 million kitchen surface factory based in Shildon. It was estimated that his fortune in 2000 was around £300 million. He purchased Darlington FC for £800,000 in 1999 and ended up investing some £27 million in all into the club. The stadium itself cost over £20 million, and was aptly named "The Reynolds Stadium". Initially the fan base thought that Reynolds was a breath of fresh air and he was extremely popular. He submitted plans for the new stadium to be built on the A66 Darlington bypass.

During the summer of 2002, Reynolds had tried to uplift the quality of players and made approaches to sign Paul Gascoigne and Faustino Asprilla. He was the Columbian player with an undeniable talent and an undeniable temper! After starting his professional career in 1988 at the age of 18 and scoring thirty five goals in his first year, he eventually came under the eye of the Italians, joining Parma. During the first season, he scored some important goals including a twenty five metre second half free kick, which resulted in his team's 1-0 victory, so ending AC Milan's unbeaten run of fifty eight matches. He joined Newcastle United in 1995 for £6.7 million and stayed with them for three seasons, scoring a hat-trick for them against Barcelona in the 1997 Champion's League game at St James Park. He was befriended by George Reynolds and agreed to sign for Darlington as a favour to him. However, on the day he was due to sign the contract, he fled the UK and has not been seen on our shores since. Strange behaviour!

When the newly constructed Stadium opened, a crowd of 11,600 watched the first game, which was a 2-0 defeat against Kidderminster Harriers. As the novelty of the new stadium wore off, the attendances settled to a mere 3,000 to 4,000 hard core supporters. The crowd would swell to over 10,000 when a local derby match against Hartlepool United was in the offing but in reality needed that attendance level every game. Although Reynolds spent millions on the ground, the working capital injections were somewhat short.

His funding dried up which then led the club into administration. He resigned as chairman in January 2004 .Sadly this was only months after the new stadium had been opened.

In 2005, Reynolds's car was stopped by the police and he was subsequently arrested when £500,000 worth of cash was found in the boot of his car with no explanation of its origin being offered. In October 2005, he appeared in Newcastle court. Here the court heard that he was now almost penniless having been forced to sell many of his assets. The police stated that Reynolds had operated a tax avoidance scam between 1998 and 2004 and it was viewed that he had run the company with "cavalier contempt". The court was told how Reynolds had emerged from

The fantastic ground at Darlington was only licensed for a maximum crowd of 10000 despite seating many more.

Boxing Day 2007 shows the crowd at Darlington still awaiting admission to the ground. Despite having a fantastic new stadium the surrounding road network cannot cope with the volume of match day traffic The kick off was delayed by 15 minutes and the final result was a 1-1 draw.

a childhood of poverty in the east end of Sunderland and had climbed the wealth ladder to be then ranked 112th in the Sunday Times Rich List 2000. It was commented by the prosecutor that Reynolds had used money from his companies' directors' expense account to fund his lifestyle stating that "In reality, he used the companies as his own personal bank account".

Any benefits that Reynolds gained from the withdrawals such as cars and houses should have been declared to HMRC as a taxable benefit on form P11D, and they weren't. He was found guilty of money laundering and was sentenced to three years imprisonment. As is common in today's prison system, Reynolds's did not serve three, but was released in December 2006 after just over a year.

Following Reynolds' resignation from the club and his convictions, the stadium's name was changed to "The New Stadium". As a clever fund raiser, the club then sold the naming rights for the stadium to sponsors. This has seen the "Williamson Motors Stadium", the "96.6 TFM Darlington Arena" and currently, "The Balfour Webnet Darlington Arena". After

Gordons Coaches still with some fans sat aboard. Rotherham United gave the coach company plenty of action over the season.

Darlington went into administration on 23 December 2003, a charity game was organised to help raise much needed cash and ex star players such as Paul Gascoigne, Bryan Robson and Kenny Dalglish were all persuaded to help the cause. The match attracted a crowd of over 14,000 and helped the club fund the period of administration. After Reynolds' departure from the club, Stuart Davies took over as chairman, heading a consortium. He was popular with the supporters as he believed in openness and participation with the fan base. This apparently had not been Reynolds' style.

After they came out of administration in September 2004, they signed a number of experienced players such as Craig Hignett (ex Middlesbrough and Barnsley), Alan Armstrong and Clyde Wijnherd. Following a poor run of form in 2006/07, manager Dave Hodgson was suspended by the club being subsequently replaced by a former Doncaster manager, Dave Penney who took over with Martin Gray as his assistant. He got off to a great start, winning the first six games then he experienced a manager's worse nightmare when some of his best players were injured. For the

2007/08 season, he had signed Neil Austin, Alan White, Steve Foster, Ian Miller, Scott Wiseman, John Braxton and Ryan Valentine. These were in addition to goalkeepers Andy Oakes and Przemysalw Kazimierczak also midfielders, Rob Purdy, Kevin McBride and Xavier Barrau. They desperately wanted promotion to league one and I knew this was going to be a tight game.

As we all mixed in the boardroom, I was introduced by one of the directors to an elderly gentleman who had been with the club through thick and thin and who was more than willing to act as a guide to take us on a tour of the ground and tell us everything we needed to know, warts and all. It was a delight for Ruth and I to accompany the gentleman around a stadium with facilities that as far as Rotherham was concerned, we could only dream of. He did explain to me that their relationship with the council was extremely strained and that despite being situated on the A66, the council had put a capping of 10,000 attendances for football matches. This was in the main due to poor access roads around the stadium. I don't know, in all honesty how the project ever received planning permission if this was the view.

When I think back to some of the "arm wrestling" I have done with local authorities on the simplest of projects, this seemed mighty strange. I did appreciate the council's point though as today's attendance was 6,965 and yet the start of the match had to be delayed as the crowds could not all be admitted safely on time. This was probably exacibated by of the high number of visiting fans from Rotherham but nonetheless, it should not have been a problem for a stadium of this size. The elderly guide informed us that the club had planned a series of music concerts as a way of increasing revenue. These were to have taken place during the summer; they were code-named "Pitch Invasion" but because of conflict with the local council again over licensing and numbers, the whole idea was cancelled. He did say that they were having a concert with Elton John the following summer. "Elton John - well, that's one place I certainly won't be visiting next summer!" I thought to myself.

On the top storey, I was fascinated to enter what was going to be George Reynolds' own state apartment. No money had been spared on the quality of the build. The lifts for example were not just lifts; they were works of art, adorned with gilding. On leaving this apartment, we went down into what was going to be a large casino. Although passed on the plans, apparently, when it came to the issue of the gaming license commissioners were not keen to allow gambling on this site. The council also decided they did not like a residential apartment situated within a football stadium.

As we walked round, we could do nothing but admire the gorgeous banqueting facilities, the restaurants and the bars .The players' facilities were also second to none. I felt slightly embarrassed thinking of the portakabin arrangements we had in place at Millmoor. The way the ground had been constructed gave potential to expand the capacity up to around 60,000 seats if the need ever arose. The whole project seemed like an over the top "Oasis" in the middle of a "Desert".

The last time the Millers had played Darlington, was back at the old ground in April 2000. That game ended in an enthralling 2-2 draw. Looking at our club's statistics in the previous seven meetings we had lost once, drawn twice and won four times. Recent form had seen Darlington play well at home, winning three, drawing two and losing only one in the last six games. However our form was good in that we had been unbeaten in our last six games with three wins and three draws. Darlington were looking to secure the final promotion place to League One. It was most certainly set up to be the match of the day.

Our team consisted of Warrington, Sharps, Mills, Joseph, Brogan, Coughlan, Ross, Harrison, Newsham, O'Grady and Holmes with Oxley, Tonge, Todd, Hudson and Taylor on the subs bench. The first half belonged to Rotherham. The lads played well, scoring through a Chris O'Grady goal in the 36th minute. Darlington seemed to rally in the second half and as the game progressed they managed to snatch an equaliser with a goal from Micky Cummins in the 68th minute. The rest of the game was a bit like being sat on the knife edge as both sides threw caution to the wind to try and secure the victory. I was disappointed that we didn't come away with all three points as I thought that Rotherham were certainly the better side of the two. I think this was reflected in the Northern Echo when I read the sports report the following morning over a northern breakfast before winding our way over to Scarborough..

CHAPTER - 37 (G.H.B.)

DINO APPEARS FROM NOWHERE

The shares of Rotherham United were wholly owned by a company called Air Estates Limited. One of the problems we repeatedly came up against with a potential sale was the fact that Dino was estranged from the rest of us and would not necessarily be as accommodating and handing over the shares he held in Air Estates Ltd to an investor if the need arose. He may have tried to stick it out for some cash and scupper the whole deal.

Since Dino's resignation as a director in December 2006, David Costin had contacted him a couple of times and had discussions with him regarding the shares. David said he would keep him talking for ages but always avoided the shares issue. At a Board meeting it was agreed we would offer him £30,000 to buy the shares so resolving the problem. We were to stump the money up personally and would recover it should a future sale take place. Dino possibly thought he was sitting on a potential goldmine; maybe he took some professional advice and was told to hold on to them in the event they would somehow generate some super profit for him in the future. We all knew that there was no opportunity of benefiting from the sale of the shares of Air Estates Limited, our relentless search was for Investors not buyers.

One problem though was that any investor prepared to inject large amounts of cash into the club would require 100% ownership. I certainly would. They would not want to inherit Dino as a fellow shareholder or want to have to buy him out. It would serve no purpose as far as going forward was concerned. To this end, we sought professional advice and it was decided that as we considered the shares were worth nothing in reality, Air Estates Limited would sell the shares it held in Rotherham United for a nominal £20,000 to a new holding company. The new holding company could then offer all its shares to a prospective investor to achieve the desired wholly owned situation. I contacted the Football League to inform them what we were planning to do and they were in approval subject to any new owners being vetted by them first. The new company name selected was Corporate Network Investments Ltd. This was simply a shell company that would leave its shares in perpetuity with us, as trustees, until an investor was found. Gavin dealt with the formation arrangements and suggested various names for the new company. He overstepped the mark when one of his proposed names was "Share World Finance Corporation" or S.W.F.C for short.

These Wednesday fans are everywhere.

Despite the financial predicament the club was experiencing, we were prepared to put the £20,000 into Air Estates Limited to effect the transaction on behalf of the new holding company ourselves. An agreement was to be put in place with Corporate Network Investment Limited that other than the repayment of the £20,000 loan back to us there would be no further payments to the Directors or shareholders. The directors would have no financial benefit from the disposal of the club and all agreed, without reservation, to hand the shares over to whoever the board of directors felt was a suitable person to take Rotherham United forward.

On 7 January 2008, a written resolution was sent to all the shareholders of Air Estates Limited confirming the sale of the shares in Rotherham United FC Limited to Corporate Network Investments Limited.

Following the recent changes in company law, it now meant this could all be done by post as opposed to having to call a formal meeting in which all shareholders are invited. This simplified things as I did not fancy chairing a meeting and trying to keep some modicum of decorum with the ill feelings between Dino and the others. We complied with the legal requirements sending out the notices confirming our intentions and voting procedures. There was 21 days notice given in which to lodge your vote for or against the resolution. There were enough other shareholders in Air Estates Limited to pass the Ordinary Resolution no matter what Dino voted so the whim of the majority would prevail.

On receiving our correspondence regarding the proposed sale, Dino appointed a solicitor in Liverpool to act on his behalf to try and coerce his way back onto the board of directors. They suggested calling an extra-ordinary shareholders' meeting, which

I thought was inappropriate as there would not be enough support from the members to call such a meeting. Section 368 of the Companies Act 1985 requires two or more members holding 10% or more of the company's shareholding, to request an extraordinary general meeting. That would mean that one of the other shareholders would have to endorse this, which was obviously not going to happen.

The letter confirmed that Dino had first contacted them back in 2007. They were very critical saying that Mr Coleman had excluded their client from the running of various aspects of the business and that he, Dino, had been made the subject of a whispering campaign against him. It went on to confirm that Mr Coleman wanted to run the business for himself without any input from or involvement of Mr Maccio. It also stressed that he was forced out of the Company against his wishes leaving his investment locked in to the business under the stewardship of the remaining shareholders in circumstances where he had no trust or confidence in their ability or willingness to best represent his interests. Leaving as a Director may not have suited him but I always say you reap what you sow. The circumstances he created overtook him.

I think the terminology "Investment" was also a little misguided; perhaps it should have said, "Shares in the company". Investment would indicate that Dino had personally invested cash funds into the club, which was not the case. Denis was quite annoyed at the tone of the correspondence and really wanted to have his right of reply, which would have no doubt included many home truths. I don't think Dino was having a brilliant time of late as he had been involved in some insolvency with the family businesses. As there was so much happening with Rotherham United particularly with the impending crisis this matter was put onto the back burner. If Dino had thought there was some money available with the share transfers he was obviously greatly mistaken.

I can not see any other reason for paying a solicitor to write to us on his behalf unless he believed this to be the case.

CHAPTER - 38 (G.H.B.)

THE AMERICANS ARE COMING

One response we had from our advert in the Financial Times for the sale of the club was from Axiom Capital in London, they were interested in receiving a prospectus on behalf of their US client. On receiving the letter, forwarded from the PO box number, I ran into Gavin's office and threw the letter across his desk. "This should prove interesting" I gloated. We decided to ring Axiom Capital to sound them out first. They seemed very reluctant to talk to us without having had the opportunity to examine all the details of the club to establish whether or not their client would be interested. As requested, we parcelled up a large package containing accounts, projections, finance agreements, lease agreements and other data about the club and duly sent it to them. It was our last piece of business before we closed down for the Christmas 2007 break.

When we returned in the New Year, we made contact with them once more and, this time, they were a little more willing to pass information to us. It turned out their client was a private merchant bank based in New York. The major shareholder and controller was just mad about English football and always ensured his trips to the UK tied up with going to see at least one game .The bank had apparently been trying to buy an English league club for some time having previously submitted bids for Blackburn Rovers and Coventry City, committing $125 million dollars to invest. They were becoming frustrated at the amounts expended on what they called "abortive bids" and their interest in Rotherham was probably a final attempt on their behalf. They had never looked at a club in League Two but we had caught their attention and they were considering us.

After a few more phone calls in answer to Axiom's questions, they passed their New York client's telephone number for us to ring and speak to them direct. Gavin and I sat in my office, put my phone on to hands free and dialled the New York number. Our call was expected and we were speedily put through to the bank's owner. What followed can only be described as a replay of a scene out of "Wall Street". The gentleman called Mark was talking to us at a hundred miles an hour, clearly pacing up and down, and he was constantly interrupted by his staff asking whether shares should be sold yet or other securities be purchased. Every time we got to something interesting, we'd hear "Sell! Sell! Sell!" booming out in the background. What could have been said in a five minute conversation with us must have taken twenty.

It was left that he wanted us to first have a meeting with the bank's representatives in London and, if that proved fruitful, he would fly to the UK and attend one of the home games. This was tentatively arranged to be against Hereford United on 2nd February 2008. We thought this would be a good advert as Hereford were third in the league.

We were, however, somewhat stunned when, right at the end, he announced that he would be expecting us to pay for his airfare and hotel bill in effecting his visit to Millmoor. As I put the phone down, Gavin and I looked at each other and thought "That's bloody odd".

A meeting was arranged for the following Friday at Axiom Capital's offices in Golders Green. They said they would like Paul Douglas (Chief Executive) and myself to attend. They did not see the point of meeting all of the board at this stage of the negotiations. Denis was a little miffed at this request as he wanted to become involved in the dialogue but we managed to persuade him to leave this to us as we were just sounding them out. After finishing work on the Thursday, Paul Douglas caught the 5.30pm train from Sheffield to St Pancras in order to meet up with me. I had travelled down to London the previous day on business and was staying at my London apartment. I met Paul at the railway station and having quickly dropped his luggage off at my place, we dived into the nearest pub, right on the bank of the Thames, to discuss our strategy for the meeting the following morning.

8.15am on the Friday morning saw us scurrying for the train down to Waterloo where we then joined the Northern Line for our journey to Golders Green. We were weighed down with briefcases full of information but despite the uncomfortable journey, we were quite excited at the prospects.

As we alighted from the tube station at Golders Green, we called their offices, as instructed, for directions and proceeded through a very Jewish part of London. Once at their offices, we were shown upstairs by a secretary who took us into a meeting room. After sometime alone, Mr David Sinclair (a Chartered Accountant) of Axiom Capital and another gentleman, the European director for the private merchant bank, entered the room.

After introductions and exchange of pleasantries, the meeting got underway. It took on the form of an interrogation. Questions and criticisms were fired at us right, left and centre. At one point, they asked Paul exactly what his duties had been the previous day. Paul gave them as honest a rundown as possible to which their response was "If my client does buy the club, the first thing we will do is sack you." Their explanation was that they wanted a chief executive to stick purely to the main role and not be prepared to get his shirt sleeves rolled up and muck in. Unfortunately, Rotherham is the kind of club where you have to; so this didn't vie very well. They also said they wished to sack the commercial manager. One thing I will say is that they had certainly done their homework on the club. They knew a lot about its history, its problems and its personnel.

They discussed a master strategy whereby Paul (obviously not now sacked) "who is the only chief executive in the football league to speak fluent Japanese" would use his language skills and contacts to communicate with the Japanese football clubs, with a view to bringing good players over here for playing opportunities at little cost to the club. They also wished to use South African players from some banking connections they themselves had. They also mentioned Steve Archibald and FC Barcelona as other fanciful plans.

They also had an idea about partial flotation of the club. The bank had many contacts who would certainly purchase shares within the club, these investors being located all over the world.

Paul managed to stop their flow to tell them that he didn't think the scheme would be possible under the constraints of the league rules. They outlined how they thought a new structure of personnel should be established for the club and doubted that many of the existing staff would retain their jobs should a takeover be effected. People should be judged on their ability and performance. If they are not up to the mark then they are out. There was only room for toughened professionals. They then went on to say that their client was interested in Rotherham

United, but he would not proceed just yet , there were problems to iron out first. They proposed to get involved with the club for a six month period, during which time they would offer various assistance and management expertise to help the club strengthen and go forward..

During this time, they also wanted to take up the case with C F Booth's. They had studied the events surrounding this case and were very interested. To this end they had a proposal. They wanted us to assign the case to the bank who, at its own cost, would use a "Quality Silk" to take another look at the brief. Through their legal connections in New York, they were proposing to use one of the international legal practices that had a large office in London. They would take the case on and come to a deal with the club as to some share of the spoils. I suppose it was a form of no win no fee. They stated that in their opinion we had used lawyers from the upper quarter of the Championship league and that C. F Booth's had used a firm in the lower quartile of the Premier league. The firm they proposed was jostling for a top position in the Premier. I thought I heard them say they were proposing Baker McKenzie, who are a huge practice with offices all over the world. They appeared as number one firm in the "Which Lawyer's global 50 firms". Paul and I looked at each other in astonishment; we were certainly not expecting this to be in the dialogue.

They went on to say that the lease with C F Booth and the associated hospitality package were completely unacceptable. It was a complete deal breaker. They didn't believe anyone in his right mind would take on Rotherham United with this hanging over it. They were concerned regarding the contingent liabilities that were attached to the lease. Although there was an exit clause on the lease in 2011, when the lease was originally taken out, there were stands on all four sides of the Ground. The Landlord's could technically ask the club to demolish the new, unfinished stand as well as remove the huge dirt mound, which had built up at the back and replace it with something similar to that which had already been demolished. The associated Hospitality agreement was viewed as being onerous and would not be tolerated by their New York Banking client. They asked us to send them full court papers and they would get underway with dealing with the lease etc immediately. It was made very clear that without the cancellation of the lease and the hospitality agreement, there would be no deal. They were very critical of the agreement ever being accepted in the first place by Millers 05.

With their message clearly spelled out the meeting ended. Paul and I left feeling somewhat bewildered to say the least. We both felt as though we had done ten rounds with Mike Tyson. We headed back to Golders Green tube station and then alighted at Hampstead for a bite to eat. Their approach was very aggressive. We worried that this hard-nosed attitude would probably work well in the streets of New York but would not wash very well with the Rotherham supporters. It appeared that the bank was very wealthy and had the financial clout to invest the funds we urgently needed but once again we were haunted by the spectre of the dreaded lease. We agreed we would not discuss the meeting with anyone until we both got back and would do a proper debriefing. I saw Paul onto the Sheffield train from St Pancras and I returned to my apartment to mull things over.

We heard from the Americans about a month later, they were still chasing up the legal papers. In a conversation with Tobin he thought we should send them off to get their proposals. Maybe he was right. They also enquired about their offer of 6 months consultancy, as outlined to us. The problem was that time was not on our side and it would be a massive risk allowing these people to call the shots without any significant financial investment at this stage. In essence we didn't have time to commit or agree anything and were in a classic Catch-22 situation. Was there a straight forward solution to our problem and would we be around long enough to find out?

Chapter - 39 (Joint)

Butch Cartledge and the Sun Tanned Kid Ride Again

Following a telephone call to Paul Douglas, there was a request to meet the board of directors by Dino Maccio, Alan Cartledge and one other (unnamed at this point). They said they were interested in the future of the club and were representing potential investors. Paul rang me and I suggested to him that he and I should meet them, as requested, to at least sound the situation out. We were all actively working very hard to try and find investors and would listen to anyone, although I have to say I was very sceptical this time considering what had happened in the past.

The meeting was arranged at our offices, in Bridge Street, on 20th February 2008, 3.30pm.

At 3.25pm, Paul and I gazed out of my upstairs window across the Bridge Street car park and could see three figures making their way across the darkening horizon. Paul suddenly said that he recognised the third party; he had met him before and his name was John Green and he knew that he'd had something to do with Chesterfield previously. They all signed the visitor's book and we went downstairs into the reception area to meet them. I then ushered everyone into the boardroom.

There wasn't much frivolity in the air and the meeting started straight away. I invited Alan to open the meeting. He explained that they were representing two parties who were interested in the acquisition of Rotherham United Football Club. They needed a lot of financial information to take away in order that this could be considered further. Paul asked Alan the identity of the parties but he was reluctant to reveal them. I thought, here we go again. This reminded me of the previous board meetings when Alan was on the verge of introducing a big hitter to the club but he would never state his identity. This was again frustrating both Paul and me. We explained to them that we could not release any information to unknown parties. In order to comply with Money Laundering Regulations and confidentiality, etc, we would require copies of passports and utility bills (as evidence as to who they were) and would also require proof of funding.

They would also have to enter into a Confidentiality Agreement. As such we could not release any information to them to discuss with unknown third parties; sorry it just could not be done.

John Green introduced himself at this point as the former chief executive of Chesterfield Football Club. He tried to back Alan up by stating that the contacts were very interested and that they were here in an official capacity to establish, in principle, whether the enquiry was worth further pursuit. I re-emphasised my previous statement; it didn't seem to be understood. John was chief executive back in 2001 when a lot of problems were rocking Chesterfield F.C. He was suspended from office but subsequently reinstated. He was obviously well familiar, dealing with clubs in trouble.

Alan then started asking all sorts of questions such as when did the club realise it was encountering difficulties. How many interested parties are there? What does the Balance Sheet look like? While Paul was fending these requests off, John Green asked me why Dino had not been notified about our intentions regarding the club's future? I stopped the meeting at this point and stated that this was not on the agenda and therefore, was not up for discussion; they were supposedly here to enquire about investors for the club. Dino then asked why a resolution was sent to him regards the sale of the club. I told him the truth; it was in order to facilitate a smooth transfer to a potential investor. It was to help secure the future of the club. I also reminded Dino that he still owed money to the club, to which he somewhat sheepishly replied that no one had written to him about it. I did state that they most certainly had on quite a few occasions. Alan then asked how much would be needed to inject into the club to continue. I again reiterated that I could not give out figures without the proper conditions being entered into. Alan then confirmed that there was no point in the meeting continuing and they would go back to their investors and contact us again if they were interested. The meeting closed at 4pm.

After they left, Paul and I had discussions as to who we thought the mystery investors could be. We muted names around such as Paul and Peter Eyre and possibly Denis Hobson the boxing promoter who we knew were contacts of theirs. The Eyre's had shown interest before, having made a very generous donation to the club in the past. Nothing was conclusive. I even wondered if there was anyone at all or were they just fishing?

We reported the meeting's events to the other directors, who were not surprised. What was so annoying about all this was that in the ensuing weeks, Dino and Alan went public, indicating through the media that the board were blocking them. The only people who were blocking their investors were Dino and Alan themselves. We had no more direct contact with them after that, we only read of their antics in the press. I know that they contacted Jeremy Bleazard to register a potential bid for the club, so there must have been somebody in the wings with some cash. I still do not know who that was though? Clearly they were interested in saving the club but why the secrecy? Just as we would've expected them to be confidential with the data we would have passed onto them, we would have been equally confidential as to the identity of the potential investors.

This confidentiality moral was put to the test when I received a call out of the blue via a city lawyer who was representing another football league chairman who was interested in acquiring Rotherham United. I was approached directly as I was the professional on the board and I agreed that the identity of this person would not be made available, even to the other directors, unless a proper offer was to be made. Obviously, a potential investor could not be involved with two football clubs and it would be dependent upon the sale of this person's shares in his existing club. This was another avenue that looked extremely hopeful to us but, unfortunately, external factors prevented the gentleman from going forward. To this day, I can confirm that none of the other directors know who the party was.

CHAPTER 40 (G.H.B.)

ARE THE IRISH COMING?

We were all running around talking to everyone trying to broker a deal to save the club when out of the blue Denis got a phone call from a contact at the Irish Football Association. The caller asked if we would meet Anthony McMullen of The McMullen Property Group. He wanted to acquire an English Football League club and Rotherham United could be ideal. McMullen had played football himself, his father and uncles were also steeped in Irelands football tradition. Denis was delighted with the call and eagerly rang the mobile number to talk to the man himself.

McMullen explained to Denis he had been looking at Gretna as a possibility but preferred an English League club if possible. A meeting was arranged two days later to try and further the talks. Denis alone drove to Newcastle to a Hotel abutting the airport to meet 26-year-old Anthony McMullen and his entourage. Denis went there in good faith and knew nothing of the man he was to meet. I had done some research on him before the meeting but there was little on him, which surprised and concerned me. In an interview McMullen told reporters he left school at 16 and started his career by buying houses in Dublin while still working in Tesco. He said he then moved into development after seeing how successful one scheme was in Bulgaria.

Five years ago, he approached his father and said that if they followed a business plan, they would be millionaires within two years. His father backed him.

He was quoted as saying "We did not stick to the plan, yet we still made 40million Euro instead" He owned and ran an Estate agency business in Ireland in addition to International property development. He apparently resided in Jamaica a good deal of the time. To me he seemed too good to be true. I mentioned it to Tobin who did his own background search. He wasn't particularly impressed either because (a) He was too young to be seriously long term, he may get bored and lose interest and (b) His public domain profile was very sparse and had little provenance.

At the meeting in Newcastle were Anthony McMullen, Roddy Collins and his brother former Boxing Middleweight and Super Middleweight world champion Steve Collins.

Roddy Collins was well known in football. He began his career at Dublin club Bohemians F.C back in September 1979. He played for two other Irish clubs before joining Mansfield Town F.C. in December 1985. He left them to join Newport County in August 1987, playing seven times in their ill-fated 1987-88 relegation from the League. Collins then went on to play only once for Cheltenham before heading back to Ireland joining Shamrock Rovers in September 1988. He was top scorer in the 1988-89 season. He subsequently played for Dundalk, Sligo Rovers, Glentoran, Bangor , Cliftonville , Larne and St Francis F.C. Collins' first venture into football management was at Bangor in 1994/95 which despite saving them from relegation, was relatively brief. In 1998 he found himself thrust into the spotlight when he was surprisingly appointed as Joe McGrath's successor back at Bohemians.

Football is a small world. When we advertised for the position of Team Manager following Alan Knills departure Roddy applied for the position and was interviewed. When Denis appeared at the meeting Roddy turned to his brother and said " This is the guy I told you about, He interviewed me for the Managers job at Rotherham but all he did was ask about you". After long discussions it was decided that they would all meet up next day at Millmoor so that they could get a feel for things. Denis and Paul showed them around the ground. As they were walking on the pitch and talking Ken Booth senior who had come for his tickets clocked them through the open gate. He stormed over to Denis and said "I hope you are not trying to sell my Ground, I will put scrap on it first". I don't think the Irish were very impressed

As the talks continued it got more serious and a meeting was set up with David Hinchcliffe at Walker Morris and Jeremy Bleazard to get down to the more serious stuff. One bone of contention was the current manager Mark Robins.

Clearly McMullen wanted Roddy Collins to be in charge but we were very happy with Mark. In the end he agreed that if successful Mark would remain in office and Collins would be made Director of football. The media were sniffing round and Denis put out a statement. "I've been dealing with Anthony for a few days now, I had a meeting with him and introduced him to the administrators the day after we went into administration." This got the media buzzing and they contacted Anthony

McMullen direct. McMullen is a property developer with property worldwide and told Radio Sheffield that he would pay any outstanding wages to staff and players as soon as he took over the club, but that would not be until April 1st at the earliest. Should the McMullen group take over the club, they said they would build the club a new ground. This was broadcast around South Yorkshire and he went on to say. "Rotherham has a great history and I want to continue to honour that I and my team along with the local council and the current chairman are committed to taking Rotherham forward. Easter weekend means that this process may not be completed until next week"

Talks continued in the wings but McMullen making these statements worried me, because at this point he had not sent any required paperwork to Jeremy Bleazard or our lawyers as promised. During talks with Denis, McMullen had said that he saw it as crucial that the fan base were behind him. He had talks previously with other clubs including Longford Town F.C, which he eventually aborted because of negative fan reactions. There were one or two groups making noises about taking the club over at this time but the crunch came when the Advertiser ran the story that "The Supporters club were backing Dino Maccio and Alan Cartledge's consortium" even though no one knew who it was. That went down like a lead balloon and the deal was off.

As time has gone on I have wondered how serious Anthony McMullen was about taking over the club. He seemed to make many attempts to buy a Football Club but it never materialised. Roddy Collins was quoted as saying " They just came to me, they said that they had followed my career, it was a call out of the blue for me to be totally honest. They had followed my career at Bohemians where they were supporters and they felt that I got a raw deal at Carlisle." and that is how he got involved.

A press report in the Irish Times reported another abortive deal as follows:

> "Sitting in a Co Meath hotel last Tuesday afternoon, Anthony McMullen was in positively upbeat form. The Dublin developer was poised to take a controlling stake in Livingston FC, the Scottish first division football club, and McMullen was keen to explain his plan to combine success on the balance sheet with results on the pitch."

He had spent the previous evening with Pearse Flynn, the Irish businessman who bought the Scottish club in 2004. Under the terms of the proposed deal, Flynn would retain a minority stake while McMullen would acquire half of the club. Within hours of finishing a lengthy interview with a newspaper, however, the entire deal had fallen apart. Late on Tuesday night, the board of Livingston issued a statement advising that McMullen Properties had failed to meet certain conditions and the deal had stalled.

A press conference by McMullen Properties the following morning announced the deal was cancelled. Livingston said they were unaware that the press conference had even been called. The sticking point, according to McMullen, was the role of Roddy Collins, the former manager of Bohemians and Shamrock Rovers. Collins had been lined up to take over as general manager of Livingston, but pulled out the day before he was scheduled to sign his contract. McMullen said his business plan had been predicated on Collins being in situ. Without Collins on board, he said it was simply not "financially sensible" to bankroll the club from his personal funds. The day before, he had outlined how he intended to redevelop the club's stadium and make millions of pounds for himself and the club in the process. He said he was going to invest £2 million in the club over two years and he expected to make £15 million in five years by utilising the club's property assets - an eight-acre site in the heart of Livingston that houses the club's stadium, Almondvale.

A spokesman for Livingston told the newspaper that the deal fell through after McMullen failed to meet a number of conditions. He said the board met on Tuesday night and decided to cancel the deal. The spokesman would not be drawn on what exactly the conditions were. However, it is understood that McMullen had not signed legal contracts or handed over the first tranche of money, a payment of £150,000, on the designated date. He said his plan for Almondvale involved knocking down two of the ground's four stands and redeveloping them into a mix of apartments, corporate boxes and retail units.

He said that the Scottish Premier League's regulations only required a 6,000 capacity and that the ground would retain that even after demolishing the stands. The plan, he said, would be "an absolute cash cow". It was the latest in a number of failed attempts by McMullen to take control of a football club. In the past six months alone, he said, he'd held talks with Longford in Ireland, Gretna in Scotland and Rotherham in England before the Livingston fiasco. No deal has ever materialised. "In my heart, I have given up on football now," said McMullen on the Wednesday afternoon. "I am going to go back to doing what I do best, development. This is the end and my heart is not in it any more" It was a dramatic turnaround for the 26-year-old father of two.

CHAPTER 41 (G.H.B.)

LIFE IN ADMINISTRATION - THE FINAL SURGE.

We had various meetings with Jeremy Bleazard of XL Business Solutions and our lawyer David Hinchcliffe of Walker Morris as it became evident that we were running out of time to clinch the deal we needed to secure the club's future. There was no threat of a winding up petition but we were running out of cash. Following legal advice on the 18th February 2008 we filed a notice of our "Intention to place the company into Administration". The Notice was a way of protecting the Club in the short term from any creditor wanting to put the screws on. This bought us a little more time for negotiations. It had been a major blow that the talks with major investors had not been fruitful as we were relying heavily on this in securing the clubs future.

We had looked into the situation regarding our "Football League share" previously and were told that even if we went into Administration for a second time we would not lose it. We briefed Mark Robins and the staff. Denis and Dave Costin went round to the Council to see Mike Cuff to advise him of what we were to do. Mike Cuff confirmed that the Council would not be deflected from their current exploratory talks about the site at Parkgate for the New Stadium.

We prepared the following press release to try and give a fair summary of the situation to the fans and others.

ROTHERHAM UNITED FOOTBALL CLUB.

Over the past two years the board have been working very hard to reduce the level of operating losses at the club. In particular cuts and savings on overheads have been made together with a thorough reorganisation of staffing in every department. At the same time the need for additional investment has remained and has in fact been an even more difficult task.

Over the past few months the Board have been involved in detailed discussions with a number of interested parties, The Board were extremely confident that one of these interested parties would invest in the future of the club and have spent a great deal of time and effort in trying to ensure this happened. However, several of these parties have now dropped out of the picture and some of our confidence has been lost. A huge stumbling block in negotiating with investors has proved to be the terms and conditions of the lease for the ground. Unfortunately, the lease was presented to the Custodian board as a non-negotiable item when they stepped in at the last minute to rescue the club. As such there have not been any opportunities to discuss more reasonable terms befitting a club of Rotherham's size and turnover.

We were very close to agreeing an investment package with a group of investors who we met in London last week which we were confident would allow the club to progress through to the time when the new Community Stadium was complete. When these negotiations fell through, again largely due to concerns surrounding our lease agreement, the directors recognised the need to seek external advice.

Our need to find new investment had become more urgent following a significant shortfall on the insurance payout after the flood, coupled with lower than anticipated match day attendances. The Club has accumulated a large debt with P.A.Y.E. We are on good terms with HMRC, with whom we have weekly discussions. They have been very sympathetic of the need for the Club to secure its future funding. We have nothing but praise for their considerate yet professional approach. However, it is plain to see that things cannot continue like this and that time is not on our side.

We are now some months down the line from beginning serious negotiations with investors and we are regrettably still not yet at a stage where a certain future for the Club can be definitely guaranteed. With the difficulties involved, a resolution could still prove to be several months away. Now really is the time for any investors to come forward.

We remain hopeful that investment can still be found and the fact that a new stadium is now in reach does make the Club a far more attractive proposition for would-be investors. Recent history has shown that new stadiums generate greater interest and support as well as additional revenue. Rotherham United and its loyal supporters are deserving of this.

But that is still some way off and in the meantime we are conscious of the need to protect the Club from any possible action from any of its creditors before the situation arises. In order to combat this, we have therefore filed a 'Notice of intention to appoint an administrator'. This does not mean the club is in Administration or even that it will necessarily go into Administration. Instead it protects the Club from possible hostile actions at a time when the Club needs to be fully focussed on finding new investment. Clearly the threat of administration will recede if a serious investor can be found . This is something we all want, and something the Club needs quickly. However, if no deal can be brokered then administration would be the only option for the Club and that would be a great shame, as it would mean another points' deduction.

The Club retains hope that there is a consortium or forum of investors/fans with the capability and financial clout to enable the Club to go forward. This is not an impossible task; other Clubs like Brentford in the same league have achieved this. The Club is one of only 72 in the Football League and represents a golden investment opportunity to enter into a traditional and cherished world. Any party who is interested in acquiring or investing in the Club should speak to Chief Executive Paul Douglas or any of the directors. The directors will either step down or work with any interested party.

It should be remembered that a lot of the hard work

has already been done for the cause. It is imperative that our fans continue to support the Club during this uncertain period in order to demonstrate to potential investors that there remains a burning desire to keep League Football in the town. Now is a critical time for the Club, and we all have to do everything we can to ensure we attract the investors we need to create another 100 years of league history for Rotherham United. Time is limited so prompt action is vital. Please show your approval and support by continuing to come through the turnstiles and be prepared to back initiatives that hopefully will arise in the next few weeks.

We all continued working furiously in the wings to find a buyer and a solution to the problems. We were confident of being able to play out the season and had done some Cash Flow projections, which were passed, to Jeremy Bleazard. It could be achieved if everyone continued with their support. All sorts of people rallied round to help. The Rotherham United Supporters trust pledged some funds. Dave Watson and Dave Nicholls announced they were to exploit commercial contacts. The "Advertiser" rallied to the cause, urging supporters to get behind the club once and for all. There was to be an auction of "Train with the Players" to raise funds.

After two further extentions to the notice period and with no sign of a benefactor emerging. We finally moved out of the "intention" and went into Administration proper on the 18th March 2008 and from that point the Nationwide hunt for a buyer intensified even more. In particular Roger Stone stepped up efforts from the Council.

On the 18th April 2008 Jeremy Bleazard issued the following press release:

"The Administrator of Rotherham United has confirmed that a number of formal offers have been received from prospective purchasers by today's 5pm deadline. Administrator Jeremy Bleazard, of XL Business Solutions, said "I am very encouraged that a number of bids have come in and I will spend the next couple of days considering each one on its merits. I hope to begin formal discussions with a 'preferred' bidder early next week."

Bleazard went on to confirm that the bids do not at this stage commit any of the prospective buyers to begin funding the club and that it is vital that supporters get behind the various fund raising efforts not to mention go along to tomorrow's game.

He stated, "Though this is good news our cash flow still does not allow me to pay the full amount of the player's or staff wages. I cannot stress enough how important our need for funds still is and hope that everyone does not simply assume that everything will now be alright".

Mark Robins had the task of persuading the players to accept a "wage deferral" until the sale of the club was finalised. This was a cash flow matter in that it meant the payment of the full wages became staggered. Chris O'Grady was the only player to reject the proposal. Mark was very disappointed in Chris.

Enquiries of a Club purchase were received from Darren Williams - A 33 year old long term fan based over in Alderley Edge in Cheshire. His Company was involved in the insurance and financial services sector, trading as the Brilliant Advice Group.

He apparently was raised in the Brecks area and had actively supported the club for over 20 years.

Speaking in a statement to the Advertiser, Williams said:

"The potential acquisition of Rotherham United is significant for the Brilliant Group. This is a further material step/change for our business."

"We aim to greatly enhance the club's capabilities and to provide a solid platform from which to build. The proposed consideration would be financed through the Group's reserves with no debt requirement to complete the transaction."

"We would also plan to invest an initial £250,000 of

working capital, which would be in part to enhance the squad. The proposed acquisition would also extend our client base and marketing opportunities. The group remains active with our expansion plans and we look forward to the next phase of our development."

"A further announcement will follow once discussions have been held with the administrators and the Booth family."

With the global calamity that hit the Insurance and Banking world a few months later I would imagine he was relieved he took it no further. To be realistic the working capital pledge was insufficient if it were to go forward and not just tread water.

Denis had been in the wings trying to get his own new consortium together. He had some success but received an unfair body blow from the Football League.

In an interview with the Advertiser it was reported;

> "Denis Coleman has slated the Football League ruling which bans him from being a football club director because he has been involved with 2 football administrations.
>
> Coleman took the club into the CVA shortly after taking over the club in 2006, which got rid of 99% of the clubs debt, however just 2 years later the club finds itself in administration again.
>
> Denis however planned to challenge the ruling, claiming that the original administration was not the fault of the current board. He confirmed that he had spoken to the Football League and had been told that no decision had been made to disqualify him but to put his feelings in writing.
>
> The administration of 2006 was not our fault, we had to put the club into administration because we didn't have time to do anything else after taking over from the Millers 05 group."

But with this League rule if no one comes in to save the club and I wanted to take it on, my disqualification means it would be forced into liquidation. The ideal situation is for someone to come in with a lot of money to throw at the club. But, if anyone thinks they can come in and take it on for nothing they are living in dreamland.

If I can, I would take the club back on but there is still a lot of work to be done and a lot of things to stack up. I would also have to be confident that the fans were behind any bid. We would have to make an initial investment of around £300,000 and then we would need a working capital from the supporters in terms of season ticket sales etc." Denis added.

I want to establish where I stand so I'm in a position to do whatever I possibly can for the club. I don't want to see Rotherham United die."

Gary Hall also did the rounds and started getting people together to form a consortium. The problem was that we knew the only way forward was with a large financial backing and that was more difficult to achieve. Even Tobin kept ringing me. He was friends with an ex Rotherham man who was connected with Huddersfield Town and he said they were considering teaming up with two others and putting a proposed bid in. Between them they certainly had the financial clout. I didn't discourage him but I hoped he did not. He was busy with a new Industrial Park he had built, amazingly named after himself and his Uncle. Sorry Tobin but I don't think you know what demands can be made on you running a football club and you would struggle to give enough time. Stay as a fan.

Jeremy Bleazard confirmed that he had considerable interest from quite a few parties.

A Russian Consortium also made an approach at the last minute. They had been stalking other Clubs but were suddenly let down and made a late leap for Rotherham United. That now meant that in the two years of our stewardship we had the Irish, the Americans, the Albanians and now the Russians.

Currently separate bids were on the table as the offers deadline came. After studying all the proposals Jeremy chose the preferred bidder to be Tony Stewart's consortium. It was not a straightforward decision as there were many things to consider. A deal had to have long term viability not just funds for today. He went public with the information the week before the last game. I told him I thought it was crucial to do this in order to give the fans some hope. The Consortium had to act quickly to start funding any shortfall that may occur in the administration period from 1st May 2008.

CHAPTER 42 (G.H.B.)

GREAT GRANDFATHER WOULDN'T HAVE BEEN HAPPY

If there was one game I was really looking forward to it was Rochdale away. So why ?

In the late 19th century the predominant team sport in Rochdale was Rugby. In the local Parks the lads kickabout was a throw and a run with the rugby ball. This was in contrast to the neighbouring towns like Bury and Bolton where association football was the dominant sports activity and their Parks were adorned with kids trying to score goals.

The town of Rochdale did not have an association football club in its presence until 1896, when the merger took place of the Rochdale Athletic Club and the Rochdale Athletic Ground Company a new Rochdale A.F.C was formed. The club joined the Lancashire Combination league for the 1896/97 season, finishing sixth. The following year they transferred into the Lancashire League, but met with less success, finishing only twelfth out of fourteen teams in the 1897/98 season. The club also entered the F.A Cup for the first time, reaching the second qualifying round. During this season future Arsenal manager Herbert Chapman played for the club, before his move to Grimsby Town.

In the next two seasons the club continued to dwell in the lower reaches of the Lancashire League, with a ninth place in 1899/1900 being their highest finish. At the end of this season the club left the Athletic Grounds to play at St. Clements, the ground now known as Spotland. The move coincided with financial hardship, and the team withdrew from the Lancashire League. The club entered the following season's FA Cup, winning two ties, but were unable to field a team for their third qualifying round tie against Workington. The club folded on 1 January 1901.

The new Rochdale AFC was formed six years later in 1907. They were accepted into the Manchester League before joining the Lancashire Combination league the following year. After winning the League in 1911 Rochdale unsuccessfully applied to join the Football League but eventually in 1921, Rochdale were recommended to be included in the new Third Division North, and played their first League game at home on the 27th August 1921, winning 6-3. However, this first season ended with the club bottom of the League, having to reapply for membership.

As a staunch South Yorkshireman I have to confess my mother's side of the family were all Lancashire born and bred, going back generations in none other than Rochdale. It was muted down the years how my Great Grandfather was one of the founders of the Rochdale F.C we see today. Against the grain he played football religously throughout his youth for various local teams mainly in other towns. His involvement with Rochdale F.C began with the new club in 1907. He was apparently there at the inaugural meeting of the club that took place in Fleece Street with the representatives of the local Council who were crucial as a ground was needed to a specific standard. I was uncertain whether he played for the new team or not. He had certainly played for the old Rochdale team though. To establish a new club of meaning there had to be a merger of existing interests. My Great Grandfather and his pals felt the citizens of Rochdale deserved league football as it was then. They met at his Trevor Street home.They secured some financial backing and great excitement was in the air.

Rochdale F.C 1920 there partly by the grace of Giles Brearley's great Grandfather .

He became involved on a day to day basis along with several others, they started work on the clubs establishment as a proper team. So now for me to be visiting the club he had helped found over a century later was very special. I looked forward to seeing their archive of memorabilia and old photographs to hopefully find something that confirmed my Great Grandfather's involvement.

The journey to the game on Monday the 28th March 2008 was horrific in that there was an accident on the M1 and another on the M62 which had blocked the usual route we would have taken. My Brother Mike, Ralph Milner and I made our way through an afternoon of sleet, rain,swirling low cloud and the odd patches of ice right over the Pennines on an assortment of A and B roads to the other side ie Lancashire and Rochdale. Ralph had not been here before and Mike and I had not visited the town since our childhoods. At the Ground the atmosphere was strange. I think the financial situation we were in at that point was starting to impact on everyone at Rotherham United from Directors, through the staff right down to the players on the field. Walking into the Boardroom you could sense an air of despondency by the look on people's faces.

Rochdale had only notched up one win in the last six home games so theoretically Rotherham should have been in a good starting position. Inside, I looked around anxiously for the traditional "Rochdale old boy" who would take me off to a closet type room somewhere under the Stand and knock dust off old pics and records and say "I know exactly where to look. Here he is, I have found him, what a great contribution "Dribbler Boardman" made to Rochdale's football, he was a brilliant little player, no one could stop him when he set off down the wing. They based "Roy of the Rovers" on his exploits. Oh and what an administrator your old Great Grandfather turned out to be after he finished playing . Just look at the family resemblance between you and him , its remarkable. Please let me introduce you to the Rochdale fans at half time" I fantasised..

No old boy appeared however and I was getting anxious as kick off time was fast approaching. I ventured up to one of the Directors and he said "the only person I think may know something may be Stan, he will be here soon." Stan did appear but I knew more of the early Club's History than he seemed to.

Action on the pitch at Rochdale on the 24th March 2008. Great Grandfather would not have been happy.

He did take me to a couple of old team pics on the wall just to show some politeness but he did not know much about them. What a dissapointment that was. Where was your archive I wondered? One of the Rochdale club's founder's great grandson's visit the hallowed ground to be fobbed off.

Great Grandfather would not have been happy...

The game was a dire event for us. We had took the lead after only six minutes when Marc Joseph headed home a Peter Holmes corner and gave us all some hope. Rochdale hit back however on the half hour when inspirational skipper Gary Jones burst into the box and rifled home a smart shot. Then in the second half, late in the game Rochdale striker Chris Dagnall, back from injury, came off the bench to score a nine-minute hat-trick and re-ignite Rochdale's play-offs chances. Dagnall had unbelievably been out of action since the end of September, having undergone surgery on a damaged knee ligament and had only been back in training for ten days. As far as manager Keith Hill was concerned, nothing ventured nothing gained and he bravely threw him back into the fray.

Wrexham's fine Trophy Cupboard. in the Directors Lounge. Why didn't Rotherham have one?

After his one man show Rotherham were a completely spent force. We showed no real spirit and the heads bowed. Rochdale were a good side and we seemed to just go through the motions. The final score was a humiliating 4-1 defeat. I felt very sorry for the loyal fans that had made the arduous journey over the Pennines showing their die-hard support. I also felt very sorry for Mark Robins whose job was now becoming twice as hard with all the financial problems of the club adding to the pressure.

On the subject of Club Archives I had great plans for organising Rotherham United's momentos into something meaningful. The local historian in me saw a great opportunity to extol this for the club's marketing image. To give the club a sense of existance with its proud history. The problem was, that what we inherited was pretty dissapointing. There were a few framed team and action photographs and some competition winners and runners up shields but where was the rest of the silverware. Despite the quip of the Chuckle brothers " Its as empty as Rotherham United's trophy cabinet" the club over the years should have accumulted plenty of collectable items. But where was it?

I even asked Ken Booth senior if he knew of its whereabouts but drew a blank there. In fairness the damage must have been done in the 1970's, as thereafter some memorabilia was in existance, but where were the old pictures, certificates and silverware? What happened to the runners up cups for 1947 and 1949 and the winners cup as third division league champions in 1951. Also succesive promotions in the Ronnie Moore era plus the Auto Windshield Trophy victory at Wembley should have produced some trophies.

As I went round various antique fairs I did notice bits of ephemeria for the club and started buying it. In an email to Tony Stewart, I suggested that he should continue doing this to help replenish the stocks. Rotherham with its past should be able to make a very credible display of its trophies and so be able to show off to visitors its long history and achievements.

Chapter - 43 (G.H.B.)

Mansfield Town – The last Away Game Blues

The directors' original intention was that we were to organise some transport and all travel together with the ladies and probably stop off somewhere on the way back for a bite to eat and have a jolly good sociable. Unfortunately, the pessimism that had crept in by now was so deep that it just fell by the wayside.

David Costin was still busy trying to sort out the state of his business following a period of nigh on two years' neglect and so didn't go at all. I ended up taking future son-in-law, George Legg and Ralph Milner as companions for the day. As we sped down the M1 on this 26th April 2008 , we were nearly involved in an accident when a solitary Millers fan, also making his way to Mansfield, decided to jump lanes and our Range Rover must have been in his blind spot. I managed to hit the brake and swerve. He realised the error of his manoeuvre and waved his hand in apology.

We arrived at the ground and parked the car ready to make our entrance. As we turned the corner of the main stand, I was faced with the outline of a figure, walking slowly towards me looking like he had ridden his horse for fifty miles and was now ready for a gun fight. He looked every inch the part. As I got near the figure, his face burst into a huge smile. I outstretched my hand and said "Well done Mark". The Club's Community Liaison Officer, Mark Hitchen, had organised the early morning departure of walkers from Rotherham all the way to Mansfield, carrying the message to the community of their determination to see Rotherham United continue. Mark led the Group of walkers off at 5-30 am. They walked out of the Ground down Moorgate past the Hospital, across Whiston Crossroads following the old road to Chesterfield.

They then picked up the Mansfield Road arriving at the ground at about 1-0pm . When I saw Mark he had just got to the ground and was as sore as sore could be. It really was a fantastic feat and brought home once again the importance of the clubs survival. It was hoped to raise about £10,000 towards the fighting fund. Printability 2000 donated a 12 foot banner and bottles of water were supplied free by DBC Food services along the route.

The Prince of Wales Pub generously paid for a coach home for the walkers at the end of the game.

After our arrival at reception, we were made very welcome and were shown into the directors' board room. Outside the boardroom, in large letters, was the sign "Welcome to Mansfield Town FC". We were the first of the Rotherham directors to arrive. We were greeted by Keith Haslam, the owner, and a couple of his colleagues. You could detect a strange atmosphere within that room but you couldn't put your finger on exactly what the problem was.

The Mansfield club had originally been founded back in 1897 and "the Stags", as they are known, entered the football league in the 1931/32 football season. Their most memorable moment was in 1969 when they beat West Ham 3-0 in the FA Cup. West Ham at the time were standing sixth in the old first division and their team fielded Bobby Moore, Martin Peters and Geoff Hurst.

Keith Haslam had been involved with the club for some ten years or more. He hit controversy when a series of loans were made from the football club into his business empire which to date, had not been repaid. The fans saw this as a huge injustice as it denied the club the right to improve the squad and compete at a higher level.

Shattered Millers fan after completing walk to Mansfield.

The 2006/07 season saw the creation of the SFFC (Stags Fans for Change), an organisation that was aiming for the removal of Keith Haslam from the club. The organisation took on many projects over the year to get their message out into the community. They even hired a plane to fly over the local derby match, with Notts County towing a banner declaring that the club was for sale and demanding that Haslam should leave. The fans' frustration hinged on the fact that sometime during the previous decade, his companies had received interest free loans from the club. In addition, he allegedly received a salary and the club had allegedly paid money into his holding company, "Stags Limited" for the purpose of buying land for an academy. The club's 2003 accounts also showed that loans to Haslam were written off as bad debts and in August 2004, the club advanced further loans, interest free despite the previous write off. A few months earlier on 29 December 2007, Haslam had rejected a bid from a James Dennis consortium, and the SFFC planned to have a TV protest against him on the BBC's Match of the Day programme.

In the directors' lounge, there wasn't much in the way of food, as was usual. We chatted happily with the people that were there and then Gary Hall and Denis arrived along with Herbie and Pedro. We directors all huddled together in what one could describe as a formation scrum, whilst we exchanged the latest gossip. We went into the directors' box seats prior to kick off and, upon gazing at the away end, were somewhat surprised at the number of Millers fans who had made the journey. We hoped they wouldn't be disappointed. As we looked round we noticed that in the away end a banner was on display protesting at the loss of Millmoor and also the Stags similar unrest with their situation .

The first half was a little lacklustre but nonetheless, we all agreed that Rotherham were the better side. Mansfield's defence was very vulnerable. Ryan Taylor was injured and was substituted by Tom Cahill. Tom missed a fine chance when he faced the keeper and shot straight at him. That was probably his lack of first team experience, you need to keep ice cool and pick your spot. Of course, with the second half, came Jamie Yates' strangely magnificent goal. The Mansfield keeper was caught totally unawares and as he raced back towards his open goal, there was a stern look of disbelief on his face. That goal of Jamie's

The walkers to Mansfield still full of spirit and getting near.

Mark Hitchens arriving at Mansfield after leading the fans on an epic walk from Millmoor on the 26th April 2008.

A fans protest at Mansfield Town F.C. Someone had been doing their homework.

The Mansfield crowd are turning ugly directing their anger at Keith Haslam who is sat at the side of the cameraman. Denis Coleman looks on in astonishment.

End of the Season at Mansfield although they had nothing to celebrate.

The Police stand on guard to stop Rotherham fans invading the Mansfield pitch, oblivious to what was happening in the board room.

George Legg and Ralph Milner at Mansfield in the Directors box at the start of the game.

The Police have just arrived and are trying to get the crowd away from the Mansfield Boardroom door. Tempers are frayed

saw the turning point in the mood of the home crowd. At first, they went extremely quiet, then suddenly burst into full vocal support for the Stags trying to rally them round to level the score and maybe edge in front. It also appeared that the referee almost wanted Mansfield to equalise.

Mansfield threw everything they had at Rotherham, so much was at stake. You could feel the heartache and emotion being felt by the home fans. If they lost today, they would be all but relegated and their days of league football would be over. Injury time seemed to last an eternity but then came the final whistle. Rotherham had won and Mansfield Town were to end their 70 years of football league membership. The mood of the crowd changed dramatically. The director's box was surrounded by seats in the main stand and people were leaning over, shouting abuse at Keith Haslam and the Team Manager. I had my camera and took a quick shot which demonstrated the hatred in their faces. There had been a lot of history and it was now going from a long term smouldering into a full scale eruption.

A lot of the police had rushed down to the pitch and made a line right across the 'Away' end to stop Rotherham fans invading the pitch.

They knew the Mansfield Town fans would do so despite being asked not to and they didn't want any problems. Whoever thought that one out was obviously no strategic genius. Why would the Rotherham fans want to storm onto the Mansfield pitch in any case? They knew it was their last game. It was their end of season tradition.

As more Security guards rushed up towards the directors' area sensing the tension they asked us to go into the boardroom. Things started to get very nasty. There were three doors into the boardroom. One was secured with a bolt and a lock and not so easily accessible but the other two now had angry mobs outside them and fists were starting to fly. A large security guard, alone, managed to hold one of the doors back – he was like a man mountain. Despite several people kicking and shoulder charging the door, they could not loosen his stance and grip. Unfortunately, the guards on the other door were struggling and could not maintain their hold. "Where are the police?" I thought. There wasn't one to be seen. Someone decided to hack down the stud wall and fists started flying through the "Welcome to Mansfield" sign. Behind that wall was the small bar serving the Directors' Lounge and the two ladies operating the bar were absolutely traumatised. They were screaming with terror. All of a sudden, one of the doors flung open and in ran three or four burly men.

They ran straight by us – they could see our Rotherham ties and had no business with us – they went straight for Keith Haslam who was at the far end of the room and a single mighty punch sent him to the deck. Haslam was on the floor as they delivered to him their message. They then beat a hasty departure. One of the other Security Guards looked to have received some painful injuries too.

The violence continued all around as the crowd felt that justice was still not yet done. Shoulder charges of the doors continued. There was still no police! By this time officers were starting to get the message that perhaps sitting watching Rotherham fans exit the Away Stand was perhaps not the best strategy, so they rushed up to the directors' boardroom. The two ladies behind the bar had now emerged and were inconsolable in their hysteria ,fear and panic. Ralph tried his best to calm them down, their screaming added to the charged atmosphere in the room. They kept asking "when are the police coming". Ralph outstretched

The Welcome to Mansfield Town Football club sign displays a fist mark where fans tried breaking down the stud walls.

his arms making himself a human shield between them and the trouble.

I strolled over to George, tapped him on the shoulder and said "Welcome to Mansfield Town".

At long last the silhouette of Police officers could be seen outside on the terrace. The crowd still persisted with real aggression. The Police had all on to persuade them to move on. They were certainly men on a mission. Eventually they managed to disperse them after what seemed like hours but was probably only fifteen minutes. Listening to people in the boardroom it seemed they knew exactly who the perpetrators were. The elderly gentleman who had introduced himself when we first arrived started to tell me why it had all kicked off and who they all were. He told me the man he believed had struck Haslam was leading a consortium to buy the club.

Keith Haslam was definitely shook up and sat on a chair alone still at the spot where he was assaulted. With the Police now in control the stewards returned to their positions. I went over to Keith Haslam to see if he was okay, he had his head in his hands. The police sergeant thought it was best that Mr Haslam be taken to hospital for a check up despite him saying he was OK. The police advised us to remain in the directors' box until the crowds had finally dispersed. After about twenty minutes, we decided to leave. On leaving I looked back at the 'Welcome to Mansfield Town' sign, now with great fist holes smashed through it.

As we went into the car park, there were still a lot of Stag fans milling around and we asked the police if they thought we would be OK. A young policeman told me how the fans had even tried to stone the vehicle taking Keith Haslam to the hospital. What price football?

We drove to the entrance and there was a heavy police presence and a large protest group had established itself chanting for Haslam to go. The police waved us through and so we set off on our way back to South Yorkshire and hopefully sanity.

As far as I was concerned, it helped demonstrate the deep, deep emotion felt by many people who had probably supported their team, boy and man, and the influence of this in their formative years moulded them for life. As we sped up the M1, we caught up with "Gordon's Coaches" the Rotherham team bus. We put thumbs up out of the windows to the team as we sped by. With the car radio on, listening to a broadcast from the Ground we could still hear there was commotion with fans kicking off in the background. They had encountered similar noise in the background as they interviewed Mark Robins for his manager's report for praise or grumble, on Radio Sheffield. I bet he was glad to be safely on the bus now and away from it all. The day's actions were something we would never ever forget. To quote Denis Coleman "The Mansfield game – I've seen some trouble over the years on the terraces but this was as bad as it gets".

As late as 30th June 2008 we were all contacted by the Mansfield Police for a statement. They told us the situation had deteriorated in that further threats were now being made on Keith Haslam's home. Also the Derbyshire village where he resided had adverse posters hung up during the night with threats on them. The guys who stormed the Boardroom all denied hitting Haslam and the matter was now going to go to Crown Court. It was classed as high profile and the Crown Prosecution Service wanted as much back up evidence as possible and we all had to make a full statement as to what we did and did not see on the day concerned.

All for Football - Unbelievable.

CHAPTER - 44 (G.H.B.)

THE FINAL HAND OVER

As April 2008 ended the directors were all quite battle scarred. The nailing down of the final purchaser of the club had certainly been a rollercoaster ride. We were all pleased that plans were now in place for the club to regroup and go forward and we could consider our work finally done.

The final match of this season was at home on 3rd May 2008 against Barnet. I rang round the other directors. David Costin was still a little reluctant to return to the ground because of the bad memories of the damage it had all inflicted on his business. However, by twisting his arm, he agreed to come along. I contacted the others and our plan was to welcome Tony Stewart into the directors' lounge to wish him well with the club. At half time, we wanted to walk onto the field with him to thank the fans for their loyal support over the last two seasons and to introduce Tony and then to leave him with the microphone and walk off the field; club officially handed over and duty done. I think that would have been a nice fitting end to it all.

The letters below were published in the Advertiser on 16th May and the 23rd May and summarise the actual events:

"Sir,

> I would like to thank the outgoing Rotherham United board of Dave Costin, Gary Hall, Giles Brearley and chairman, Denis Coleman for all their efforts over the past two years.
>
> They put a lot of time and effort into the club and although they made mistakes, at least they kept it alive.
>
> If it were not for them, we would not have a team to support now. At the end of the day, they are not millionaires and needed someone to come in who was.
>
> That has now happened although at the last match of the season, these four men were not allowed to go in the directors' lounge to pass on their good wishes

to the incoming board and wish them all the best for the future and also to say goodbye to the staff who worked in there and have a drink with them.

I don't know the reason behind this but, as it was the last match of the season, why not meet them and accept their good wishes? It just put a dampener on the day as far as myself and my friends were concerned.

Surely these men deserved better and was it too much to ask at possibly the last game at Millmoor to allow them to do that?

I personally think they should have been invited onto the pitch with the new board so the crowd could show their appreciation for them. I am sure they would have had a good reception."

Peter Wainwright, Kimberworth Miller

"Sir,

I read with interest the letter by Peter Wainwright (Advertiser, 16 May) regarding the "ban" imposed on Denis Coleman, Dave Costin, Giles Brearley, Gary Hall at the final Rotherham United game of the season.

I wonder at the time of the ban being imposed whether Tony Stewart and his colleagues at the club were aware that had it not been for Denis, Dave, Giles and Gary, there would have been no marquee or hospitality to bar them from. When the previous board took over at Millmoor, there was no hospitality to offer to sponsors at all and without their hard work and tireless efforts, that would have remained the case.

Dave Costin, in his role as stadium director, took on the task of building up the marquee, calling on business associates to sponsor televisions, carpets and bars to make the place look as good as possible, often with the help of his wife, working late to get the place clean and ready for match days.

Maybe if Mr Stewart and his associates had come

along to help the existing board of Denis, Gary, Giles and Dave before administration then the team would not have been deducted the ten points and who knows, could have gone on to gain promotion but that is something we will now never know.

So Mr Stewart, perhaps instead of banning these guys from the marquee, you should have been offering them thanks for the their efforts along with lifelong membership of the Executive club at Millmoor, should they wish to take you up on this of course."

A disappointed Rotherham Fan

"Sir,

I would like to echo Pete Wainwright in his letter (Advertiser 16 May) in thanking the previous board of Denis Coleman, Dave Costin, Gary Hall and Giles Brearley for their work for Rotherham United. Had it not been for Coleman and Dino Maccio coming forward to take over when they did, there would not have been a club because it would have folded in 2006.

A big thank you also to Mark Robins and John Breckin for their handling of a very tricky season."

Alan Charlesworth, Sheffield.

Tobin my secret confidant rang and left a message at the office that he was appalled at what had happened and he would be in touch soon.

Tony Stewart had still not signed any agreement for taking over the club when this incident occurred and indeed, was many weeks away from completing the deal. He did not become a Director of the company they were to use as the new club (Rotherham United Football Club (RUFC) Ltd),(co number 06550400) until the 23rd May 2008 .The other investors in this new consortium did not and still have not become Club Directors.

The shares for this company were issued on the 5th May 2008.

The owners of the new Rotherham United club from hereon are;

Anthony Stewart	150,000 shares	60.00%
Ronald Hull	33,333 shares	13.33 %
Brian Beckett	33,333 shares	13.33%
Leslie Wilson	33,333 shares	13.33%

Whilst we were all disappointed with the events of that last game we genuinely wish the new consortium and club every success. We only did what we did because we believed in Rotherham United continuing for another 100 years. With the dreaded lease now out of the way and with the move to Don Valley, at least they stand a good fighting chance.

We had all worked very hard for the club over the last two years at great personal and financial cost and you could not have asked any more of anyone involved. Tony Stewart's initial strategy did seem to be to charge into things. When they went to clear the Training Ground in readiness for the move to Doncaster's facilities, a tractor mower was also removed. Denis and David had bought this themselves and loaned it to the Club, this was in addition to the free van's and minibuses provided by AFP to the club over the past two years. It got quite heated and David threatened that if his equipment was not returned by the end of the day he would inform the Police.

All a little unnecessary really, but why throw kindness back in someone's face? David had all his receipts of purchase as back up evidence if needed. When the mistake was realised Tony Stewart resolved the matter immediately and returned the equipment to its rightful owner. An old boardroom table from Millmoor was put into storage at Denis's offices after the floods. Denis got a stern letter asking for it to be returned to the club. Denis said "it was ridiculous, they knew where it was and only had to ask me for it, no need for all that heavy stuff."

The path through administration into the new company was not without its moments. The problem that occurred was that part of the Football League's rules on Football insolvencies is that the exit from Administration must be via a Company Voluntary

Arrangement (C.V.A). One was drawn up and proposed to the creditors but was unfortunately rejected by the H. M .Revenue and Customs and by the C.F Booth Group. HMRC had adopted this rejection policy nationally some time ago, so it was disappointing but not personal to Rotherham. It seemed the only way it could go through was if the Football Stadia Grant Trust that had re-emerged once more would enter a claim and vote in favour of the CVA. They were on a hiding to nothing whichever way they voted "for" or "against". If they voted for it they would get virtually nothing, if they voted against it they could bring the club down. This "Football Debt" inherited by the Club, from the Millers 05 regime, which has haunted us ever since may now have suddenly become a useful negotiating tool.

While all this was being considered an alternative strategy emerged. This meant that the new club of Rotherham United would have to make an application for the Football League share under the "Exceptional Circumstances Rule" If successful the League would decide how many points would be deducted. As we all know this was 17 points in the end. A tall order but considering the fate of Luton Town and Bournemouth, with their points deduction also, it gave great hope for the Millers staying in the league by the end of the 2008/09 season. The deal was finally done and I would praise Tony Stewart and his legal advisors for the first class negotiating and lobbying they did.

All attention now turned towards the Stadium problems. As the weeks went by the news oscillated like a pendulum. The deal is done and Millmoor will remain the Club's ground until the new stadium is built, but just a few more matters to iron out with the landlords. Then it is all off, Tony Stewart has not managed to broker a proper deal with C.F Booth's and so Sheffield (and the DVS as it is now referred to) here we come. The League and Football Stadia Trust threw their "penny's worth " in by insisting that a bond of £700,000 be lodged as an act of good faith, as long as the proposed new stadium is built in Rotherham within 4 years. The Council came to the rescue and put the bulk of the money up (I hope it was drawn out of their Icelandic Account just in time)

During the debacle over the move from Millmoor I have one unpleasant memory. In early May 2008 when conversations about this were rife, one Friday night I was out with friends at the

"Pals again" John McNamara and Giles Brearley.

Tony Stewart

Travellers Rest in Swinton having a beer, when my long term friend and retired client John McNamara came in . He was a lifelong R.U.F.C supporter and was getting quite fuelled up as to the future possibility that Millmoor may be abandoned. John lashed into me saying that the Club's future was at Millmoor and that the whole problem emanated from us Directors making it a personal vendetta with the Booth's. He shocked me as to how strong he felt. I tried to explain that the lease as it was would make things very difficult and the Hospitality Package had a price tag attached far too extravagant for a Club Rotherham's size. John remonstrated that it was only tickets for otherwise empty seats and an advertising board. I reminded him of the crucifying nature of the high rental lease with full repairing clauses for a Ground that was falling about around our ears. He believed that the new owners would fare a lot better by keeping the Club rightfully where it should be. We parted on not too good terms. On the last Wednesday in June I was in the Travellers Rest doing the Pub's Quiz when John walked in once more. He came over with a large beam on his face, greeted me and said "Yon bloke couldn't do it either, then". Alas normality and our friendship restored.

Meeting Tony Stewart in October 2008 with Gavin we asked him why we were prevented from entering the ground on that last game. He said that when he took the club over he was very judgemental and suspicious of everyone who had been involved with the club previously. He wasn't prepared to listen to any advice or offers of help from us and instead decided to do everything in his own way. He admitted that as time had gone by he had mellowed somewhat and realised how difficult it was running a football club unlike his very successful lighting business. He had established there were some very good people who had been associated with the club. I got the impression he wanted to move on from the past and wished us all to harmoniously look to the future. Which we whole heartedly agreed to do "in the best interests of Rotherham United".

Chapter 45 (G.H.B.)

So how did we compare? – Giles's finance notes

As I have stated in this book previously, whenever I came into contact with Finance Directors of other clubs I always entered into a bit of an interrogation with them to see how they were faring. I became well known for this and one or two of them came to Swinton to see me and asked for my ideas in a few matters. As much as members of the league do meet through the Finance Meetings twice a year, I feel that it would pay for all the clubs to talk together on financial matters more often. By pooling ideas a lot of good could come out of it. Since I finished my duties with Rotherham United I have had "whispers in the ear" from two other league Clubs to see if I will "come on board" but have declined to get involved. I think I need a break, considering the state of most Club's finances it would become another thankless task and after the Keith Haslam incident potentially life threatening too.

I want to share with you the other League Two clubs finance reports, which I have collected from their previous year's data, and then look at Rotherham United's to see just how we compare. Before I go into individual Club's accounting performances I will define the common areas and relevance's I used to extract on my trips.

Working Capital - This is the "at the year end" position of available resources to trade. Working capital shows the relationship between the plusses ie Cash in hand, Cash at the Bank, Monies owed to the club, and Stocks held less the minuses ie the who has to be paid creditors, any outstanding overdrafts, short term finance commitments. Ideally a club should have a positive figure of at least two months of its expenditures. A negative Working Capital means there is not enough to pay the creditors and may spook future suppliers. These figures are some times misleading, as monies injected in the club by directors are shown as a loan to be repaid and is included in the current liabilities. This is often problematical in that if the club does get some cash, the last thing the fans want to see is the directors whipping the cash out again. This occurred in Rotherham

United's history; when the Sky Digital lump sum payments were made to the league clubs in 2001, £2.1 million was taken back by the directors to repay monies they were owed. The great debate would be whether the prioritising of that debt endangered future trading.

NET ASSETS – This is the Balance Sheet "snapshot in time" of just what the club and its finances consist of. A measure of its overall wealth. In essence it is the total fixed assets (land, buildings, equipment) plus the working capital but then less any long term liabilities owing. One must remember that the value of the squad is not included in the Balance Sheet other than fees paid and written down.

ANNUAL PROFIT/LOSS – These final trading figures show us just how the club has fared. Losses can not be sustained indefinitely.

SHARES ISSUED IN THE LAST ACCOUNTING YEAR - to try and waylay crisis, some clubs issued more shares for cash to help fund the losses. This was instead of treating them as a loan to be repaid as mentioned earlier. I felt this was important to be aware of as it explains how some of the clubs managed to survive.

DIRECTORS SALARIES - One common feature of most clubs (as with Rotherham), was that the directors offered their services for no pay throughout the season.

SEASON TICKET MONIES - Depending on the time of the club's year end, season ticket money collected in advance of games being played will be shown as a liability in working capital. It would not contribute to the insolvency as it is a pre-payment by the fans. A club with a year end say 30th June will most likely contain a larger figure than say a 31st May year end.

So now below I will highlight my league two notes for 2007/2008 season: (Please note at times the figures are rounded to the nearest thousand. A figure in brackets means a negative. The following figures are all after player sales.

ACCRINGTON STANLEY	31st may 2007 year end
Profit	102000
Working Capital	(49934)
Net Balance Sheet	256820
Average attendance	1633

A small club, operating on a very tight budget with only a small working capital deficit. They were obviously a little short of cash. There is not much room for a large players' budget which could impact on them. Their attendances are only low so someone must be working very hard on the sponsorship front. They have a lot of competition for fans. At least though, the club is solvent. There is a backer behind the club; whether he can stay the course with the higher cash demands now they are out of the Conference and in the League will be seen in due course.

BARNET F.C	30th June 2007 year end
Profit	122000
Working Capital	164184
Net Balance Sheet	286227
Average attendance	2108

A well run club with a good working capital and profit. When I met Mr Kleanthous the owner I was impressed at his attitude to the Players budget and the controlling of players wages and football as a whole. He did advise me of some Ground limitations because of planning issues with the local council but have made a good start.

BRADFORD CITY	30th June 2007 year end
Trading Loss	(501000)
Working Capital deficit	(1293539)
Net Balance Sheet	(114850)
Shares issued in year	2000000
Average attendance	13756

I met Bradford Chairman Julian Rhodes a few times and admire him for his football gusto. He took the gamble of cheap season tickets to put bums on seats which did give him some success. Just look at his attendance figures. The highest in the league. Once people are through the turnstile they are a captive audience for programmes, snacks and the likes. As with RUFC they have also been through the insolvency mill over the last few years. It is believed that the working capital deficit is exasperated in its accounts by including cash loaned to it by the directors. I don't know when they are likely to be repaid. They have a huge ground rent to find and there was talk of trying to bring the rugby club on board to share the ground and costs. They are quite tight financially despite the share issue during the year, their Directors loans were partly converted into shares at the year end so not all cash was received. It does state in the accounts that the club is reliant on the directors for its continued support.

BRENTFORD F.C   31st May 2007 year end
Trading Loss   (152658)
inc 91k grant write off and 700k player sales
Working Capital deficit   (1187093)
Net Balance Sheet   1876367
Average attendance   4469

I met Chairman Greg Dyke ex BBC a couple of times. He like the Barnet Chairman had some good ideas and views as regards controlling League 2 football costs. Attendances had come down about a thousand on the previous year, he told me, which was obviously a great concern. Like RUFC they have had financial problems in more recent times. Allowing for £528k of deferred debt, the working capital deficit is still huge. The club is best described as Asset rich and Cash poor. There were plans to sell the ground which is valued at some £10 million and move to a new stadium site and free up some cash. They certainly need it. The working capital deficit appears huge and will endanger the club once again if not attended to.

BURY F.C	31st May 2007 year end
Trading Loss	(43000)
Working Capital deficit	(323000)
Net Balance Sheet	36799
Shares issued during year	68000
Average attendance	2601

Although the trading loss is small the true Working capital deficit is probably about a 150k which will need some juggling to keep all the balls in the air. The deficit of 323k includes some brewery finance and mortgage payments. They obviously need to return to profit as quickly as possible to repair the cash flow. They are lucky in that like Brentford they own their ground which is probably worth more than the written down value on the balance sheet. One presumes the £68000 of shares issued bailed out a cash crisis. Cash is clearly very tight. Without prudent management the balance Sheet can easily drift into insolvency. They are in stiff competition for crowds and times ahead may be hard.

CHESTER CITY	Year end 31st May 2007
Profit	48000
Working Capital deficit	(2484544)
Net Balance Sheet	(2583402)
Average attendance	2479

The adverse net assets confirms that the club stays alive mainly because of the support of the directors Mr Allan and Mr Gray whose outstanding loans made to the club over the years are included in the creditors. Again one wonders when these sugar daddies may ever get their money back. The small profit shows someone is trying but there is a long way to go. Cumulative losses to date amounted to £2.5m which will take some clawing back.

CHESTERFIELD F.C.

No information made available to me. All I got was they were hoping to do a deal for a New Stadium to be partly grant funded.

Average attendance	4103

The referee takes control of a possible on pitch flare up between Rotherham's Dale Tonge and Barnet's Puncheon. We lost the game 2-0.

Brentford's Griffin park was a nice little stadium but like Rotherham they had been through the Finance wars in the previous few years.

Shot taken from the Directors box at Grimsby. A whole host of ships made their way up the Humber during the course of the game. Grimsby's ground is actually In Cleethorpes.

Wrexham's ground. They own the Land at the side where they hoped to build on a Hotel and conference facility . I wonder how relegation will effect that.

DAGENHAM and REDBRIDGE F.C.

No Information made available. As new kids on the block they are certainly very cost conscious. Strangely the attendances went down after their promotion from the Conference League. Being situated in the middle of a large North London Housing Estate the Pub type bar they operate at the Ground generates them a good profit. There is virtually no competition.

Average attendance	2007

DARLINGTON F.C.	Year end 31st May 2006
Trading Loss	(1,895,000)
Working Capital deficit	(745,645)
Net Balance Sheet	(2,494,589)
Average attendance	3818

The magnificent Stadium they play in is not theirs. The finances are in a precarious state. They are ultimately owned by Executive Care Group Ltd. Mr G Houghton Director had issued personal guarantees of £181k to creditors on the clubs behalf. They only trade by the support of the directors. Their loan accounts are included in working capital as repayable. The above losses are a serious deteriation from the year before. Clearly they only continue because of the support of the Directors. The Trading Loss was one of the highest. During my visit I felt morale at the club was low. Something seriously has to be done.

GRIMSBY TOWN F.C	Year end 31st May 2007
Trading Loss	(857,513)
Working Capital deficit	(992,312)
Net Balance Sheet	(565,264)
Average attendance	4114

Their actual trading loss was about £284k as they wrote off £574k of abortive new stadium costs spent over the previous years. This was a demise from the previous year when they had a £400k profit. They told me the Council was very anti the Club and seemed to put up obstacles for them all the time. Their guest when I went was long term supporter Austin Mitchell. I thought that he should have been able to mediate for them with the council. The Club turned over about £2.3m during the year which was about £750k down on the previous year. The reductions had come about following a fall of some £500k+ on match day receipts and a £230k reduction in sponsorships, which was very worrying. The Working capital deficit does not include Directors loans. Some of it is hardcore debt, included in the figures is a £588k overdraft at the bank. They are another example of a Club formerly Asset rich cash poor but they have now run out of reserves. The losses were at a dangerous level and needed urgent attention. The Directors very bravely offered personal guarantees to the bank for the £588k overdraft at the time. Director and ultimate owner Mr J S Fenty had also offered Personal Guarantees of £325k to finance Companies for Hire Purchase contracts. The only way that Grimsby F C continues is with the support of the Directors. If anything happens to Mr Fenty he may well be tough to replace.

HEREFORD UNITED (1939) F.C.	Year end 31st May 2007
Trading Profit	164,214
Working Capital	336,293
Net Balance Sheet	(652,568)
Average attendance	3421

They turned over £1.6m compared with only £1.0m the year before. A substantial increase, I wonder how they did it ? The club is a wholly owned subsidiary of Hereford United Football Club (1982) Ltd.The ground is held on a lease that cost them £4700 for the year.(what a dream). The club also has the benefit of large loans from the B.S Group Ltd with no interest being charged. The loans crystallised back in 1997 to enable the club to pay its creditors. The attraction to B.S Group was that they would keep 25% of the proceeds of the eventual sale of the Ground (rented to the club) when the quest for a new stadium is successful. As I spoke to them it turned out this was somewhat renegotiated but I didn't glean the final outcome. With a bank balance in excess of £400k and debtors of some £288k this leaves the club in an enviable trading position considering most other clubs.

LINCOLN CITY F.C   Year End 30th June 2007
Trading Profit   822
Working capital deficit   (255567)
Net Balance Sheet   (1733374)
Shares issued during the year   145000
Average attendance   4078

The Club had in the past incurred serious losses but at least things now appear to be under control. Even though they own their own ground which has obviously helped in obtaining back-up finances overall they look deep in debt. They have accumulated debts up to £650k which they keep chipping away at. It is not a director's loan and to me is a bit of a mystery. It is included in the short term debts for working capital purposes. While it remains semi-dormant the cash flow is manageable. They own their ground and the adjoining all-weather pitch complex.

Cash is tight for the club with a sizeable working Capital deficit. It was even worse the year before being some (£333k). They told me they hoped to increase the profits in future years which will then ease the situation. The share issue obviously greatly helped the cash flow and seems to be a regular event at the club they issued £47.5k worth the year before.

MACCLESFIELD TOWN F.C   Year End 30th June 2007
Trading Loss   (565000)
Working Capital deficit   (294742)
Net Balance Sheet   (197531)
Shares issued during the year   1070000
Average attendance   2297

The Club was in serious trouble the year before, when the balance sheet was insolvent by some (£703K). The huge influx of share capital helped absorb some of the loss for the year and put the balance sheet back to some kind of order but none-the-less it is still showing as insolvent. The money owed to the parent company was some £1.5m but was reduced by £519k after the share issue. Cash is tight and the negative working capital will be hard to control.

They own their ground, which is great, but they need to take serious action and bring more cash in if they are to survive long term as losses at this level will quickly take there toll,. The club is owned by Ramy Ltd which is 80% owned by Mr A Alkadhi.

MANSFIELD TOWN F.C.	Year End 30th June 2007
Trading Loss	(44000)
Working Capital	687444
Net Balance Sheet	1206922
Average attendance	2820

The Club trades very well in essence for its size. It should be stronger on the balance sheet than these figures are showing after some of Keith Haslam's loan write-offs. The loss is only small in essence. So the club is relatively well run but the lack of expenditure on players cost them their place in the League. I do have sympathy for the club in that the Finance Director is probably (excluding the loan write-offs) quite happy with the performance; the Fans however were not. The Accountant's lament. The strong working capital is only because it includes the loans still outstanding by Mr Haslam and his company. If they become bad it will greatly impact on the figures and probably show a level of working capital that would need strengthening.

M.K, DONS F.C.	Year End 30th June 2007
Trading Loss	(3153024)
Working Capital deficit	(5290011)
Net Balance Sheet	(5103962)
Shares issued during the year	600000
Average attendance	9456

One has to ask how they are still here. There turnover was £2.49 million while their costs were nearly £5.5 million. They had lost £1.6 million the year before. So what is the price of promotion. They had one of the largest player's budgets in the league. It will be interesting to see if the Division one will be more favourable to them.

The key to their existence lies with Peter Winkleman the club Chairman and an agreement between Inter M.K ltd (the club's 90% shareholders, who are property developers) and the club whereby Inter M.K have provided an undertaking to make available such funds as are needed by the company and not to seek repayment of amounts made available. There is a total injection to date into the club of £4.92m.

The amount of £1.95m was pumped in during the year. The debt to the parent is shown as a liability on the balance sheet but even if you accept that it is supporting the club it still appears (£183k) insolvent. It is at least a two part gamble as the financial benefits of promotion to league 1 are hardly a lifeline (a 50% rise of little). It is not until you can climb into the Championship league (over a 700 % increase) that you can really have some meaningful cash to do something with. This is a great example of the power of the drug of football. Some £600k worth of shares were issued during the year to take the strain a little off of the balance sheet.The cumulative trading losses on the profit and loss are some £6.7 million.

MORECAMBE F.C	Year End 31st May 2007
Trading loss	(428,000)
Working Capital deficit	(277,050)
Net Balance sheet	7,887
Shares issued during the year	325,000
Average attendance	2811

A Trading loss occurred that the club can ill afford. The Shares issue cash that was injected was crucial to take the sting out of the cash flow but even so the year end working capital figure was still a negative (£277k). Unless the losses are stemmed the sale of Shares will have to become an annual event. Cash is very tight. They own their Ground which is some comfort The Balance sheet was "propped up" into looking more solvent by the revaluation of the ground, increasing its value by £109k. This is only cosmetic and is not real working capital improvement. The club has struggled and has suffered cumulative losses to date of (£1.3m)

NOTTS COUNTY

No information given other than confirmation of minimal annual rent of £18000 charged by Nottingham City Council the stadium owners.

Average attendance 4732

PETERBOROUGH UNITED   Year End 31st May 2007
Trading loss   (1079000)
Working Capital deficit   (4193948)
Net balance Sheet   (3235292)
Shares issued   1600
Average attendance   5994

Up to this point the financial performance has been disastrous. The cumulative losses to date are some £6.5m. The Auditors also put a warning in the accounts that despite re-assurances of ongoing support from the directors and the bankers there was still some concern over the uncertainty of this with the respective consequences of them not doing so. The directors were owed loans they had made. Barry Fry £520,258 and A H Hand £344,520 they also guarantee the overdraft personally. You may recall a fly on the wall documentary followed Barry Fry around while he ran the club.

How anyone traded with the "Posh" without concern is amazing. It was obviously a big gamble by the club with the high players' budget but at least they got promotion into League 1.

The Shares were subsequently purchased by football fanatic Darragh MacAnthony (who was born in Dublin on 24th March 1976.) He is the Chairman of the MRI Organisation, which sells overseas property to British and Irish clients. He wishes to become sole owner of the club and is to inject some much needed cash into it. He has announced plans to invest more in the squad and advance into the Premiership as well as build a new 30,000 seater stadium, all within the next 7 to 10 years. Very ambitious

ROCHDALE F.C. Year End 31st May 2007
Trading Loss (148670)
Working Capital Deficit (325471)
Net Balance Sheet 145765
Shares issued 225000
Average attendance 3051

The issuing of shares obviously bailed out the club for that year and gave a little bit for next year. They turned over £1.7m which was up on the £1.6m achieved in the previous year. The loss was reduced by the sale of players which generated £221k. The club has built up unrelieved tax losses of £4.52m which shows how precarious past trading has been. The directors loan account outstanding was £61k This is reflected in the working capital figure. Taking this out of the equation still leaves a large deficit. The club had a £65k overdraft which they did not have the year before. The adverse Working capital must make ongoing trading difficult. It was reduced to (£325471) from (£391867) the year previous but non the less is a bitter pill to swallow..

They paid £57000 rent for the Stadium during the year. The Directors had given personal guarantees to the bank of up to £10000 each on these figures

Great Grandfather would not have been happy.

SHREWSBURY TOWN F.C Year end 31st May 2007
Trading Profit 33,315
Trading Profit after saleo f Stadium 12,010,235
Working Capital 1,516,535
Net Balance Sheet 13,760,357
Shares issued 638,438
Average attendance 5658

The sale of the old stadium "Gay Meadows" propelled the club into one of high cash holdings. It had, in years gone by, struggled but now the future looks much brighter They traded at a small profit of £33k so none of the cash reserves was depleted propping up trading losses. The average attendance was at the high end for League Two giving them gate receipts of some £1.3 million.

They turned over £2.4m just slightly up on the year before. With cash at the bank of £1.5 m a new stadium acquisition of £10.7m (partly grant funded) with careful management they can plan ahead positively. They also issued more shares in the year . Owning the Ground has been the saviour. Like so many other clubs Rotherham's death knell accelerated in reality after it lost ownership of Millmoor.

STOCKPORT COUNTY F.C   Year end 30th June 2007
Trading Loss   (230,000)
Working capital deficit   (445,474)
Net Balance Sheet   (4,324,780)
Average attendance   5642

The seriously high creditors must make trading very difficult. The club can only trade on with the support of the Directors, Bankers and Creditors as it appears seriously insolvent. The cumulative losses to date are £4.8 million. Director's loans are only £150k (some £25k was paid back during the year). The loss of £230k is after a ground share as well. The main Shareholder and beneficial owner was Stockport County Supporters Society Ltd. Some £3.8m of long term finance hangs there in the balance presumably which will have to be paid back at some point. They have had some good crowd attendances but boy do they need it.

WREXHAM F.C   Year end .30th June 2007
Trading Loss   (199,000)
Working capital deficit   (1,143,211)
Net Balance Sheet   (98779)
Average attendances   4234

They turned over some £2.7m. Of this £1.2m was from attendances. Their player's budget excluding management was £1.1m. This was overshadowed by £2.2m spent on other operating staff. The bank overdraft of £296k was covered by the personal guarantees of Neville Dickens (Chairman) and Geoff Moss, (Director). The club were looking to sell land at their "Racecourse

Ground" to settle the bank debt. Both these Directors had between them also loaned the club £2.8 million in the past. These loans were secured on the Ground. A John Marek has also loaned the club £500k interest payable at 6%. Again it was hoped a sale of land would wipe these debts off. This Marek loan figure is included in the working capital deficit. If taken out it still leaves the club with a £600k deficit to trade with. With a £300k overdraft they are desperately short of cash. Clearly the club only continues because of the directors support. The ultimate share controlling parties are the same two directors.

Relegation to the Conference League will clearly cause further problems to contend with.

WYCOMBE WANDERERS F.C.	Year end 30th June 2007
Trading Loss	(699,000)
Working Capital deficit	(1,790,776)
Net Balance sheet	(2,236,785)
Average attendances	4746

They turned over some £4.7 million (with no player sales) which was very good. This was up £500k on the previous year. For the league the turnover is at the high end. There had obviously been some cutting back as the losses were £1.9 million in the previous year. To keep the cash flow alive the club have borrowed another £1.7m during the year. Past trading has established unused Trading Losses for tax purposes of £7.47 million. The plus side is that they own their Stadium. The Directors are included in the long term creditors as being owed £4,175,556. Clearly the club only trades because of their ongoing support. The working capital deficit is quite hardcore in its nature. With an overdraft standing at £1.1 million and creditors awaiting immediate payment of £320K it can't make life easy. The Directors feel that the way forward is to sell the existing ground and release some cash on the back of a new Stadium development.

Our Own illustrious results during the same period were:-

ROTHERHAM UNITED F.C   year end 31st May 2007
Trading Profit   51331
Working Capital deficit   (331803)
Net Balance sheet   538635
Average attendances   4201
Turnover   2,781,452

One of the reasons in our own case for the working capital deficit is because we held a fair chunk of season ticket money for the forthcoming campaign and we could not claim it as an asset until the season unfolded. This may also have affected the other clubs. Despite this we still showed reasonable trading figures for the year end considering the initial problems we had experienced. Obviously the player sales were the main reason for us returning a profit, but the deficit from the previous year under the Millers 05 was still reduced by £1m, which is a great achievement by a board with no obvious benefactor to hand.

We were in a reasonable position for the start of the new season albeit in League Two.

Table of Net Profit Findings of Each League Two Club:

PROFIT only 7 clubs filed a profit; Accrington Stanley, Barnet, Chester, Hereford, Lincoln Shrewsbury and Rotherham United.

LOSSES were incurred by the others as follows :-

£ Between	
0 - 100000	Bury and Mansfield
101000 - 250000	Brentford, Rochdale, Stockport and Wrexham
251000 - 500000	Morecambe
501000 - 750000	Bradford, Macclesfield, Wycombe.
751000 - 1000000	Grimsby
1000001 - 1500000	Peterborough
1500001 - 2000000	Darlington
2000001 - 3000000	None
3000000 - 4000000	M.K Dons

Summary of the Net Balance Sheets of the Clubs

£ Clubs with Net Assets	
10000000 to 15000000	Shrewsbury Town
5000000 to 10000000	None
1000000 to 5000000	Mansfield Town
500000 to 999000	Rotherham United
250000 to 499000	None
100000 to 249000	Rochdale
0 to 99000	Bury, Morecambe
Clubs with Net Liabilities	
0 to (249000)	Wrexham
(250000) to (499000)	None
(500000) to (1000000)	Grimsby, Hereford
(1000000) to (2000000)	Lincoln, Macclesfield
(2000000) to (3000000)	Chester, Darlington, Wycombe
(3000000) to (5000000)	Peterborough and Stockport
(5000000) to (6000000)	M.K.Dons

LEAGUE TWO PLAYER SQUAD SIZES

Squad sizes	2007/08	2006/07
Darlington	41	43
Wrexham	41	41
Accrington	38	38
Brentford	38	35
Macclesfield	38	38
Stockport	36	37
Mansfield Town	35	31
Shrewsbury	34	32
Rochdale	34	40
Wycombe	33	-
Bradford City	33	36
Chesterfield	33	33
M.K Dons	32	35
Chester City	32	34
Peterborough	31	38
Bury	31	38
Notts County	30	25
Dagenham and Red	30	-
Rotherham United	30	32
Hereford	29	34
Lincoln City	29	36
Barnet	28	26
Morecambe	28	-
Grimsby town	26	36
Boston Utd	-	39

Rotherham's squad size was in the bottom half of the above table. Whilst squad size is relevant it is the individual player's wages within, that is the determining factor.

IN SUMMARY

Out of all this Rotherham fared very well. Especially considering the huge losses incurred during 2005/2006.

So what went wrong in 2007/2008 as far as Rotherham United was concerned.?

1) Rotherham did not have a "benefactor" loaning money to the club to bail it out each year despite all the efforts. Trevor Smallwood had helped us before but we could not rely on him each time.

2) The lease and its onerous repairing liability really hit us once more .It was heavy during the 2007/2008 season when over a £100,000 was spent on essential repairs alone.(£164,000 year before)

3) The floods insurance claim settlement left us with an overall shortfall in our budget of approx £200,000.

Unfortunately Hereford did not fetch many away fans. A big problem for our cash flow in both League 1 and 2.

4) Falling crowds. These were down from an average of 4762 in 2006/07 to an average of 4201 in 2007/08. This was even more weighted towards the end of the season. The Brentford game saw a crowd of only 2979. The previous season had seen home crowds as high as 7,800 against Notts Forest. The fall in attendances slashed revenue by over £220,000.

5) We were still burdened with the overlap of League One player contracts

6) Poor cup runs and poor draws.

7) Rising Match day costs way above inflation.

8) No Tangible assets (ie No Stadium or Training Ground) to approach a Bank with as proper security so to get loan/overdraft facilities to help the cash flow out. We traded with no overdraft facility whatsoever.

9) The length of time it took to find an investor to eventually takeover.

In the Rotherham Advertiser of the 3rd October 2008 the back page ran an article stating that Tony Stewart claimed the Club was; "Back in the Black". The club's bank account may have been in the "black" but so was ours. It also stated that the business plan in place should get the Club back into profit within 3 or 4 years which was always our goal. The article went on to say that we had lost £1.2 million, which again was reported incorrectly. This was a quote from the statement of affairs prepared by the Administrator. The figure of £1.2 million included:

A) Monies owed to the new investors for financing the administration.

B) A claim by C.F Booth's under the terms of the lease.

C) Football League debts.

D) Other contingencies which only materialise in a cessation scenario. i.e. Breach of Contract claims as the company will not be able to honour these to the end of the specified term.

All in all the actual trading deficit when we finally stepped down in April 2008 was less than half of that which was quoted. There were also unrealised funds to consider from player sales of Oxley and O'Grady which put some funds back into the pot.

When we put the Club into Administration it was because it was running short of cash and we didn't between us have a spare £500k to throw into the mix, which unless you are a multi millionaire is a lot of money to risk in football, passion or no passion.

Considering the circumstances I think we did quite well. With a few more bums on seats and a bit of luck in the Cup competitions we could have perhaps avoided Administration, one will never know.

We never professed our master plan to be the long term answer to Rotherham's plight or any other Football League club for that matter. Football today is a very expensive hobby. When Denis Coleman stepped into the breach in March 2006, he did so to save the club from extinction by putting his neck on the line and constantly reiterated in the media that he would try everything he could to get the club back on its feet again but never claimed to have millions to throw at it. Tony Stewart has been reported as saying "This is my yacht" after finally taking over as chairman. We wish him well, but have no doubts the maintenance costs of his new "yacht" are going to seriously test his passion for the game.

Further information from my notes on discussions with the League Two clubs:

SOURCES OF INCOME

> Ticket sales continue to be the most important source of revenue for most of the clubs. About a third expected the ticket sales to rise in the current season. In the previous year, I was told this by around 50% of the clubs so it demonstrated an overall fall in attendance .Was it a reflection of less free money in the economy.

BROADCASTING

Every financial director I talked to felt that League Two did not receive adequate broadcasting revenue and that the League should make better representation.

There was talk of an initiative whereby there was to be more regular screening of League 1 and League 2 clubs.

SPONSORSHIP REVENUE

Two out of three directors felt that they would receive an increase in sponsorship revenue during the current season. However, most felt that the increase would be outweighed by respective overhead increases. With everyone and their Grandfather chasing sponsorships it is not an easy feat any more.

BANK PRESSURES

Most of the clubs I spoke to felt they were coming under increasing pressure from their bank and 2 clubs in particular had had very serious run ins. This was a big swing from the year before and perhaps reflects the banks' nervousness at the amount of money spent by many clubs. One in five clubs had had to renegotiate facilities with their bank during the year. Over 50% of Directors had put up personal guarantees but of these most thought they wouldn't be called upon.(So why give one in the first place? Who are their Accountants?). This tended to be with new finance in particular (car leases etc).

FINANCE DIRECTOR PRESSURE

About half of my fellow colleagues in division two felt they were under pressure to sanction greater spending than the club could afford. I sympathised with this as I certainly had that at Rotherham.

Player Costs

Despite the increasing financial burdens surprisingly, only one in four directors was trying to reduce the size of the first team squad. About half said they were trying to keep the squad the same size as of the previous season whilst the rest confirmed they had a bigger budget for first team squad this season. One area of contention was the player related bonuses. At Rotherham we seemed to have more than our fair share, putting us in the minority of clubs. We had inherited much of this. My own view is I think they are good for the game but not at the levels they are being paid. If we had got promoted last season we would have had to have found over £125000.

Transfer Budgets

Despite the general financial gloom of being in division two, I was somewhat surprised that around a third of the clubs were looking to increase money spent on transfer fees during the season. How could they justify this, one wondered? I did wonder about the wisdom of that as a strategy considering the restraints of the league we were all in..

Football Agents

An increasing number of directors I spoke to felt that agents did not assist the clubs and hindered and added costs. I could certainly relate to this from Rotherham's experiences. About half of the Directors felt that agents were useful compared with a near majority when I enquired in the previous year. People were obviously changing their minds.

Stadium Improvements

Just above half of the directors I asked indicated they were planning to spend money on their grounds in the following seasons. This was a fall from the previous season when around 75% indicated they were to spend on their Stadium. A few (including ourselves) did confirm attempts were continuing to obtain a new stadium. The majority of stadium owning clubs were looking to invest with a view of providing extra commercial income like at Wrexham where Hotel expansion was being planned.

What were the Club's biggest Concerns

For both of the seasons we were involved, players' salaries were cited as being the biggest concern for finance directors. It is an area that can so easily get out of control. No matter what your plans, it never happens, there are always reasons. A player may become injured and then you have to find the wage and hotel expenses of a Loan Player. Collectively the League could do something about it. Many of the wage demands I felt were obscene considering the league we were in. For clubs relegated there is not the commercial opportunity to make a huge difference. There I often thought it and now I have said it... Some of the League One and Two players' wages were at far too high a level to be justifiable. Stricter wage capping may assist.

Question: So how do you make a Football Club in the Lower leagues successful?

Answer: Find a Sugar Daddy.

It will now be interesting to see how Rotherham fares financially. I think Tony Stewart will find out that Football is like no other business. No matter how good your business experience, you will be put to the test in an environment where most events are outside of your control. Players injuries, Poor performances on the pitch, falling crowds, adverse weather causing rearranged fixtures, essential services increasing their costs, take it or leave it. Tony Stewart told David Ness he would line up the costs with the level of income. That will take some time.

I sincerely wish him "Good Luck".

CHAPTER 46 (JOINT)

MATCHDAY AND OTHER ANTICS

VISITING BOARDROOMS AT WAR

The football league indicates standards for the treatment of visiting Directors and their guests.

First and foremost there should be free parking at the football ground, a bar and a hot drinks facility available on arrival accompanied by a hot meal, a free programme and team sheet, a seat in the directors box, a hot drink at half time and soup and finger buffet to enjoy at the end of the game while the crowd disperses.

What I found a little surprising was how in both leagues we did occasionally get requests to ensure seating was specifically provided so that certain visiting Directors sat together whilst others were kept as far away as possible. Not always easy in our marquee but we endeavoured to oblige. Their Boardrooms were so split I wondered how they managed to function properly.

A Home Director should always greet the visitors and make them feel welcome. These split boardrooms would put you right on the spot as you were in a no win situation. Whichever group you went to first the other felt they had their nose's pushed out. Each side would give you their opinion as to the state of their club and the problems. Neither side acknowledged each other throughout the game.

Sometimes, although not at war, a visiting Chairman would not even grace your doorstep with his presence. Magically appearing when the match kicked off and disappearing again at half time.

Re-appear for the second half then shoot off at the end of the game without so much as a "hello or goodbye". This noticeably happened when we played Peterborough. Director of Football Barry Fry did a sterling job representing the club in his absence I must add. What a character. The T.V did a documentary on him about how he nearly lost everything he owned to keep Peterborough F.C alive. Perhaps their Chairman Darragh MacAnthony thought Barry might outshine him and so he lay low.

VISITING TEAM MANAGERS

The majority of Team Managers spent most of the time during the match on the touchline or in the dugout. They saw it as a key part of team management. There were however some exceptions. When we played Millwall on 30th September 2006. Team Advisor Ray (Butch) Wilkins, former England player from the 80s, came with the Directors and their Chief Executive into the marquee. What was even stranger was that he sat with us at our table talking about the ups and downs of the game over the years. As an ex-England star he was still recognised and he was accosted by a lot of young supporters all asking for his autograph. When he came back in he told us that those kids did not fool him. He noticed it was their Dad's pointing him out and sending them off in pursuit. The autographs were obviously for the Dads benefit.

During that game he sat with us in the Directors box. He may have been talking to the team manager via radio and if so he was being very discreet. His Directors were not showing any interest in him at all. The next day a press release was issued by Millwall F.C saying they had removed Butch Wilkins as their advisory team manager despite them actually winning the game 3-2.

He must have known it was coming. I felt a little sorry for him.

When we played the M.K Dons, their manager Paul Ince came and sat at the side of his Chairman (Peter Winkleman) in the directors' box. I couldn't help thinking that Ince looked to have clapped a bit of weight on. He kept standing up as some action manifested itself , be it their initiative or ours. He was clearly communicating with his touchline staff and would then be leaning over still half standing explaining the situation to Peter Winkleman After a while people seated immediately behind him started asking him to sit down, which he ignored. The stewards then politely asked of him the same. In the end he was given a final warning "Sit down sunshine or you are out". We all smiled. He went back to the dugout. I think he liked the attention of the fans.

I also noticed some Chairmen got quite involved in influencing the Team Manager with decisions which I think shows a mistrust of the manager's ability in controlling his team. One Chairman seemed to be never off the radio set, constantly gaggling down it like some possessed lunatic. At half time he was down in the dressing rooms barking out the orders again.

ILICIT TICKET SALES

During September 2007 we were tipped off by a few people (including my good friend Colin) that someone had been seen in the Prince of Wales, The New Inn and The Millmoor selling match day tickets for just £10. We were puzzled where these could be from. Ticket control was pretty tight, so we would have known if there was a problem with rogue or forged tickets. We did wonder whether they were from the pile of tickets that Mr Booth collected for his employees before each match as part of the hospitality package. I could certainly not see the Booth's trailing around the town centre pubs to get a few quid, but maybe some of their employees were doing just that. We armed a couple of supporters with some money to try and buy any offered so we could solve the mystery. They called in randomly over the next few months into the different pubs but to no avail. Whilst our undercover lads were sat in the "Prince" we were told they had been in the "Millmoor". To make things even harder it didn't seem to be happening at every home game. Despite our efforts we were never able to solve this alleged abuse.

WARRING MASCOTS

In one of the early home games of 2006/7 I was down at the Players tunnel talking with David Costin .The teams assembled in line, ready to run onto the pitch when the announcer welcomed the teams to Millmoor. Our mascot was now in the guise of a gangster, and was at the front already whilst the visiting mascot was running a bit late. With costume donned, the visitor then ran down to the front almost knocking our mascot flying. Ours reacted by giving him a mighty shove backwards, and then that was it. If you have ever seen two mascots all costumed up throwing fists at each other, then you have seen a sight worth beholding. It was meant to be vicious but the constraints of the outfit did not really allow it. It reminded me of the game show "Jeux Sans Frontier" hosted 30 years ago by Eddie Waring.

As all the lads ran on the pitch so did the mascots. Our Gangster was the quickest and he ran onto the pitch then headed back towards the dugouts. The other mascot did a similar route, then as they approached each other they went back into flying fists. The crowd though it was just larking about but I knew it was not. I collared one of the Stewards who shot down and intervened dragging the pair of them apart. The feud continued when they disrobed but our security men managed to calm them both down. They eventually started laughing about it and finally gave each other a big hug.

THEY MORE THAN DANCED THE GAME AWAY

Lisa Costin had, for a while, thought that it was a shame that the club didn't have its own dance troupe as was common at some other clubs we visited.

Cherry O'Grady, usually accompanied with her baby, liked to watch husband and player Chris in action on the pitch. So she was not sat alone in the stand we offered her accommodation up in the marquee and a seat with us in the Directors part of the stand. She soon struck up a rapport with Lisa and part of their conversation got round to the subject of there being no dance troupe at Milmoor. They decided they would pool their resources and attend to the matter forthwith. An advert was placed on the club's website for volunteers and sufficient youngsters came forth to answer the call.

Lisa and Cherry mapped out various dance routines and training took place two nights per week. This was a tall order over the winter period because the insufficient heating in the Tivoli suite meant the girls were trying to concentrate and practice whilst being freezing cold. As the girls were of mixed ages it made the teaching and practice a little harder. Lisa's two daughters Whitney and Danielle were part of the troupe and a friendship between the girls quickly developed.

The parents bought the dance outfits for their child and in the form of a sponsorship deal, David Costin, through his company, AFP, acted as overall sponsor. That meant that in return for his company name at the back of the blouses, he would provide all the additional pieces of kit required, such as pompoms, etc over the season. The girls all worked very hard and I did feel at times that the crowd were not appreciative enough of them and the efforts that they made. It takes a lot of guts to go out in all weather in front of a large crowd and strut your stuff.

One funny incident that occurred was the first time the new kit was being worn. David brought all the directors out at half time from the marquee to stand and watch the troupe. He was eager we all saw the new kit with his company logo and name being proudly displayed for all. As they filed onto the pitch we all fell about laughing, most of the girls had long hair and their locks covered over any mention of AFP! He was so uptight and frustrated, strutting up and down saying "I can't believe it"

Lisa and Cherry gave David two options from hereon in; one - that either the girls would have to tie their hair back and wear ponytails or two- to swap the name to the front. David, not wanting to interfere in the external appearance of the troupe, opted for the name to be re-embossed on the front of their blouses instead.

Another thing the girls had to contend with was the shocking weather. They danced through it all: rain, sleet, snow and wind. One amusing incident was when they all donned white tights and the ground was very muddy after intense rain. They finished their first routine by dropping down onto their knees. When they stood up they all had two distinctly visible black circles. They continued the show, and as the marks were so vivid it looked like part of their costume's decoration.

One thing that we noticed from observing the troupe in action was that after each dance, one of the girls unknowingly went to scratch her behind. As soon as the troupe had finished and they were all stood in a final pose you could see one pompom moving up and down as the dancer scratched away vigorously. Apparently, this had also manifested itself in training but was hard for the girl to control as she was doing it subconsciously.

By March of 2008 it had also become difficult with the training etc for Cherry, as her husband, Chris O'Grady, was not the most popular team member following his sole rejection of the wages deferment for the Administration, which his teammates had accepted. Chris missed that weekends defeat at Morecambe and failed to report for training on the Monday, Mark Robins told the Sheffield Star: "He has kicked his team-mates in the teeth and also the fans who have supported him. "He has been looked after here like royalty, on and off the field, and then this happens.

"He is under contract at this football club and was ordered to report for the reserve team game.

"I will not let this club be walked all over if I can help it and I shall try and do the best I can to ensure that no-one takes advantage of the club in its current predicament."

Unfortunately, the girls were denied their last dance. The girls had put a lot of effort into their routines and rehearsals and it's a shame that it all came to such an abrupt end. They had given their "all " and deserved better. Perhaps the new board should try to get the dance troupe re-assembled. I am sure there will be plenty of volunteers to pick up the mantle from Lisa.

GAVIN GRABS ALL THE GLORY

Gavin Mackinder and John Hesselden business partners at Brearley & Co and both decent players in their younger days were invited to represent the club's staff in a fundraising football match at Millmoor versus a team made up of the club's sponsors. The staff consisted of a few ex pro's including Mark Robins, Mark Todd, Simon Tracey, Nick Daws, Ian Bailey who were all working at the club in one way or another and a few other staff members, Paul Douglas, Ian Herbert (Herbie), David Hall and Carol Rockett's son Gavin who worked in the ticket office. During the second half and despite his advancing years Gavin the elder was brought on and made an immediate impact getting scythed down in the penalty area at which the guest referee Howard Webb blew his whistle and pointed straight to the spot. Mark Robins who was the team captain for the day walked towards the crumpled body lying on the ground and shouted "Go on you take it Gav" but as he got up and dusted himself down, joy turned to despair when Carol's son, his name sake obviously thought Mark was referring to him, grabbed the ball placed it on the spot and gleefully dispatched the penalty with aplomb. To this day young Gav still doesn't realise what eternal damage and suffering he caused, denying old Gav his moment of truth on the big stage at Millmoor, much to the amusement of his wife Lynn and two children Tom and Katie who were watching from the stand.

GETTING PAST THE OLD GUARD

On match days I would pick up my tickets and passes and make my way with any guests into the Ground to go on up into the Directors Marquee. The route you would go would tend to be the same. As you became better known, fans would stop you to ask questions regarding the club. Questions were not always easy to answer for many reasons. Not that you were becoming evasive but confidentiality had to dictate. Even though we often arrived quite early some fans came in even earlier and sat in their aisle seats, on guard, blocking your access. By August 2007 there were no routes left for me to go without being nobbled. Every stairway was now covered by well meaning inquisitive fans. What astounded me was the knowledge they had on current matters and problems. The various websites would often state as a matter-of-fact many things, which were often wildly exaggerated, but these all seemed to have good intelligence on the various issues.

They had most likely been attending games from being small boys often a third generation spectator following in the footsteps of their Father's and Grandfathers. The club was as much a part of them as their family were. Joking apart I personally valued their opinions. I listened to them and respected their views and suggestions. On one occasion I had just got onto the top landing when a small boy of about 5 years of age approached me and he said "Can I have your autograph Mr Chuckle". I duly obliged and once back inside the others roared with laughter. What with similar haircuts and a moustache, the resemblance had been jokingly mentioned at the board meetings several times. When I next saw Paul Chuckle and told him of the mistaken identity I told him to be prepared as people may well be approaching him to enquire of the clubs finances." I will just tell them were getting by and keep supporting us if they do" he responded laughingly.

DAGENHAM AND REDBRIDGE F.C AWAY GAME HOSPITALITY

We were all looking forward to this game. As "new kids on the block" it was always a pleasure to network and mix with other like-minded people. I was in London on business that week so I stayed over to see the game. I took my son Alex and future son in law George with me. As stated previously the league set the standards for hospitality but D and R had not took much heed. When we entered the Boardroom we were offered nothing at all. No drink, no food only a "Hello". After about 15 minutes one of the Directors approached and asked if we were okay. Quite cheekily I asked him if it would be possible for us to have a lager. About 5 minutes later an elderly gentleman appeared with a tray containing a single can of Fosters and three glasses, which we had to share between us. He apologised that there were no biscuits or anything to eat. Maybe they had got it right. They were obviously making significant cost savings.

ENGLAND UNDER 18 CALL UP

We were ecstatic when goalkeeper Mark Oxley had his call up to the England U-18 squad. Considering all the doom and gloom it was nice that some good news surfaced from within.

The Millers youngster received the call up from U-18 coach Brian Eastick for the friendly on April 16th 2008 at Hartlepool United's Victoria Ground. Oxley was to be part of an 18 man squad for the match against Austria, which included players from Premier League giants Manchester United, Arsenal and Tottenham Hotspur. He was proving to be a very saleable asset for the future.

Mark Oxley had come through the youth scheme at Millmoor and had been making great strides this season. He featured on the Millers first team substitutes bench several times to deputise for the injured Steven Cann.

A SURPRISE PRESENTATION

We were a little taken aback when we hosted Notts County on the 22nd September 2007.

Their Chairman had been doing his research on us and presented the Directors with a lovely Commemorative Shield to celebrate 100 years of us playing at Millmoor. We never expected it. Considering all the problems the ground was causing us, we had not really organised much to celebrate the anniversary landmark in this light. It was like when your wife presents you with a present and a card on the wedding anniversary that you have forgotten. But still a lovely gesture by them. Paul Douglas

Pete Winkleman, M.K Dons Chairman and backer in the Directors seats at Millmoor for the 5th February 2008 game. We lost 1-0 but the crowd was encouraging at 5421..

The Dagenham stadium. It was their first year in the football league.

Dagenham and Redbridge's ground. Strangely the crowd attendance figures went down following their promotion into the league 2 from the Conference.

Tony Styles our intrepid stadium announcer.

Despite injury following a clash of heads Chris O'Grady plays on. The match was on the 27th October 2007, we won 2-0.

Gavin Mackinder in the Directors Lounge at Millmoor.

Paul Douglas (right) sat with his dad and brother David (Upper left) and friend Ian Haffety at Chesterfield.

The on pitch flare-up at Chesterfield that eventually cost us a fine from the league. The Chesterfield goalkeeper appears to be threatening Rotherham's Danny Harrison. The match was on the 5th December 2007 on a freezing cold night. We won 2-0.

Heading out through the tunnel at Scunthorpe 17th February 2007. we eventually lost 1-0.

The "United Rotherham" game where the Advertiser was good enough to get behind and provided all the posters.

Team Captain Graham Coughlin.

Directors guests Ian Herbert, Pete Wainright, Mel Beaumont and Ralph Milner pose at Grimsby on the 12th April 2008.

YOU'VE WON THE THOUSAND POUNDISH: Paul Douglas greets the Grimsby directors at Millmoor. They bought some 50:50 draw tickets but were not as lucky.

EARACHE AT BARNET: Football and violence should be kept apart but we were nearly driven to it by the gentleman (top left) shouting a running commentary and criticism for the full 90 minutes at Barnet. We believe a relative was playing. His voice was permanently pitched at 120 decibels. The ladies retreated inside in the second half because the noise hurt their ears.

Ruth and Amy Brearley accompanied by George Legg arriving in the knick of time at Barnet's Underhill Stadium following an accident on the North Circular 29th September 2007.

THE BIGGEST CROWD: Inside Notts Forrest ground for the 9th April 2007 game. It was the biggest crowd Rotherham United played in front of during all 2006/07 and 2007/8.

to be fair had organised some celebrations and Trevor Swift, Roy Lambert and Trevor Womble all made guest appearances being hero's from our illustrious past.

We managed to find the club's photographer and saved the day.

AN INNOCENT ERROR

It was just a slip of the tongue when Tony Styles goofed announcing the "minute's applause" tribute to former manager Ian Porterfield. He actually said " Jimmy Armfield" ex Leeds and England player who is still alive. It was a simple human error, which we all make from time to time. The Press and media were on his case most unfairly. The Star in particular gave an almost hysterical coverage in their editions. They also lambasted us for not including an obituary notice in the match day programme. We had in fact planned a special dedicated tribute and produced a programme in his honour for the RUFC v Mansfield game on the 6th October 2007. Ian had been the club's manager between 1979 and 1981 and will be remembered as the man behind the Millers Third Division Championship winning side in 1981. This had to be researched more thoroughly and people from his past contacted so that we could do him justice. We issued a statement apologising for the human error, but it just shows the length some people will go to stir up a hornet's nest.

Tony did a good job for the club as Stadium announcer and knew how to keep things flowing.

Unfortunately "you are only ever remembered for your worst act and none of your best".

PAUL HURST'S RECORD BREAKER

Pressure was put on Mark Robins to make sure that he played Paul Hurst in the oncoming game against Shrewsbury on the 24th November 2007. He had equalled Danny Williams's club record of 492 league appearances and he was now in a position to beat it. He had been with the club for 14 years. What a consistent, one club player he had been .It may be debatable who has given better service to Rotherham United's cause over the years but Paul for me is at the top of the tree.

The media had picked up on this impending feat and Les Payne and Gerry Somerton kept referring to it over the ensuing months. In fairness to Mark Robins he is his own man when it comes to the team and although he will listen he does what he feels is the best. Paul was included in the squad but starting out the game on the bench. He was however brought on as substitute and so the old club appearance record fell. Mark Robins had just been named as Coca Cola Division 2 Manager of the month so it was celebrations all round. The game was a win for Rotherham with a 2-0 victory but sadly for us the crowd was a disappointing 3832. Where were all the fans we wondered?

THE KIDS FOR A QUID

The New Years game 1st January 2008 was against Macclesfield Town who we knew had a lowly following. We wanted it to be a full house, party time so Denis and Gary started pushing the publicity machine into gear to gain some momentum. The offer was made available for the Community Stand only and a paying adult had to attend with the child. We set the definition of

"A Kid" as being 12 years old with a maximum of 4 tickets per full paying adult. The League had been pushing this type of action under the "Fans for the future "initiative. We said tickets had to be purchased from the Ticket Office prior to match day in order to vet the unbelievable six-foot tall kids who claimed to be only 12 years old. The game was a great success for us as we won 3-0. Ryan Taylor played really well showing good skills on his continuing meteoric rise up the pecking order. The crowd that day was 4464 the previous 4 home games had been; 2754, 3832, 3808, 3773. So it had worked somewhat although we did hope for a higher figure. In his match report Mark Robins commented that to the players it made a big difference when there were more bodies passing through the gate filling up the empty stands. The impetus did seem to continue though as for the game against M.K Dons the attendance went up to 5421.We issued a statement thanking everyone for their support on this event, the atmosphere was amazing. The following home game against Wycombe saw our highest crowd of the season 6709.

M.K DONS AWAY- A Bad Day at the office. 9th February 2008

I had been working in London and Ruth and I decided we would stop over and drive to the game on Saturday lunch time so getting to the Stadium M.K Dons in good time. Perhaps it was an omen on the way up, as we were delayed with three separate traffics jams due to accidents on the M1.

I am not a big fan of Milton Keynes as a place, the traditionalist in me finds the landscape pretty bland and soulless without a proper centre to it. I have to say though the ground is magnificent. What a Stadium. That did make me green with envy. Chairman Pete Winkleman makes a good host and the facilities were very good. They had only moved in on the 18th July 2007 so everything was still new. We were very optimistic of a great game that afternoon.

The game started well enough with both teams getting the feel of each other at first. We were presenting a 4 4 2 formation. Some 14 minutes into the game Kevin Gallen of M.K Dons scored first with a great shot after some sloppy defending. Then for the rest of the first half we did not shine too well and M.K Dons dominated the field of play. At half time though, Mark Robins gave them a structured talk and managed to lift their confidence. They always say, "If you believe in yourself you can achieve anything".

Then in the second half came that shocking injury to Stephen Brogan after his collision with the Dons keeper Willy Gueret only 8 minutes into the second half. I could tell by the way he rolled around on the ground that it was serious. He was only 19 and starting to make a name for himself. It turned out to be a double fracture of the lower leg. As he was stretchered off I went down to the medical room with Denis to see how he was. He was heartbroken and saying that his football career had now been finished. I felt awful for him. He went to the hospital with his parents our physio and Paul Hurst accompanying him. Little did we know he would be there several days with multiple operations? It was a bad break.

Back in the game Ryan Taylor and Jamie Yates seemed to rally. From then on the team was a different animal. They wanted to get a result for Stephen's sake. M. K Dons were a good side with a lot of experienced players but non-the less Danny Harrison hit home a belter of a equaliser on 82 minutes. This was a half volley following a cross from Ryan Taylor. The game ended up a 1-1 draw. There were 7 minutes of added time to the game following Stephen's injury. It seemed to last 7 years. It was a great salvage job from the wreckage of his injury. On leaving the Ground we went up to the General Hospital on Standing Way to enquire about Stephen. It was a well-equipped Hospital and we knew he was in good hands. The medical staffs were great. We said our goodbyes and ventured back up the M1 to South Yorkshire.

I mention this incident, as it was emotional for us all as a Board. We really felt sickened by Stephen's plight. We sent him well wishes and kept in touch. Denis Circuit and others went down to Milton Keynes to see him. Stephen had screws inserted into the bone to hold it all together. A further operation was needed later to remove this. Then some four days later some complications set in called "Compartment Syndrome". This is where pressure builds up within the body and Stephen had to go back to surgery and have an incision to release this. The wound was then left open and re stitched later on. For only the second time in the season Rotherham faced their next game without Stephen. They certainly missed him .The game was a disaster in that we lost to Stockport 4-1. This was the start of a poor run which despite the financial problems virtually finished off our challenge for automatic promotion.

I was as pleased as punch when Stephen turned up on crutches at our home game against Chesterfield on the 15th March 2008. I had a quick word with him and wished him a speedy recovery. Hopefully all this will just become a bad memory and he can get on with his playing career. I am sure he will make a top grade professional one day.

BEWARE IN SHEFFIELD

As part of the Watford deal for Hoskins and Williamson we were to get the free loan of a young midfielder Toumani Diagouraga . Alan Knill was talking to the Club Directors at our offices on Bridge Street when his phone rang. It was Toumani making contact for the first time. "So where are you" asked Alan? "You are at Sheffield Railway Station, Okay just wait there and I will send someone to pick you up" Alan told him. "How will we recognise you" Alan enquired? "You are 6 feet 2 inches and you are wearing black leather jeans and a Pink shirt," "My god " said Alan " stay right where you are and do not speak to anyone, particularly any men who will appear to be very friendly towards you." We all burst out laughing.

Toumani Diagouraga was a 19 year old when he came to Rotherham. He was of French nationality and was a central midfielder. Having been spotted by a scout in Paris, Diagouraga was signed by Watford's Academy. He signed professional terms in November 2004 then aged 16. He made his first team debut in the League Cup game against Wolverhampton Wanderers on 20th September 2005. His first team league debut was against Burnley in Decmber 2005. He was loaned to Swindon Town for the rest of the 2005/06 season.

His time at Rotherham was not very prolific and he returned back to Watford who re-loaned him out to Hereford United. He signed a three year deal with them in July 2008 and apparently was instrumental in gaining Hereford their promotion to League One.

CHRIS OGRADY ON TARGET

Chris was in a rush; he had come back to the ground to pick up Cherry and was late. She was assisting Lisa Costin with the dance troupe .He tore into the Car Park, parked his car and jumped out. As he walked off, to his horror he saw his car careering down the slope and watched in vain as it crashed through the Ticket office wall. At the training session next day the players hung a big sign saying "Ticket Office" in the goal . Team Captain Coughlin thought it was a way to perhaps get Chris scoring goals again cause he's proved he can hit that.

AN EXPENSIVE GAME

The match against Chesterfield on the 5th December 2007 proved to be an expensive evening out. Listening to the pre-match radio phone-ins on the drive down from Swinton it was apparent that most Spireites supporters were confident that we'd be well beaten this cold and windy evening.

The game at Chesterfield's Saltergate Stadium was certainly

lively. As a local Derby you could say that it was at the very least played with spirit. The game ended up being our seventh successive league victory and it was without doubt very satisfying.

We started off playing good football and were from the start the better of the two sides. Brogan should have been awarded a penalty when he appeared to be brought down by Niven but the referee bottled it and awarded a corner instead. Derek Holmes scored early doors after the keeper fended off a fine long ball from Chris O'Grady. In the second half former Chesterfield player Mark Hudson fired home a second goal at close range right in front of the Chesterfield fans amassed in the cop behind. They had booed him right from the start of the game. Then there was a controversial challenge and the pent up tension of Chesterfield's players burst out in protest and havoc prevailed. The Referee was struggling to contain the incident as shoving and jostling was going on all around. It was our players who bared the brunt of it but they still behaved like gentlemen.

About a week later a letter arrived at Millmoor from the Football league. They were fining both Chesterfield and us £2000 for misconduct on the pitch. We all watched the official Video of the incident and thought what a miscarriage of justice this was. We decided to appeal setting out all our reasons. We were the victims in all this. About a week later a letter came back from the Football league. They had considered our request but the decision stood, oh and by the way the fine for you is now £2500. More money up in smoke.

BARRY HEARN HUMOUR

The game against Leyton Orient on the 23rd September 2006 was at their Brisbane Road ground. The stadium was officially known as the "Match room Stadium" after Chairman Barry Hearn's sports promotion company. The ground had undergone extensive redevelopment in recent years, not withstanding that finance for some of the redevelopment had already been raised by selling off the four corners of the stadium for residential blocks of flats. An increase in costs however and a weakening of the Balance Sheet meant that an emergency general meeting was called in April 2005. It was agreed that the club should sell a c.999-year lease on the West Stand for £1.5 million to a consortium led by Barry Hearn. The consortium then leased it back to the club on a same-length lease basis, all of the stand, except the office space , for an annual rent of only £1. The additional funds generated by this arrangement were used to complete the building of the West Stand ready for the 2005/06 season. The stand has a single lower tier of seating, while further up the structure are directors' and corporate hospitality boxes, club offices and player facilities .We were shown into the Directors Board room in the West Stand.

The atmosphere was welcoming despite the fact that Orient had just lost seven matches on the bounce. The game itself was lively and one where you lost your voice. Sharps scored first after 19 minutes, Orient then equalised just one minute later with a goal from Chambers. Just before half time Hoskins banged away another goal putting Rotherham 2-1 up. The second half saw further action when Orient's Miller scored an equaliser in the 68th minute. We managed to clinch the game though when Wiseman got a third goal winner in the 82nd minute giving us a 3-2 victory.

Denis was quite interested in the Stadium development and when back in the Boardroom asked if it was all right if he had a look around before heading off. Barry Hearn at the other side of the room overhearing shouted, "Someone go with them Northern CxxxS we don't want them nicking anything else, they've already pinched three points".

BARRY FRY HUMOUR

The 13th November 2006 saw us confronting Peterborough United at their London Road Stadium in the F.A Cup. On entering the Directors Board room we were greeted by Barry Fry Director of Football. "Come on in lads, come on in, the Footballs shit here, but the food is magnificent and the drinks are great.

They stuffed us 3-0 so it wasn't that shit!

THE DOCTOR GETS CALLED AWAY BEFORE I COULD NOBBLE HIM.

The 17th February 2007 saw us playing Scunthorpe away at their Glanford Park Ground. Another new stadium for us to envy. As part of our cost cutting it had been mentioned at Board meetings that Paul Douglas should approach the Club's match day Medics to see if he could persuade them to cut their costs for a while to help the club. Whether Paul did not want to be the bearer of these tidings I am unsure but he never seemed to drop on the main man at the right time. He did however tip me off the Club doctor was going to the away game, which was a bit of a one off for him. He also thought it better for me to pull him regards the cut in pay.

As regards the game despite a magnificent second half display that was dominated by the Millers totally, Scunthorpe took all three points with a 1-0 win. My opinion was that Rotherham were by far the better team and it was certainly rough justice. We were near the bottom of the league looking at relegation and Scunthorpe were near the top looking for promotion, yet we were the far better side on the day.

Scunthorpe's Jermaine Beckford (on loan from Leeds), put them in the lead in the 17th minute, when he found the back of the Millers net with a shot from the edge of the penalty area. Richie Partridge took the ball round Foster and stormed towards goal before crossing the ball to Martin Woods only to see his effort seized on by Crosby in the 22nd minute. Martin Woods had another go 5 minutes later with a belting shot that was cleared just short of the goal by defender Lee Ridley.

In the Directors box I sat next to the Doctor and was busy chatting to him all about the club, slowly edging my way round to costs. Then just as I was about to strike. ...bang...Goalkeeper Neil Cutler was hurt in a clash while trying to win the ball. He looked to be concussed. The game ground to a halt and the Doctor ran out of the box and down to join Denis Circuit on the touchline, amazingly the Referee did not give them permission to come on the pitch for quite a few seconds. Eventually the Referee waved them on. Neil appeared to be suffering from concussion and it was decided to take him to hospital to get him checked out. He was placed on a stretcher and carried out after a 5minute delay. A very unfortunate incident. But as much as we love the game nasty accidents always leave a knot in your stomach. The Doctor went off with him and I never had the opportunity of nobbling him again.

Cutler was replaced for the second half by team substitute goalkeeper Gary Montgomery. Neil Cutler had joined The Millers jut before the start of the 2005/06 season. He played over 60 games for the club before we released him at the end of 2006/07-season. His contract expired and re-negotiations were not fruitful.

UNITED ROTHERHAM DAY

The idea for this came about from Gary and Denis discussing the club over a beer. They had decided patriotic action was needed. The rationale behind it was to try to fill Millmoor and prove to the people of Rotherham that the Council were behind the project of the New Stadium. The idea was discussed with Rotherham Council who gave it their blessing. The day was a great success with Millmoor being almost sold out. There had to be a lot of hard work done behind the scenes to organise the event. The Advertiser paid for all the printing of the posters and gave it great coverage in their paper. Gary Halls's dad, Alan, helped immensely by taking posters round the borough getting as many shops etc to back the campaign. The game selected for this demonstration of unity was the match against Wycombe Wanderers which would normally have had a poor attendance. The crowd was 6709 including 288 away supporters. The minute that we all walked on to the pitch and saw the crowd lift up the cards will stay with us all forever. The game ended up a 1-1 draw with goals from Steve Brogan after 14 minutes who blasted home a superb free kick from 25 yards. In the 55th minute McGleish equalised for Wycombe from a freak pass that was caught by the wind.

YOU'VE WON THE THOUSAND POUNDISH

We played Grimsby away on the 26th April 2008. As with most clubs we would always buy tickets for the half time draw, particularly away from home. Whilst I was talking to their chief executive a gorgeous ticket seller waved a wad of tickets in front of my nose. "How many would you like sir?" She enquired. The chief executive told me that to win this one was well worthwhile, not like other clubs where you end up with a fraction of the prize. The draw here gets great support. With a large Thousand Pounds blazing away on the ticket front and with his reassurances I bought £20 worth. During the half time interval we were joined by Grimsby M.P Austin Mitchell who was very supportive of the club. I was just talking to him about his time as a TV reporter when the announcement went out. The winning ticket is 056498. I cut Austin short to grab the pile out of my back pocket. Yes it was my ticket. I had bloody well won... You must be my lucky mascot I told Austin. As we were just about to go back to our seats a young man entered and said I understand the winner is in here. "Tis I" came my reply. "I will come back and see you shortly, okay." He said..

At full time he was nowhere to be seen. I hung on but my guest Ralph was wanting to be off sharply to meet someone in "The Plough" at West Melton. I went to find the mystery Draw promoter.

When I did track him down he was a bit sheepish. The prize is only £240 this week. "What?" I said.

"Poor take up this week I am afraid. It does say on the ticket in the small print a prize of up to £1000" he said in a low voice. Oh and I couldn't take the cash away with me as it had all been locked up. I had to wait for a cheque in the post. Ah well, these things happen.

Alas we are almost at the end of our jouney, a snapshot in time with Rotherham United. We hope you have found our story both informative and enlightening, as we consider our mission is accomplished. We hope the club's long and illustrious history will continue under Tony Stewart and his new board of directors and would like to wish the club and its supporters the very best for the future and urge all concerned to continue the fight in "keeping Rotherham United".

Chapter 47 - Rotherham United Statistics

Goal Scorers Season 2006/2007

Player	FL1	CUPS	TOTAL
Will Hoskins	15	1	16
Delroy Facey	10	1	11
Lee Williamson	5	1	6
Eugen Bopp	5	0	5
Chris O'Grady	4	0	4
Martin Woods	4	0	4
Richie Partridge	3	1	4
Marc Newsham	3	0	3
Ian Sharps	2	1	3
Dave Hibbert	2	0	2
Justin Cochrane	1	0	1
Pablo Mills	1	0	1
Michael Keane	0	1	1
Ian Henderson	1	0	1
Scott Wiseman	1	0	1

FL1 = Coca-Cola Football League One
CUPS = Carling Cup/Johnstone's Paint Trophy North

Home Attendances

Highest	Opponent	Lowest	Opponent	Average
7809	Nottm Forest	3223	Gillingham	4762

Completed Saturday, 5th May 2007	Pld	Home W	Home D	Home L	Home F	Home A	Away W	Away D	Away L	Away F	Away A	Overall W	Overall D	Overall L	Overall F	Overall A	Pts	GD
1 Scunthorpe United	46	15	6	2	40	17	11	7	5	33	18	26	13	7	73	35	91	+38
2 Bristol City	46	15	5	3	35	20	10	5	8	28	19	25	10	11	63	39	85	+24
3 Blackpool	46	12	6	5	40	25	12	5	6	36	24	24	11	11	76	49	83	+27
4 Nottingham Forest	46	14	5	4	37	17	9	8	6	28	24	23	13	10	65	41	82	+24
5 Yeovil Town	46	14	3	6	22	12	9	7	7	33	27	23	10	13	55	39	79	+16
6 Oldham Athletic	46	13	4	6	36	18	8	8	7	33	29	21	12	13	69	47	75	+22
7 Swansea City	46	12	6	5	36	20	8	6	9	33	33	20	12	14	69	53	72	+16
8 Carlisle United	46	12	5	6	35	24	7	6	10	19	31	19	11	16	54	55	68	-1
9 Tranmere Rovers	46	13	5	5	33	22	5	8	10	25	31	18	13	15	58	53	67	+5
10 Millwall	46	11	8	4	33	19	8	1	14	26	43	19	9	18	59	62	66	-3
11 Doncaster Rovers	46	8	10	5	30	23	8	5	10	22	24	16	15	15	52	47	63	+5
12 Port Vale	46	12	3	8	35	26	6	3	14	29	39	18	6	22	64	65	60	-1
13 Crewe Alexandra	46	11	4	8	39	38	6	5	12	27	34	17	9	20	66	72	60	-6
14 Northampton Town	46	8	5	10	27	28	7	9	7	21	23	15	14	17	48	51	59	-3
15 Huddersfield Town	46	9	8	6	37	33	5	9	9	23	30	14	17	15	60	63	59	0
16 Gillingham	46	14	2	7	29	24	3	6	14	27	53	17	8	21	56	77	59	-21
17 Cheltenham Town	46	8	6	9	25	27	7	3	13	24	34	15	9	22	49	61	54	-12
18 Brighton & Hove Albion	46	5	7	11	23	34	9	4	10	26	24	14	11	21	49	58	53	-9
19 Bournemouth	46	10	5	8	20	27	3	8	12	22	37	13	13	20	50	64	52	-14
20 Leyton Orient	46	6	10	7	30	32	6	5	12	31	45	12	15	19	61	77	51	-16
21 Chesterfield	46	9	5	9			3	6	14			12	11	23			47	
22 Bradford City	46	5	9	9			6	5	12			11	14	21			47	
23 Rotherham United (-10)	46	8	4	11			5	5	13			13	9	24			38	
24 Brentford	46	5	8	10			3	5	15			8	13	25			37	

Date	KO	Venue	Opponent	Comp	Result	Score	Attendance
August							
Sat 5	15:00	H	Brighton	FL1	L	1-1	4,998
Tue 8	19:45	A	Huddersfield	FL1	L	0-3	10,161
Sat 12	15:00	A	Blackpool	FL1	W	1-0	5,677
Sat 19	15:00	H	Scunthorpe	FL1	W	2-1	4,708
Tue 22	19:45	H	Oldham	LGCP	W	3-1	3,065
Sat 26	15:00	A	Bradford City	FL1	D	1-1	8,669
September							
Fri 1	19:45	H	Northampton	FL1	L	1-2	4,971
Sat 9	15:00	A	Chesterfield	FL1	L	1-2	4,803
Tue 12	19:45	H	Tranmere	FL1	W	2-1	3,732
Sat 16	15:00	H	Doncaster	FL1	D	0-0	6,348
Tue 19	19:45	H	Norwich City	LGCP	L	2-4	3,958
Sat 23	15:00	A	Leyton Orient	FL1	W	3-2	4,063
Tue 26	19:45	A	Oldham	FL1	L	1-2	4,880
Sat 30	15:00	H	Millwall	FL1	L	2-3	4,977
October							
Sun 8	14:00	A	Port Vale	FL1	W	3-1	4,810
Sat 14	15:00	H	Brentford	FL1	W	2-0	4,722
Tue 17	19:45	A	Hartlepool	JPT(N)	L	1-3	1,832
Sat 21	15:00	A	Bournemouth	FL1	W	3-1	5,544
Sat 28	15:00	H	Crewe	FL1	W	5-1	5,407
November							
Sat 4	15:00	A	Carlisle	FL1	D	1-1	7,247
Sat 11	15:00	A	Peterborough	FACP	L	0-3	4,281
Sat 18	15:00	H	Nottm Forest	FL1	D	1-1	7,809
Sat 25	15:00	A	Gillingham	FL1	L	0-1	6,201
December							
Sat 2	15:00	H	Yeovil Town	FL1	W	3-2	4,823
Sat 9	15:00	H	Bristol City	FL1	D	1-1	4,862
Sat 16	15:00	A	Cheltenham	FL1	L	0-2	3,525
Sat 23	15:00	A	Swansea City	FL1	D	1-1	12,327
Tue 26	15:00	H	Oldham	FL1	L	2-3	6,512
Sat 30	15:00	H	Leyton Orient	FL1	D	2-2	4,715
January							
Mon 1	15:00	A	Tranmere	FL1	L	1-2	6,675
Sat 13	15:00	H	Chesterfield	FL1	L	0-1	5,188
Sat 20	15:00	A	Millwall	FL1	L	0-4	9,534
Sat 27	15:00	A	Doncaster	FL1	L	2-3	12,126
February							
Sat 3	15:00	A	Brighton	FL1	D	0-0	5,444
Sat 17	15:00	A	Scunthorpe	FL1	L	0-1	5,978
Tue 20	19:45	H	Huddersfield	FL1	L	2-3	4,448
Sat 24	15:00	A	Northampton	FL1	L	0-3	5,464
Tue 27	19:45	H	Swansea City	FL1	L	1-2	3,697
March							
Sat 3	15:00	H	Bradford City	FL1	W	4-1	4,568
Sat 10	15:00	H	Port Vale	FL1	L	1-5	3,854
Sat 17	15:00	A	Brentford	FL1	W	1-0	4,937
Sat 24	15:00	A	Crewe	FL1	L	0-1	5,675
Tue 27	19:45	H	Blackpool	FL1	W	1-0	4,025
Sat 31	15:00	H	Bournemouth	FL1	L	0-2	3,657
April							
Sat 7	15:00	H	Gillingham	FL1	W	3-2	3,223
Mon 9	15:00	A	Nottm Forest	FL1	D	1-1	27,875
Sat 14	15:00	H	Carlisle	FL1	L	0-1	4,428
Sat 21	15:00	A	Yeovil Town	FL1	L	0-1	5,878
Sat 28	15:00	H	Cheltenham	FL1	L	2-4	3,876
May							
Sat 5	15:00	A	Bristol City	FL1	L	1-3	19,517

Goal Scorers Season 2007/2008

Player	FL2	CUPS	TOTAL
Derek Holmes	11	0	11
Chris O'Grady	9	2	11
Mark Hudson	9	0	9
Ryan Taylor	6	0	6
Danny Harrison	4	1	5
Marc Newsham	4	0	4
Marc Joseph	4	0	4
Stephen Brogan	3	1	4
Jamie Yates	3	0	3
Ian Sharps	2	1	3
Peter Holmes	2	0	2
Jamie Green	1	0	1
Graham Coughlan	1	0	1
Pablo Mills	1	0	1
Marcus Bean	1	0	1

FL2 = Coca-Cola Football League Two
CUPS = FA Cup/Carling Cup/,Johnstone's Paint Trophy North

Home Attendances

Highest	Opponent	Lowest	Opponent	Average
6709	Wycombe	2979	Brentford	4201

	Completed Saturday, 3rd May 2008	Pld	Home W	D	L	F	A	Away W	D	L	F	A	Overall W	D	L	F	A	Pts	EP
1	Milton Keynes Dons	46	11	7	5	39	17	18	3	2	43	20	29	10	7	82	37	97	+45
2	Peterborough United	46	14	4	5	46	20	14	4	5	38	23	28	8	10	84	43	92	+41
3	Hereford United	46	11	6	6	34	19	15	4	4	38	22	26	10	10	72	41	88	+31
4	Stockport County	46	11	5	7	40	30	13	5	5	32	24	24	10	12	72	54	82	+18
5	Rochdale	46	11	4	8	37	28	12	7	4	40	26	23	11	12	77	54	80	+23
6	Darlington	46	11	7	5	36	22	11	5	7	31	18	22	12	12	67	40	78	+27
7	Wycombe Wanderers	46	13	6	4	29	15	9	6	8	27	27	22	12	12	56	42	78	+14
8	Chesterfield	46	9	8	6	42	29	10	4	9	34	27	19	12	15	76	56	69	+20
9	Rotherham United (-10)	46	12	4	7	37	29	9	7	7	25	29	21	11	14	62	58	64	+4
10	Bradford City	46	10	4	9	30	30	7	7	9	33	31	17	11	18	63	61	62	+2
11	Morecambe	46	9	6	8	33	32	7	6	10	26	31	16	12	18	59	63	60	-4
12	Barnet	46	10	6	7	37	30	6	6	11	19	33	16	12	18	56	63	60	-7
13	Bury	46	8	6	9	30	30	8	5	10	28	31	16	11	19	58	61	59	-3
14	Brentford	46	7	5	11	25	35	10	3	10	27	35	17	8	21	52	70	59	-18
15	Lincoln City	46	9	3	11	33	30	9	1	13	28	30	18	4	24	61	77	58	-16
16	Grimsby Town	46	7	5	11	26	34	8	5	10	29	32	15	10	21	55	66	55	-11
17	Accrington Stanley	46	7	1	15	20	39	9	2	12	29	44	16	3	27	49	83	51	-34
18	Shrewsbury Town	46	9	6	8	31	22	3	8	12	25	43	12	14	20	56	65	50	-9
19	Macclesfield Town	46	6	8	9	27	31	5	9	9	20	33	11	17	18	47	64	50	-17
20	Dagenham & Redbridge	46	6	7	10	27	32	7	3	13	22	38	13	10	23	49	70	49	-21
21	Notts. County	46	8	5	10	19	23	2	13	8	18	30	10	18	18	37	53	48	-16
22	Chester City	46	5	5	13	21	30	7	6	10	30	38	12	11	23	51	68	47	-17
23	Mansfield Town	46	6	3	14			5	6	12			11	9	26			42	
24	Wrexham	46	6	7	10			4	3	16			10	10	26			40	

Date	KO	Venue	Opponent	Comp	Result	Score	Attendance	
August								
Sat 11	15:00	A	Hereford	FL2	D	0-0	3,566	
Thu 16	19:45	H	Sheffield Wed	LGCP	L	1-3	6,416	
Sun 19	14:00	H	Peterborough	FL2	W	3-1	4,291	
Sat 25	15:00	A	Stockport	FL2	D	2-2	5,764	
September								
Sat 1	15:00	H	Chester City	FL2	D	1-1	4,036	
Tue 4	19:45	A	Mansfield Town	JPT (N)	W	1-0	1,578	
Sat 8	13:00	A	Darlington	FL2	L	0-2	3,988	
Sat 15	15:00	A	Wrexham	FL2	W	1-0	3,711	
Sat 22	15:00	H	Notts County	FL2	D	1-1	4,181	
Sat 29	15:00	A	Barnet	FL2	L	0-2	2,088	
October								
Tue 2	19:45	A	Macclesfield	FL2	D	1-1	1,715	
Sat 6	15:00	H	Mansfield Town	FL2	W	3-2	3,881	
Tue 9	19:00	H	Grimsby Town	JPT(N)	L	1-1	2,362	aet 2-4 on pens
Fri 12	19:45	A	Brentford	FL2	D	1-1	3,841	
Sat 20	15:00	H	Morecambe	FL2	W	3-1	4,181	
Sat 27	15:00	A	Dagenham & Red	FL2	W	2-0	2,091	
November								
Sat 3	15:00	H	Grimsby Town	FL2	W	2-1	4,162	
Tue 6	19:45	H	Bury	FL2	W	2-1	3,425	
Sun 11	15:00	A	Forest Green	FACP	D	2-2	2,102	
Sat 17	15:00	A	Accrington	FL2	W	1-0	1,918	
Tue 20	19:45	H	Forest Green	FACP	L	0-3	2,754	
Sat 24	15:00	H	Shrewsbury	FL2	W	2-0	3,832	
December								
Wed 5	19:30	A	Chesterfield	FL2	W	2-0	5,417	
Sat 8	15:00	H	Rochdale	FL2	L	2-4	3,808	
Sat 22	15:00	H	Wrexham	FL2	W	3-0	3,773	
Wed 26	15:00	A	Darlington	FL2	D	1-1	6,965	
Sat 29	15:00	A	Notts County	FL2	W	1-0	5,290	
January								
Tue 1	15:00	H	Macclesfield	FL2	W	3-0	4,464	
Sat 5	15:00	H	MK Dons	FL2	L	0-1	5,421	
Sat 12	15:00	A	Lincoln City	FL2	W	3-1	5,016	
Sat 19	15:00	H	Wycombe	FL2	D	1-1	6,709	
Sat 26	15:00	A	Chester City	FL2	W	1-0	2,536	
Tue 29	19:45	A	Peterborough	FL2	L	1-3	5,152	
February								
Sat 2	15:00	H	Hereford	FL2	L	0-1	4,746	
Sat 9	15:00	A	MK Dons	FL2	D	1-1	9,455	
Tue 12	19:45	H	Stockport	FL2	L	1-4	4,004	
Sat 16	15:00	A	Wycombe	FL2	L	0-1	4,610	
Sat 23	15:00	H	Lincoln City	FL2	W	3-2	4,321	
Tue 26	19:45	A	Bradford City	FL2	L	2-3	13,936	
March								
Sat 1	15:00	H	Accrington	FL2	L	0-1	3,683	
Sat 8	15:00	A	Shrewsbury	FL2	D	1-1	5,265	
Tue 11	19:45	A	Bury	FL2	L	0-3	1,957	
Sat 15	15:00	H	Chesterfield	FL2	W	2-1	4,550	
Sat 22	15:00	H	Bradford City	FL2	D	1-1	4,157	
Mon 24	15:00	A	Rochdale	FL2	L	1-4	2,985	
Sat 29	15:00	A	Morecambe	FL2	L	1-5	2,171	
April								
Sat 5	15:00	H	Brentford	FL2	L	1-2	2,979	
Sat 12	15:00	A	Grimsby Town	FL2	W	1-0	3,583	
Sat 19	15:00	H	Dagenham & Red	FL2	W	2-1	3,203	
Sat 26	15:00	A	Mansfield Town	FL2	W	1-0	5,271	
May								
Sat 3	15:00	H	Barnet	FL2	W	1-0	4,834	

Rotherham United squad 2006-2007

Rotherham United Squad 2007-2008